Lecture Notes in Computer Science 3263

Commenced Publication in 1973
Founding and Former Series Editors:
Gerhard Goos, Juris Hartmanis, and Jan van Leeuwen

Mathias Weske   Peter Liggesmeyer (Eds.)

Object-Oriented and Internet-Based Technologies

5th Annual International Conference on Object-Oriented
and Internet-Based Technologies, Concepts, and Applications
for a Networked World, Net.ObjectDays 2004
Erfurt, Germany, September 27-30, 2004
Proceedings

 Springer

Volume Editors

Mathias Weske
University of Potsdam, Hasso Plattner Institute
Prof.-Dr.-Helmert-Str. 2-3, 14480 Potsdam, Germany
E-mail: Mathias.Weske@hpi.uni-potsdam.de

Peter Liggesmeyer
Fraunhofer Institute Experimental Software Engineering
Sauerwiesen 6, 67661 Kaiserslautern, Germany
E-mail: peter.liggesmeyer@iese.fraunhofer.de

Library of Congress Control Number: 2004111955

CR Subject Classification (1998): D.2, H.4, H.3, C.2.4, I.2.11, D.4

ISSN 0302-9743
ISBN 3-540-23201-X Springer Berlin Heidelberg New York

Springer is a part of Springer Science+Business Media

springeronline.com

© Springer-Verlag Berlin Heidelberg 2004
Printed in Germany

Typesetting: Camera-ready by author, data conversion by Olgun Computergrafik
Printed on acid-free paper   SPIN: 11325536   06/3142   5 4 3 2 1 0

In Memoriam

In memory of Mario Jeckle
who died in a tragic car accident
in June 2004.

We will miss your optimism,
your friendly attitude,
your cooperativeness,
your commitment,
your compassion and
the smile on your face even in turbulent times.

Preface

Based on the Net.ObjectDays tradition of bringing together researchers from academia and industry on the one hand and system architects, developers, and users from industry and administration on the other hand, this year's conference took an international research perspective, so that we see the first volume of Net.ObjectDays main conference proceedings published in the Springer Lecture Notes in Computer Science series. This volume consists of 16 papers carefully selected in a rigorous reviewing process by an international program committee; to provide a concise overview, these papers are briefly described.

In the Languages and Models session, Beate Ritterbach proposes a new language element for object-oriented programming languages that supports arbitrary value types. In her contribution *Support for Value Types in an Object-Oriented Programming Language* she describes the corresponding keywords, syntax, and consistency checks, thereby giving an impression of the look and feel of value types from an application programmer's perspective. Walter Binder and Jarle Hulaas look at portable CPU accounting and control in Java, which is based on program transformation techniques. In their paper *Self-accounting as Principle for Portable CPU Control in Java* periodically the threads of an application component aggregate the information of their respective CPU consumption within a shared account; scheduling functions make sure applications do not exceed their allowed CPU share.

The Agents and Semantic Web session features the use of Semantic Web technology in a particular application domain as well as in agent communication. Robert Tolksdorf and Elena Paslaru in their paper *Organizing Knowledge in a Semantic Web for Pathology* investigate the organization of knowledge in pathology based on Semantic Web technology. The system introduced combines text and image information and offers advanced content-based retrieval for diagnosis and teaching. Matthias Jöst, Matthias Merdes, and Rainer Malaka in their contribution *Listening to Agents – Transparent Representation and Presentation of Agent Communication in Mobile Systems* look at agent communication in mobile systems. In particular, they introduce an XML-based ontology for mobile multi-agent systems as well as a uniform mechanism for transforming agent communication into a format readable by human users.

In a session on Software Processes, Ander Altuna1 et al. in their paper *Cooperative and Distributed Configuration* look at multi-component product configuration based on Semantic Web technologies. In their contribution *Micro-measurements for Dynamic Aspect-Oriented Systems* Michael Haupt and Mira Mezini introduce a first step towards a benchmark suite for dynamic aspect oriented programming. Schahram Dustdar and Stephan Haslinger in *Testing of Service-Oriented Architectures – A Practical Approach* look at automated testing of service-oriented applications, and they provide a case study in the telecommunications domain. Kai Blankenhorn and Mario Jeckle (†) introduce *A UML*

Profile for GUI Layout for expressing GUI layout information, which allows for modeling the static representation of graphical user interfaces.

In the Software Product Lines session, Valentino Vranic in his contribution *Reconciling Feature Modeling: A Feature Modeling Metamodel* aims at providing an integration of feature modeling approaches based on a meta-model. Periklis Sochos, Ilka Philippow, and Matthias Riebisch in *Feature-Oriented Development of Software Product Lines: Mapping Feature Models to the Architecture* provide an analysis on the state of the art of feature-oriented software product line methodologies, focusing on the linkage between feature models and architecture. The use of the pattern paradigm in managing software product line variability is introduced by Jürgen Meister, Ralf Reussner, and Martin Rohde in *Managing Product Line Variability by Patterns*. It is shown how the management of product line variabilities can be improved by introducing a pattern-based architecture and an associated pattern language to complement it. The Software Architectures session looks at frameworks for component specification and nomadic desktop computing. Sven Overhage proposes *UnSCom: A Standardized Framework for the Specification of Software Components*, which provides the basis for development, discovery, and composition of components. Stefan Paal, Reiner Kammüller, and Bernd Freisleben introduce *A Cross-platform Application Environment for Nomadic Desktop Computing*. This paper proposes an approach to nomadic desktop computing based on dynamically deploying and executing personalized applications on the desktop system. A cross-platform application environment is presented that automatically adapts itself to a nomadic desktop application by enabling the execution and migration of applications across heterogeneous desktop computers.

In an industry case study, Rainer Burkhardt and Volker Gruhn report on *Agile Software Engineering: A New System for an Expanding Business Model at SCHUFA*, a large financial institution in Germany. The paper discusses how agile process elements and model-driven technologies can be combined in order to achieve a lightweight, flexible and incremental software engineering process. In a visionary paper, Oliver Imbusch, Falk Langhammer, and Guido von Walter introduce *Ercatons: Thing-Oriented Programming* as an emerging programming model that aims at overcoming some of the limitations of current practice in software development.

Finally, we thank the Business Process Technology research group at the Hasso Plattner Institute, including Hilmar Schuschel and Mirko Schulze, for their help during the reviewing process and Arnd Schnieders for the preparation of the camera-ready copy of this Springer LNCS volume. We acknowledge the excellent cooperation with Alfred Hofmann of Springer and his colleagues in the preparation of this volume.

Potsdam and Kaiserslautern, July 2004   Mathias Weske
                                                         Peter Liggesmeyer

Program Committee

Table of Contents

Software Architectures

Case Study and Visions

Semantic Web Services –
Fundamentals and Advanced Topics

Christoph Bussler

Digital Enterprise Research Institute (DERI)
National University of Ireland, Galway, Ireland
Chris.Bussler@DERI.org

Abstract. The 'traditional' Web Service triple SOAP, WSDL and UDDI, while widely praised as the next Silver Bullet, has been heavily criticized at the same time as being just the most recent replacement technology for remote procedure calls. The main criticism lies in the syntactic nature that SOAP, WSDL and UDDI retain compared to previous solutions: Enterprise Application Integration (EAI) and Business-to-Business (B2B) Integration are possible on a syntactic level only; however, the biggest problem – the Semantic Integration – still cannot be solved by traditional Web Services at all, whatsoever. The goal of Semantic Web Services is to change exactly that. Fundamentals of Semantic Web Services are discussed as well as advanced topics that are necessary for Business Integration in the real sense.

1 Introduction to Web Services

SOAP [1], WSDL [2] and UDDI [3] are the 'traditional' set of Web Service standards. While SOAP defines XML-structured message layout and allows its binding to synchronous as well as asynchronous transport protocols like HTTP and SMTP for message transmission, WSDL and UDDI are a bit more interesting.

1.1 WSDL

WSDL is an interface definition language based on the fundamental idea that communication endpoints receive and return individual XML messages. WSDL provides a simple model for accessing server entry points. The messages are defined using XML schema [4] as the definition language. Communication endpoints expose so-called operations that take a message as input and return at most one message as return message. In a synchronous transmission style this is equivalent to a remote procedure call. In an asynchronous transmission style this implements message queuing with return messages.

Since the messages are defined with XML schema, their meaning is everybody's best guess. Imagine a purchase order message is defined that contains a price field without further qualification. In an actual transmission this field might contain the value 500. While the sender might interpret this price as the price of the ordered goods including value added tax (VAT), the receiver might interpret it as the price

M. Weske and P. Liggesmeyer (Eds.): NODe 2004, LNCS 3263, pp. 1–8, 2004.
© Springer-Verlag Berlin Heidelberg 2004

excluding VAT. Both are right in their interpretation since not more has been specified in addition to the price. No qualification has been made that the price includes or excludes VAT. If in addition the price is specified as an integer data type, a value of -500 (minus 500) can be interpreted as the seller owing the buyer if neither the buyer or the seller actually checks that the price is equal or larger than 0 (zero). While one might think this is a ridiculous example, one cannot really assume that it does not happen. In summary, XML schema only allows the definition of a message structure, not its semantics as XML is a language lacking semantic concepts unlike Semantic Web Languages such as RDF-S [5] and OWL [6].

WSDL has as model the client/server approach whereby the server exposes interfaces, but the client is not defined at all. Therefore, message exchange patterns that consist of a sequence of messages sent back and forth cannot be described in WSDL at all. This is one of the reasons why interoperability is not necessarily given between a requester and a provider as it is not possible to formally define the message exchange sequences between both.

1.2   UDDI

UDDI defines the interface for registries that can store Web Service definitions (i.e., WSDL-defined interfaces). The basic idea is that UDDI can serve as a repository of Web Services that can be searched. If a requester that wants to invoke a Web Service providing a specific functionality does not know an appropriate one already, it can go to a UDDI repository and search for ('discover') a suitable one. Once found, it can be invoked by the requester if the message definitions of the requester and the Web Services match.

Of course, the fundamental problem is finding a suitable one, i.e. one that implements the desired functionality. In terms of the above example, a buyer can look for a seller and find one. However, the different interpretation in price cannot be taken into consideration during the discovery process since the semantic interpretation is not part of the Web Service's interface definition. The discovery process returns a seller where it should not due to mismatching semantics.

UDDI assumes a homogeneous environment as the Web Services are stored as defined. For example, if the seller's message includes 'price', however, the buyer's message the synonymous 'total_value' instead, the discovery process would not return the seller's Web Service, even if it should. The fact that 'price' is synonymous to 'total_value' would be unknown since this semantics is not described in UDDI.

2   Web Service Processes

Individual message exchanges are an important functionality; however, in real environments this is rarely enough to conduct a complete series of business operations. Usually a significant series of message exchanges needs to be executed in order to achieve the desired goal. For example, a buyer purchasing goods usually expects back a purchase order acknowledgement message. In addition, as networks are inherently unreliable, transport level acknowledgement messages are necessary. Once a purchase order has been acknowledged, goods have to be received, invoices issued and payments made. All these messages are necessary to completely execute the buying process [7].

As WSDL does not allow defining this, various language proposals are available for defining these processes. Amongst them are BPEL [8], ebXML [9] and WS-CDL [10]. All these process definition languages allow the definition of message exchange patterns from a workflow-like viewpoint. The sequence of message exchanges is defined.

However, no semantics is addressed at all. For example, it cannot be defined that after a specific message there is no point of return possible any more in the sense that the transaction can be easily aborted. This usually happens when purchases are being made. Once the purchase happens, it is not easily possible to return the goods for a full refund unless explicitly agreed. Purchasing airplane tickets is of this nature, too. Non-refundable tickets are just that: not refundable. However, unless it can be specified in the process, the process definition does not reveal it. And that might cause a mismatch between the web service requester and provider having different expectations regarding refunding.

3 Semantic Web Services – WSMO

Semantic Web Services have as goal to overcome the syntactic nature of the current Web Service standards and solve the semantics requirements. Major efforts in this space are WSMO [11], OWL-S [12] and PSL [13]. In the following WSMO is used to introduce the concept of Semantic Web Services.

WSMO stands for Web Service Modeling Ontology and, as the name says, is an ontology that defines the concepts necessary for defining and executing Semantic Web Services. Not only does WSMO provide a sound conceptual model based on the WSMF (Web Service Modeling Framework) [14], it also uses an ontology language to formally specify the concepts and relationships itself.

The main concepts of WSMO are

- **Ontology.** An ontology enables the definition of domain concepts. This includes concepts like price, VAT, product identification, purchase order, and so on. Every concept that is required in a communication between communication partners is described semantically through an ontology. This means that the semantics is machine processable and semantic mismatches are detected automatically.

- **Web Service.** A Web Service defines the functionality of a communication partner. This not only includes the individual message exchanges, but also the message exchange pattern as well as the processes. WSMO defines them as choreography and orchestration. Orchestration is the problem solving process like the overall purchase process. This is the domain specific logic in order to achieve an overall business goal. Choreography is the definition of the message exchange pattern between two partners that defines individual message conversations like the exchange of a purchase order and its acknowledgement. Choreography is about the actual message exchange pattern. An orchestration might require several choreographies with different partners as it executes. In addition, a Web Service defines its capability. This is important for discovery when certain capabilities are required by potential Web Service requesters. Goal match capabilities and that is the basis to relate a Web Service requester to a Web Service provider.

- **Goal.** To enable semantically correct discovery a Web Service requester can define its requirements formally as a goal. A goal states the desired functionality a Web Service requester is looking for. Goals are matched with Web Service capabilities. Matching goals and capabilities establish a successful discovery.
- **Mediator.** The concept of mediator allows overcoming the heterogeneity problem. A mediator can state, e.g., that 'price' and 'total_value' are equivalent or that the price of a Web Service requester is equivalent with the price plus VAT of a Web Service provider. Mediators ensure that misinterpretations of similar concepts are eliminated by precisely defining their relationship. Goals themselves might be subject to mediation to overcome different ways of expressing the same or similar goals.

The concepts of WSMO support the semantic definition of interfaces instead of syntactic definitions only. It is possible to define that a price includes or excludes VAT. Using the mediator it is possible to define that 'price' and 'total_value' are equivalent thereby matching perfectly. This functionality allows to semantically defining Web Services. With the explicit definition of choreography and orchestration it can be ensured that Web Service requester and Web Service provider match also in terms of the message exchange sequence. This is important to ensure that no message is dangling or an expected message will never be sent.

The concept of goal and capability ensure that discovery can return semantically matching Web Services ensuring that no mismatch can occur. This is of utmost importance when relying on dynamic matching. Dynamic matching occurs at Web Service execution time. In this case Web Services are discovered at run time and are executed after having been discovered. The Web Service definition does not predefine specific Web Services in this case. Needless to say, in order to trust such a mechanism, the discovery has to work flawlessly.

WSMO is implemented by the WSMX (Web Service Model Execution Environment) [15] prototype in order to clearly show that Semantic Web Services are not only defined on a conceptual model but can be implemented for real. As WSMO progresses and include concepts for advanced topics as discussed below WSMX will implement those accordingly.

4 Advanced Topics

Integrating businesses is the final goal of Semantic Web Services, no just invoking computational functionality. There are advanced topics that need to be addressed in order to integrate businesses. While current Semantic Web Service efforts propose the essential and fundamentally required functionality they do not yet address business level requirements. However, it is only a matter of time when this will happen and WSMO has taken first steps into this direction. A few more advanced topics are discussed in the following in more detail.

This is not to say that all that no work is being done in these areas, however, it is done in context of the traditional Web Services triple and not in context of Semantic Web Services, thereby not addressing the semantic aspects and the semantic interoperability problem.

4.1 Process Discovery

Discovery today is proposed based on the matching of Web Service interfaces with goals and capabilities. However, if a seller is capable of selling machine parts it is not guaranteed that the processes of the buyer and the seller match. Both, orchestration as well as choreography might mismatch. In the buyer's orchestration he might plan to execute a request for quotation while the seller does not provide this functionality as the seller expects only purchase orders directly without the quotation process. The buyer's process of how to buy and the seller's process of how to sell have to be in lock step so that all sent messages are received and all returned messages are expected. This requires that mismatches are detected at discovery time as a mismatching seller should not be discovered.

4.2 Commitments

Web service requesters and providers enter commitments when agreeing on business interactions. A buyer when buying a product commits to pay. A seller commits to delivering the goods and demands payment. In addition to the normal case of engagement, exceptional cases have to be agreed upon, too. For example, the buyer might expect the seller to pay a 'fine' when the seller delivers late. However, this needs to be committed upfront by both, the seller and the buyer, otherwise a dispute is likely. If the seller is not willing to pay a fine when delivering late the seller must be able to find out if the buyer expects this. Only a semantic definition of the commitments along the way allows detecting any disagreement or the need for special deviation.

4.3 Compensation

Sometimes already executed Web Services require being 'undone'. This is the case when one of the Web Service requester or provider changes its mind. For example, a buyer buys several products, however, later finds out that it only needs half of the number of purchased goods. In this case the other half has to be 'undone' or compensated for. In the easiest case the seller might not have manufactured it yet and no problem arises (except releasing scheduled manufacturing time). However, in the worst case the products have already been shipped. It now depends on the commitments how the compensation is executed. One possibility is that the seller takes them back without requesting payment. Another possibility is that the buyer has to pay for them since they have already been shipped. Many other scenarios are possible, too, of how buyers and sellers deal with this case.

4.4 Policy

A policy is a definition of business behavior that has to be ensured. Policies are set to ensure specific properties and also uniformity. For example, a policy is that a company always conducts a request for quotation process before purchasing any goods. A related policy might be that the quotation process must result in at least three quotes before making a purchase decision. This behavior can be directly modeled into the orchestration of a Web Service requester. However, this also means that it has to be modeled in all cases where the policy applies. Needless to say that if this is modeled directly no conceptual and explicit representation exists, instead, the policy is encoded in conditional statements and other process constructs. Any change would require a redesign and that might not be consistent across all occurrences. The requirement is that policies are separate concepts that govern the actual execution and ensure consistency across all possible occurrences. Changes in policy will be achieved by changing policy object directly without redesign of choreographies or other artifacts.

4.5 Constraints

Constraints are similar to policies, however, more on a system level. For example, the constraint that all communication has to be SSL secured is more a system constraint then a business policy. Another constraint is that there shall be no more than 25 open connections to partners at any point in time. This is irrelevant on a business level, however, very relevant in context of the infrastructure execution Semantic Web Services. Like in the case of policies, it is important that constraints apply, no matter what has been defined specifically otherwise. Only then it can be ensured that constraints are obeyed.

4.6 Dynamic Change

Web services can be carefully designed and executing perfectly. However, at some point in time due to changes in the business environment changes might be necessary. For example, it might be required that specific incoming parts need to be checked according to criteria that were not applicable required before. This might require a change in the Web Service definition as result, for example, the involvement of an external partner that performs the checking and sends the result back to the buyer. This in turn means changing the orchestration. While not yet started purchases can follow the new definition without problem, already executing Web Services have to be changed while executing. This requires the dynamic change of the executing Web Services in order to comply with the new criteria.

4.7   Real Automatic and Dynamic Composition

A Web Service requester does not request Web Services from providers in isolation. Through orchestration a Web Service requester can request a series of Web Services from different providers in order to achieve its objective. This composition of Web Services in an orchestration is usually predefined by the requester. For example, a purchase process is defined in phases like quotation, ordering, shipment, and payment. However, it would be a lot more efficient if the orchestration could be dynamically and automatically composed at runtime itself based on the Web Service requester's goal. If a requester has as goal to purchase a product and if it is known how to buy products then the actual necessary orchestration should be derived from that instead of manually encoding it. This requires providing knowledge in such a form that the composition can be dynamically composed. In addition, the concrete process discovery can ensure that only matching requesters and providers are the result of the automatic and dynamic composition.

4.8   Verification and Correctness

When defining Web Services the provider defines the Web Services according to his understanding and capability it can provide. Web Service requesters define what they need in terms of Web Services to achieve their objective. Through discovery matching partners are detected that based on the semantic definition can understand each other through matching ontologies as well as processes like orchestration and choreography. Mediation might be necessary to overcome heterogeneity problems, of course. However, in addition to the matching, it is necessary that the combined requester and provider do not run into inconsistent execution states that cause stalling of the interaction or even data inconsistencies. For example, it is important to check upfront if life locks or deadlock can occur. Also, it is necessary to ensure that all data are mediated in case of a mediation situation. It should be impossible to only map a subset of a message without detection.

4.9   Summary

These are only a few advanced topics that require to be considered by Semantic Web Services in the future to better reflect the needs in real integration environments like Business-to-Business integration. All these are advanced functional topics. Of course, there are non-functional ones like transactions, service guarantees, reliability and so forth that require being addressed.

There is no doubt that these advanced topics will be addressed in order to further strengthen the functional capabilities of Semantic Web Services.

Standards organizations like [16] are working on many of the above aspects. [17] reports on a impressive array of standards in the space. However, these standards are isolated efforts not addressing semantics. It is essential that all aspects are integrated in one conceptual model and that semantics is addressed for the benefit of semantic interoperation.

References

1. SOAP. http://www.w3.org/TR/soap/
2. WSDL. http://www.w3.org/TR/wsdl
3. UDDI. http://www.uddi.org/
4. XML Schema. XML Schema. http://www.w3.org/XML/Schema
5. RDF-S. http://www.w3.org/RDF/
6. OWL. http://www.w3.org/2004/OWL/
7. Bussler, C.: B2B Integration. Springer, Berlin Heidelberg New York, 2003
8. BPEL. http://www.oasis-open.org/committees/tc_home.php?wg_abbrev=wsbpel
9. ebXML. http://www.oasis-open.org/committees/tc_home.php?wg_abbrev=ebxml-bp
10. WS-CDL. http://www.w3.org/2002/ws/chor/
11. WSMO. http://www.wsmo.org/
12. OWL-S. DAML Services. www.daml.org/services/
13. PSL. http://www.tc184-sc4.org/ SC4_Open/SC4_Work_Products_Documents/PSL_(18629)/
14. Fensel, D.; Bussler, C.: The Web Service Modeling Framework WSMF. In: Electronic Commerce Research and Applications, Vol. 1, Issue 2, Elsevier Science B.V., Summer 2002
15. WSMX. http://www.wsmx.org/
16. OASIS. http://www.oasis-open.org/
17. Coverpages. http://xml.coverpages.org/

Support for Value Types
in an Object-Oriented Programming Language

Beate Ritterbach

Logimod GmbH, Birkenweg 20, 25436 Moorrege, Germany
`b.ritterbach@logimod.de`

Abstract. Values and objects are two different logical concepts. Objects can be created and changed, values, in contrast, exist per se and are immutable. Current object-oriented languages support mainly objects and classes of objects. Classes cannot be used to simulate value types in a satisfactory way.

The paper proposes a language element that supports arbitrary value types and that can be embedded in an object-oriented language. It describes the corresponding keywords, syntax, and consistency checks. Thereby, it gives an impression of the "look and feel" of value types from an application programmer's perspective.

1 Introduction

Current object-oriented languages support only objects. That means, that an application programmer can define and use arbitrary objects, or classes of objects, but values and value types are not supported in the same way.

Many object-oriented languages support values indirectly, or in a limited way. Eiffel [12], Java [4], C++ [16], and C# [10] comprise built-in types, i.e., primitive data types like numbers, characters and booleans. The language Smalltalk [3] supports only classes of objects, but some of the library classes - Character, Integer, Symbol, etc. - are programmed in a way that makes their behavior rather value-like. This indicates that values are indispensable also in object-oriented languages. The value concept needs some kind of support. If a language does not provide it directly, the values come "through the back door". However, if values could be programmed explicitly, and if they could easily be identified in the code, the conceptual clarity and expressiveness of a language would be improved.

2 Objects and Values as Logical Concepts

2.1 Differences Between Objects and Values

B. J. MacLennan was one of the first who pointed out that values and objects must be regarded as two logical concepts: According to [11], values are timeless abstractions, they exhibit referential transparency. Objects, on the contrary, simulate entities of the real world, they exist in time.

Objects are the central abstractions of all object-oriented languages. The concept of an object comprises the notions of creation and mutability:

M. Weske and P. Liggesmeyer (Eds.): NODe 2004, LNCS 3263, pp. 9–23, 2004.
© Springer-Verlag Berlin Heidelberg 2004

- Objects do not exist per se. They are created, and they can be destroyed.
- Objects have a mutable state. That means that the properties of an object can change in its lifetime, nevertheless, the object remains the same object.

In every domain, we may find some abstractions which do not fit into that scheme. For example let's consider a date. We may use a date, e.g., "March 10th, 2005", to describe the scheduled end of a project. Does it really make sense to assume that the date is created before it can be assigned to the project? Let's imagine that this date will also be used in another context, e.g., for describing the day when the project manager intends to travel to Paris. Is "March 10th, 2005" reused then? Or do we have to create a second instance of "March 10th, 2005"? In what respect could the two dates be different? The idea of creating a date does not make sense at all. The notion of "date" already encompasses "March 10th, 2005". It is much more natural to act on the assumption that dates are not created, neither destroyed, they simply exist.

The idea of a mutable state can be questioned in a similar way. Indeed, a date does have a state: We can find out its corresponding year (2005), its week-day (a Thursday), its day of the year (the 69th), etc. However, that state is not mutable. In the example above, let's assume the project's scheduled end date is put off by two months. Sometimes we say that the date is "changed to May 10th, 2005". But these are merely imprecise terms. We do not change the date, but we do change the project, by assigning another end date to it. What could the sentence "March 10th, 2005 is changed to May 10th, 2005" be supposed to mean? Taken literally it is pure nonsense. "March 10th, 2005" and "May 10th, 2005" are two different dates, neither of which can change.

Dates are values, just like numbers, booleans, characters, strings, monetary amounts, points, etc. We can summarize that values are characterized, and distinguished from objects, by two basic properties:

Value Universe
Values can neither be created nor destroyed, they simply exist.

Immutability
Values cannot be changed.

These two characteristics can also be regarded as a double immutability of values: every single instance is immutable, and the value type - interpreted as a set - is immutable as well, since it is not possible to add or delete members from it. All other differences between values and objects can be inferred from the two characteristics above:

Cloning
Objects can be cloned, i.e., copied. This is not possible for values.

Abstract Versus Concrete
Values are abstract things that cannot be located in space or time. Objects may be both concrete or abstract, but even abstract objects are usually related to some concrete things, e.g., a course is held by a teacher, in a room, for a group of students.

Presence in the Real World
Values cannot be observed in the real world directly. You will never encounter the color red, or the number 4. However, you may come across an object that can be described by the value, for example a red rose, or a clover with 4 leaves.

Stand-Alone Instances
One single object can yield information about the world, even if it is isolated from its context. For example, the object "Henry Rose" tells us, that a person called Henry Rose exists, it informs, depending on the other properties modeled, about his eye-color, his weight and so forth. Conversely, one stand-alone value does not yield sensible information.

2.2 Commonalities of Objects and Values

Despite their fundamental differences, objects and values have a lot in common.

Abstract Data Types
Objects and values can be described by abstract types. The type specification comprises operations, and rules that apply to the operations, i.e., invariants, pre- and post-conditions.

Encapsulation
When defining a type in a programming language, the interface and the implementation should be separated. The user of the type only needs to know the type's interface, i.e., its public operations. The internal representation is encapsulated. This applies to both object types and value types.

Business Dependency
Like objects, values represent abstractions from the business that is being modeled. For example, "MonetaryAmount" may be required in a financial application, or "Point" in a graphical application.

Usage
Objects and values are used in the same way:

- as an input parameter or return parameter of an operation.
- inside an operation, e.g., by binding it to a local variable.
- as a member variable for another type.
- if the language provides parametric polymorphism then both object types and value types can substitute the generic parameter.

Sharing
Both objects and values can be shared, i.e., one instance can be part of more than one context. As an example, an employee can be referred to as a member of a department, or as the manager of a project. A monetary amount, say, "4213,50 Euro", can be used to describe an account balance or the monthly salary of a person.

If an object is changed, this change will be visible in all contexts that include that object. Since values are immutable, there are no changes that could be seen in other contexts. Thus, sharing of objects and sharing of values have different qualities.

Note that everything stated in this section depicts the logical level. The underlying technical implementation may be completely different.

3 Programming Value Types

3.1 Value Types in Programming Languages

This subsection gives a brief survey of the support for value types in current object-oriented programming languages. A comprehensive support for value types implies that the programming language provides the means for defining arbitrary value types, and that the language ensures the conceptual properties of values: once a type is declared as a value type its instances cannot be created or changed.

Many object-oriented languages (Eiffel, C++, Java) provide primitive types, such as numbers, characters, or booleans. Though primitive types describe values, they do not provide a general support for value types. The number of built-in types is limited, there is no way to define arbitrary value types.

Many languages support enumerations, (C++ [16], C# [10], Java from version 1.5 [17], and also procedural languages like Pascal [5], or C [8]). In an enumeration, each single value is declared by a separate identifier. Some languages only permit the declaration of the enumeration elements, some also allow for the definition of arbitrary operations (Java 1.5). Again, enumerations are a special case of value type, they do not support value types in general.

C# [10] supplies so-called value types, but except for the name they have nothing in common with the logical concept proposed in this paper. Neither the value universe nor immutability are supported by the language. The purpose of C# value types is to allow programming of lightweight types in a very efficient way, i.e., with allocation on the stack instead of the heap.

In Eiffel [12] an object type, or even a single variable, may be declared "expanded". This affects the semantics of assignments and comparisons. It makes the type behave similarly to a value type in some respects. Yet the instances of expanded types are objects, they can be created and changed. This approach shifts the responsibility for the value-like behavior from the type itself to its variables. Additionally, mixing expanded variables and non-expanded variables in an assignment, or in a comparison, or in a call, can get rather complicated and makes the code hard to understand.

The situation is similar in C++ [16], where a variable can hold an object, or a primitive value, "immediately" or it can hold a reference to it.

Sather [15] provides a separate type constructor for "immutable classes". Instances of immutable classes cannot be changed. However, instances of immutable classes must be created, hence only one characteristic of the value concept is fulfilled.

Blue [9] introduces "manifest classes". Instances of manifest classes are not created but they exist per se; therefore they satisfy the "value universe" characteristic. However, Blue does not support arbitrary manifest classes. Only enumerations can be defined by the programmer. The basic manifest classes - Integer, Boolean, etc. - are provided as predefined language primitives.

Functional languages include only values and functions, but no concept of object, creation, assignment or mutable state. Since we want to extend object-oriented languages with value type support, purely functional languages will not be the solution we are looking for. There have been approaches to combining the object-oriented and the functional paradigm in one language, for example in Scala [13]. Scala comprises object-oriented concepts, such as classes, subclassing and polymorphism, and concepts typical for functional languages, such as pattern matching and higher order functions. Yet, it does not support the definition of arbitrary value types.

Summary: The object-oriented languages outlined above do not explicitly support value types by a dedicated language element. They plainly do not comprise the notion of value types as described in section 2. As shown in the next subsection, there are modeling techniques that simulate a value-like behavior to a certain extent. However, that is not the demanded language support but merely a way of manually putting together the value-likeness using other language elements.

3.2 Modeling Value Types with Classes

If an object-oriented language is used, and a system requires domain specific value types, e.g., Date or Point, they are usually modeled using classes. There are some approaches and patterns that can make a class behave more like a value type. Some of these will be outlined in this subsection.

Client Responsibility

According to this simple approach the implementor of the "value type class" does not need to take care of any of the conceptual properties of values. The instances of the class can be created and are mutable. That approach was used, for example, in the Java-class java.util.Calendar, or in the Smalltalk String class.

In order to make the class behave in a value-like manner, the clients have to clone an instance before it is changed, or every time it is passed on to another context, for example when an instance is a return value of an operation. If two variables are compared, the customary identity operator ("==" in Java and Smalltalk) won't work as expected. The client has to use a special operation provided by that class ("equals" in Java), or a different operator ("=" in Smalltalk).

Clearly, this approach shifts the burden for the value-like behavior from the implementor of the "value type class" to its clients. The value logic is not coded in a central place, which makes the approach error-prone. Some refinements can help to reduce unnecessary copies of instances, e.g., the body-handle-pattern (Coplien [1]), yet this does not remedy the client's responsibility.

Immutable Classes

Immutability of instances can easily be obtained by writing a class without modifying operations. For example, the class java.lang.String was implemented in this way. Thus clients do not have to copy an instance before passing it on to another operation. Because instances of the class can be created, the problem of multiple copies of the same conceptual value remains. Again, clients have to use an equals-operation which must be provided by the "value type class". Using the customary identity operator for comparing two expressions can fail and is a well-known source of errors.

Framework Support

More sophisticated approaches can indeed simulate a value-like behavior completely. Often these approaches are part of a framework. For example, the JWAM-framework, version 1.x [6,7] realizes values as flyweights [2], and it uses a factory-pattern [2] to create and store the instances that represent the values. As in the previous approach, the "value type class" must not contain modifying operations.

In some respect all approaches involving classes resemble a one way street: the "value-likeness" of a class can be obtained with patterns or conventions; the code works correctly, but it is hard to understand its meaning. The situation can be compared to the concept of a loop and its realization in an assembler language: it is easily possible to code a loop by using labels for the start and the end of the loop and appropriate jump statements. But when reading the code it is hard to recognize the loop. Furthermore, the meaning can easily be destroyed by changing just one line.

The reason for these drawbacks is the use of an inappropriate language element. Classes are unsuited for modeling values:

- The concept of an eternal value universe is not supported by classes. All instances of a class must be created. Thus, it is possible to create more than one instance with the same state, which contradicts the value concept. It requires using another operation for comparing two value variables (e.g., "equals") unless the language provides a way to overwrite the customary identity-operator.
- The immutability of class instances cannot be guaranteed. A programmer can omit modifying operations, but another programmer may fail to understand the meaning of the class and destroy its value-like behavior by adding modifiers.

The approaches outlined above solve that problem, with more or less complexity. This paper does not aim at solving but at avoiding the problem. Values must be supported on the programming language level.

4 Language Support

This section proposes a language element supporting value types in an object-oriented language. The purpose is to demonstrate that a dedicated language element for value types is possible, and to show in what respects it differs from an object class. Obviously, this proposal is just one way of designing such a kind of language support. Alternatives are conceivable and will be mentioned where possible.

In order to describe a language element completely, 3 perspectives must be taken into account:

1. The perspective of the programmer who uses the element as a client.
2. The perspective of the programmer who declares and implements the element.
3. The perspective of the programmer who develops the respective language environment, i.e., implementation issues for compiler, runtime environment, virtual machine.

The main focus of this paper, especially of this section, is perspective number 2. Therefore, the following subsections describe how to declare and implement a value type and how this task is supported by the language.

The first perspective has already been described in section 2 by elaborating the conceptual properties of values. When using a value type, the client programmer can rely on these properties to be fulfilled. He does not have to take care of them himself.

The third perspective, i.e., implementation issues, is an area of current work, but it is not in the focus of this paper due to limitations in the length of this presentation.

In the following, a hypothetical language is used for illustration purposes. It is strongly typed, it borrows some of the syntax from Java, for example the braces and the visibility modifiers, and it uses ":=" as the assignment-symbol and "=" as the operator for comparing two expressions.

4.1 A Dedicated Type Constructor

A value type is declared with a dedicated type constructor, different from the type constructor for object types. In the proposed language, *valclass* is the keyword for declaring a value type. The counterpart *objclass* is the keyword for declaring an object type, i.e., the equivalent of a conventional class. Thus, the declaration of a value type "Point" may look like this:

```
valclass Point {
   private real _x;
   private real _y;

// operations for Points
 ...
}
```

The keyword valclass has been chosen because, like a conventional class, this type constructor is used to specify both interface and implementation for a value type. The same refers to the keyword objclass. Using prefixes for both type constructors - "val" and "obj" - emphasizes that none is a special case of the other.

Except for the different keyword, this valclass resembles a normal class. It contains member variables - _x and _y in the Point example - and operations for points. The member variables represent the immutable state of a value. They should be visible only inside the valclass. Operations may have arbitrary visibility.

4.2 Value Selectors

A value type has no constructors. Since values exist in their value universe forever and cannot be created, a call to a constructor statement such as "new Point(...)" makes no sense conceptually. However, a client programmer needs a way to access a particular value. The operations doing this will be called "value selector". The declaration of a value selector for valclass "Point" may look like this:

```
Point pointForCoordinates(float x, float y) {...}
```

and it can be called, for example,

```
Point p := pointForCoordinates(3.1, 0.5);
```

A valclass may have more than one value selector, just like an objclass may have many constructors. Yet, "value selector" and "constructor" are not just two different names for the same thing. Calling a constructor twice always yields two objects by definition. Two calls of a value selector can return the same value. This is especially true if two calls to a value selector involve the same actual parameters.

In the body of a value selector, the implementor must specify which value to pick out of the universe. This is supported by the keyword *value*:

```
Point pointForCoordinates(float x, float y) {
   value._x := x;
   value._y := y;
   return value;
}
```

"value" is a pseudo-variable, only available inside the body of a value selector. Its type is "Point", or in general, the valclass the value selector belongs to. "value" must only be used by assigning something to its member variables, it cannot be the parameter of an operation call, or the right or left side of an assignment. By assigning whatever is appropriate to the member variables of "value", the programmer specifies which Point, or in general, which value to select. When the specification is finished, "value" is returned to the caller.

The name of a value selector may be chosen freely. It is not necessary to adhere to some naming convention, and no additional keyword is required, neither for declaring a value selector nor for calling it. This is another difference from constructors. In object-oriented languages, the name of a constructor is usually fixed by the language design or by convention. Eiffel uses "Create", Smalltalk uses "new". In Java, C++ and C#, the name of a constructor must be the name of the class. A similar restriction for value selector names would cause problems if you needed another value selector for the same valclass with the same number and the same types of parameters. In the Point example, lets assume we need a second value selector with polar coordinates as input parameters. We can easily define it, like this for example:

```
Point pointForPolarCoordinates(float x, float y) {...}
```

That would have been impossible if the language would have forced us to name all value selectors, e.g., "Point" or "Create". In any case, a special naming convention for value selectors is not necessary. A value selector can be recognized by its return type, which is the valclass in which it is specified.

Every valclass must have at least one value selector, otherwise no value of that valclass would ever be accessible. The existence of a value selector can be checked statically, i.e., by the compiler.

4.3 Immutability

Member variables of a valclass behave as if they were implicitly declared final. In the body of a value operation, the member variables can be read only, they cannot be assigned. Here are some examples for operations of valclass Point:

```
float getX( Point p) {
  return p._x;
}

float distance (Point p1, Point p2) {
  return sqrt((p1._x-p2._x)**2 + (p1._y-p2._y)**2);
}
```

Conversely, an operation like

```
move (Point p, float x, float y) {
  p._x := p._x + x;   //wrong
  p._y := p._y + y;   //wrong
}
```

will cause a compiler error, because it contains assignments to member variables. Conceptually, this would mean changing a Point, or in general, changing a value, which is not possible. However, if the operation is coded like this:

```
Point move (Point p, float x, float y) {
  return pointForCoordinates(p._x + x, p._y + y);
}
```

it will be accepted. Syntactically, it only reads p's member variables, and conceptually, instead of moving (changing) p, it yields another point.

The only exception to the assignment rule are assignments to member variables of the pseudo-variable "value". In that case, no existing value is changed. The expression "value" is interpreted as an empty template, and the assignments to its member variables specify the value that has to be selected.

Note another feature that has been chosen for valclasses: syntactically, value operations are defined and called like functions in that all operands involved in a value operation are specified in the parameter list. (Indeed, it can be argued that all value operations conceptually *are* functions.) This is different from defining and calling an object operation, where one object is marked as the "receiver of the message", and zero or more other operands are regarded as parameters of the operation. In the case of valclasses, the familiar receiver-parameter-syntax from object operations would have led to some disadvantages:

Firstly, it does not make sense to regard a value operation as an action for one dedicated value. In the Point example, why should one input point be interpreted as the value "on" which the operation "distance" is operating, whereas the other input point is only a parameter? In a way, both parameters are equivalent. In the case of "distance", they happen to even be symmetrical.

Secondly, the functional syntax avoids the necessity of a special keyword or syntax for calls to a value selector. This makes the code more homogeneous. The proposed syntax reflects the fact that a value selector is a normal value operation. Like any other value operation, it maps the input values to an output value.

4.4 Enumerating Values

The Point example represented one special case of valclasses. It was a valclass that internally was composed of member variables, just like objclasses. In general, valclasses, unlike objclasses, can also be defined by enumeration. Here is an example for a definition by enumeration:

```
valclass Weekday {
  enum {monday; tuesday; wednesday; thursday;
        friday; saturday; sunday;}
  // operations for Weekday
  Weekday successor (Weekday someday) {
    if (someday = monday) return tuesday;
    ...
    if (someday = sunday) return monday;
  }
  ...
}
```

This means that the identifiers within the enum clause - monday to sunday in the example - are expressions that denote mutually different instances of the valclass "Weekday". They can be used both by clients and within the body of the valclass. There is no need - and no possibility - to code an implementation for the values monday to sunday. It is sufficient to declare them. Arbitrary operations may be defined for the enumerated values.

Definition by enumeration syntactically looks completely different from defining a valclass based on member variables. Conceptually, there is no difference. The expressions inside the enumeration - monday to sunday - are nothing but value selectors: A constant can be regarded as a borderline case of a function, it is a function without parameters. When calling the function, because of the missing parameters the parentheses may as well be omitted. That is a syntactic idiom also used in Eiffel [12]. Thus, the expression "monday" is a call to a value selector, returning an instance of the valclass "Weekday". Since two calls to the same value selector with the same parameters always yield the same value - "no parameters" is a special case of "the same parameters" - each occurrence of the expression "monday" denotes the same value.

The Weekday example was very simple. Defining a value type by specifying its member variables, and defining it by enumerating its instances, is not mutually exclusive. Both can be done within one valclass. This will be illustrated with another example, a possible implementation for the valclass String:

```
valclass String
  enum {empty;}
  char _first;
  String _rest;

// operations for String
  String concat (String s1, String s2) {
  if (s1 = empty) {
    return s2;
  }
  else {
    value._first := s1._first;
    value._rest := concat (s1._rest, s2);
    return value;
  }
  ...
}
```

In this String example, the empty string is defined in an enumeration with only one element, the identifier "empty". All other instances of String are internally composed of two member variables, _first and _rest. This composition makes the coding within the valclass slightly more complicated. The member variables _first and _rest are only available for instances of "String" that are not "empty", or in general, not defined in the enumeration. This is something the implementor of the valclass "String" has to bear in mind to avoid runtime errors.

The example operation "concat" is a value selector. It returns a String, and in the body it uses the pseudo-variable "value".

The code above sketched only a small fragment of the valclass "String". In particular, "String" has more value selectors not shown in the example. If "concat" were the only value selector then "empty" would be the only value available.

Also note that the member variable "_rest" and the operation "concat" are defined recursively. Thus, this example illustrates that recursion is possible for valclasses.

The concept of "definition by enumeration" is related to enumerations known from languages like Pascal, C, C#, etc. However, there are some major differences:

- In this paper, an enumeration is not a separate type constructor, but it is one way of defining values within a valclass. It can be combined with other value definitions, i.e., representations based on member variables.
- In the languages mentioned above, enumerations have an underlying type, usually an integral type such as Integer. The enumerated identifiers can be cast to Integers, in C they can even be used like Integers. This is not possible for the value types proposed in this paper.

4.5 Sum Types

In general, a valclass can contain more than one representation based on member variables. Here is an example:

```
valclass Figure
   circle {
      Point _center;
      float _radius;
   }
   triangle {
      Point _p1;
      Point _p2;
      Point _p3;
   }
// operations for Figure
   Figure getCircle {...}
   Figure getTriangle {...}
   float area (Figure f) {...}
   ...
}
```

The example illustrates that, in the most general case, a more elaborate syntax is required. In order to separate the variants from each other - circle and triangle in the Figure example - the member variables of each variant must be grouped under the corresponding name. In the other examples only one variant with member variables existed, hence the additional name and the grouping could be omitted. In practice, simple cases like these constitute the majority of all valclasses.

Types that can be defined in more than one way, using the possible definitions alternatively, are known as "sum types" in some functional languages, or "union types" in some procedural languages. For example, see the specification of sum types - and product types as their counterparts - in OPAL [14].

The general rules for specifying a valclass make evident that enumerations are not another stand alone type in the type system. An enumeration is a borderline case of a sum type: each enumerated expression is a variant without member variables, therefore it comprises one value only.

4.6 The Identity Operator

In this paper, the operator "=" is termed identity operator in order to emphasize what it does conceptually: it tells whether the two expressions involved yield the same thing, i.e., the same object or the same value.

As stated above, two value selector calls with the same actual parameters must yield the same value. Thus, in the code snippet

```
Point p1 := pointForCoordinates(3.1, 0.5);
Point p2 := pointForCoordinates(3.1, 0.5);
if (p1 = p2) ....  // true
```

the expression "p1 = p2" yields true. In the case of valclass "Point", the identity operator must work as if it were implemented like this:

```
// compare Points p1 and p2
return p1._x = p2._x AND p1._y = p2._y ;
```

In general, the identity operator for valclasses works as follows:

1. If the values involved belong to the same variant, and all corresponding member variables have the same content, then it is the same value.
2. If the values belong to different variants, then they are always two different values. This is especially true if one value is represented by member variables and the other is defined by enumeration.
3. If the values are defined by enumeration, a check is performed to determine if the enumeration expressions are the same. After all, this is only a special case of "belonging to different variants" or "belonging to the same variant".

Furthermore, comparing expressions of two different types, such as a String and a Point, is invalid and results in a compile error.

This behavior is part of the language, i.e., it is performed by the language environment. It need not be coded by the implementor of each single valclass. This reduces the amount of code the application programmer has to write, and more importantly, it removes a potential source of errors.

The description above specifies only the externally visible behavior of the identity operator. It does not determine the underlying technical implementation. E.g., it is possible that the runtime environment allocates many representations of one (conceptual) value, and compares them according to the rules 1. to 3. It is also conceivable that every value has one physical representation at most, which is referred to each time the value is used.

The specification of the identity operator is based on the tacit assumption that the representation of a value always is unique within its valclass. This is true for many valclasses like Point, Weekday, and String. However, it need not necessarily be true in any case. Consider the following valclass "Rational" which represents rational numbers and their arithmetic:

```
valclass Rational {
    private _numerator;
    private _denominator;
    public Rational getRational (Integer n, Integer d)...
    public Rational add (Rational r1, Rational r2)...
    public Rational subtract (Rational r1, Rational r2)...
    public Rational multiply (Rational r1, Rational r2)...
    public Rational divide (Rational r1, Rational r2)...
}
```

A rational number, for example 1/2, may have more than one representation. It can be represented with numerator 1 and denominator 2, with numerator 3 and denominator 6, and many more. Since the language environment simply compares the member variables, the two representations 1/2 and 3/6 will be regarded as two different values. This is false if the valclass Rational is meant to model rational arithmetic.

As a solution, the programmer of the valclass must ensure that the representation of a value becomes unique. In the Rational example, the implementor has to write code in which numerator and denominator always are coprime, i.e., the fraction must always be reduced. Calling the value selector:

```
...  getRational (3,6) ...
```

will then result in an internal representation with numerator 1 and denominator 2, thus the identity operator will work as expected.

The implementor of valclass "Rational" must remember to do this in every value selector. Of course, the routine for reducing the fraction can be implemented once only, say, as a private operation, and then it can be called from every value selector. Yet, forgetting the call to that routine in one of the value selectors is a potential source of error and will lead to an unsound behavior of the valclass "Rational".

The algorithm for finding out a value's unique representation is another potential hurdle. In the Rational example, the numerator and denominator can be divided by the greatest common divisor, which can be calculated using the Euclidean Algorithm. It is not proven that such an algorithm exists for every valclass with a potential non-unique representation. Nevertheless, this problem is merely a theoretical issue. In practice, valclasses with a non-unique representation of their values are quite rare. Two more examples are "Length" (a distance which can be measured in meters, yards, or inches) and "Timestamp" (including the timezone). For both examples an algorithm for a unique representation can easily be found.

The Rational example shows clearly that a programming language cannot prevent all logical errors. The language element "valclass" only ensures a behavior according to the value type concept. This also refers to the valclass "Rational" if it were coded wrongly, i.e., without reducing the fraction. Even then it would be a value type. However, the identity operator would yield unexpected results. It is always possible to write code that does not reflect the situation that was actually intended.

The potential difficulties concerning valclasses and the correctness of the identity operator are no weakness of the design of valclasses. They are caused by the conceptual differences between objects and values:

For objclasses, the identity operator must be independent of the state of the objects, because firstly, an object's state can change, and secondly, two objects with the same state can exist and must be distinguishable. Therefore an object's identity is managed by the language environment - transparently for the application programmer - as well as the identity operator which is based on that internal identity. Since the language takes care of both, no problem will occur. (Note that this is no longer true if the identity operator of objclasses can be overridden by the application programmer, or if the identity is managed by the application programmer manually.)

In contrast, a value is determined completely by its immutable state. That is why for valclasses the identity operator must be based on the state of the values, just as described above. The language provides the identity operator but not the state - the state is specified by the valclass' implementor (unless the valclass is defined by enumeration only). Therefore, in the case of valclasses, the programmer can indirectly influence the behavior of the identity operator, which is the reason for complications in some special cases like Rational.

5 Conclusion

Values and objects represent two fundamentally different concepts, independent of any programming language aspects. Both are needed to model abstractions of the real world. Most object-oriented languages support objects only, thus they compel the programmer to use roundabout ways whenever a value type is required. There are several approaches to modeling value types with object classes, but none of them express the value concept in the code clearly.

In short, one benefit of value types is overcoming the drawbacks described in subsection 3.2. By explicitly supporting both value types and object types, a programming language will gain expressiveness and clarity: Every type can immediately be recognized as a value type or an object type. The "value-likeness" of a type is coded in a central place, i.e., in the type itself. It is neither a quality of its variables, nor is it delegated to the type's clients. Explicit support for value types also enhances safety. Code changes cannot accidentally destroy the value characteristics of a type. The language guarantees that the conceptual properties of values - value universe and immutability - are fulfilled. Several consistency checks become possible, many of them at compile time.

Indeed, the integration of value types makes a programming language more complex because it leads to a dual type system. On the other hand, the existence of value types can also simplify some aspects, for example the question of different kinds of equality. With both objects and values supported by the language, only one kind of equality is required on the language level: identity. For both objects and values it is provided by the language, and conceptually, it works the same way.

The integration of value types in an object-oriented language entails numerous consequences and requires careful design-decisions. Both are subject of a separate paper, and in this context, they can only be mentioned briefly. They include, for example, impacts on the language model, the question whether a common abstraction over values and objects should be introduced, if and how the concept of subtyping is applicable to value types, and many more.

One advantage of a value type support that should not be underestimated, is the way it may influence the programmer's conception of the world. The effect of a programming language on the programmer's way of thinking is well known, yet often unnoticed. A Java programmer probably will not perceive any difference between "String" or "Date" on one side, and "Student" or "Vehicle" on the other side. From his - and the language's - point of view they are all classes. Conversely, a programmer using a language with explicit value types and object types may be inclined to regard the conceptual difference between the two as rather obvious.

References

1. Coplien, J.: Advanced C++: Programming Styles and Idioms, Addison-Wesley, 1992
2. Gamma, E., Helm, R., Johnson, R., Vlissides, J.: Design Patterns: Elements of Reusable Object-Oriented Software, Addison-Wesley, 1996.
3. Goldberg, A., Robson, D.: Smalltalk-80: The Language, Addison-Wesley, 1989.
4. Gosling, J., Joy, B., Steele, G.: The Java Language Specification, Addison-Wesley, 1996.
5. Jensen. K., Wirth, N.: PASCAL User Manual and Report, Second Edition, Springer Verlag, 1978
6. JWAM - A Framework to Support the Tools & Materials Approach, http://www.jwam.org

7. JWAM Value-Framework, http://sf.net/projects/jwamdomainvalue
8. Kernighan, B., Ritchie, D.: The C Programming Language, Second Edition, Prentice Hall, Inc., 1988.
9. Kölling, M., Rosenberg, J.: Blue - A Language for Teaching Object-Oriented Programming, SIGCSE '96, Philadelphia, Pennsylvania; in SIGSCE Bulletin, Vol. 28, 1, 1996.
10. Liberty, J.: Programming C#, 3rd Ed., O'Reilly, 2003.
11. MacLennan, B. J.: Values and Objects in Programming, Languages, ACM SIGPLAN Notices, 17:12, pp. 70-79, 1982
12. Meyer, B.: Eiffel: the Language, Prentice-Hall, New York, 1992.
13. Odersky, M. et. al.: The Scala Language Specification, Version 1.0, Draft 2004, http://scala.epfl.ch/index.html
14. Pepper, P.: Funktionale Programmierung in OPAL, ML, HASKELL und GOFER, Springer Verlag Berlin, 1999
15. Stoutamire, D., Omohundro, S.: The Sather 1.1 Specification, ICSI Technical Report TR-96-012, International Computer Science Institute, Berkley, CA, 1996.
16. Stroustrup, B.: The C++ Programming Language (3rd edition), Addison Wesley, 1997.
17. A Typesafe Enum Facility for the Java Programming Language, http://jcp.org/aboutJava/communityprocess/jsr/tiger/enum.html

Self-accounting as Principle
for Portable CPU Control in Java

Walter Binder[1] and Jarle Hulaas[2]

[1] Artificial Intelligence Laboratory, EPFL, CH–1015 Lausanne, Switzerland
Walter.Binder@epfl.ch
[2] Software Engineering Laboratory, EPFL, CH–1015 Lausanne, Switzerland
Jarle.Hulaas@epfl.ch

Abstract. In this paper we present a novel scheme for portable CPU accounting and control in Java, which is based on program transformation techniques and can be used with every standard Java Virtual Machine. In our approach applications, libraries, and the Java Development Kit are modified in order to expose details regarding the execution of threads. Each thread accounts for the number of executed bytecode instructions and periodically the threads of an application component aggregate the information of their respective CPU consumption within a shared account and invoke scheduling functions that are able to prevent applications from exceeding their allowed CPU quota.

Keywords: Bytecode rewriting, CPU accounting and control, Java, program transformations

1 Introduction

Accounting and controlling the resource consumption of applications and of individual software components is crucial in server environments that host components on behalf of various clients, in order to protect the host from malicious or badly programmed code. Java [9] and the Java Virtual Machine (JVM) [11] are being increasingly used as the programming language and deployment platform for such servers (Java 2 Enterprise Edition, Servlets, Java Server Pages, Enterprise Java Beans). Moreover, accounting and limiting the resource consumption of applications is a prerequisite to prevent denial-of-service (DoS) attacks in mobile object (mobile agent) systems and middleware that can be extended and customized by mobile code. For such systems, Java is the predominant programming language.

However, currently the Java language and standard Java runtime systems lack mechanisms for resource management that could be used to limit the resource consumption of hosted components or to charge the clients for the resource consumption of their deployed components.

Prevailing approaches to provide resource control in Java-based platforms rely on a modified JVM, on native code libraries, or on program transformations. For instance, the Aroma VM [12], KaffeOS [1], and the MVM [7] are specialized JVMs supporting resource control. JRes [8] is a resource control library for Java, which uses native code for CPU control and rewrites the bytecode of Java programs for memory control.

M. Weske and P. Liggesmeyer (Eds.): NODe 2004, LNCS 3263, pp. 24–38, 2004.

The Java Resource Accounting Framework J-RAF [4] is based completely on program transformations. In this approach the bytecode of applications is rewritten in order to make the CPU consumption of programs explicit. Programs rewritten by J-RAF keep track of the number of executed bytecode instructions (CPU accounting) and update a memory account when objects are allocated or reclaimed by the garbage collector.

Resource control with the aid of program transformations offers an important advantage over the other approaches, because it is independent of a particular JVM and underlying operating system. It works with standard Java runtime systems and may be integrated into existing server and mobile object environments. Furthermore, this approach enables resource control within embedded systems based on modern Java processors, which provide a JVM implemented in hardware that cannot be easily modified [5].

CPU accounting in the initial version of J-RAF [4] relied on a high-priority scheduling thread that executed periodically in order to aggregate the CPU consumption of individual threads and to adjust the running threads' priorities according to given scheduling policies. This approach hampered the claim that J-RAF enabled fully portable resource management in Java, because the scheduling of threads within the JVM is not well specified and the semantics of thread priorities in Java is not precisely defined. Hence, while some JVMs seem to provide preemptive scheduling ensuring that a thread with high priority will execute whenever it is ready to run, other JVMs do not respect thread priorities at all. Therefore, scheduling code written for environments using J-RAF may not exhibit the same behaviour when executed on different JVM implementations.

To overcome this limitation, the new version J-RAF2[1], the Java Resource Accounting Framework, Second Edition, comes with a new scheme for CPU accounting. In J-RAF2 each thread accounts for its own CPU consumption, taking the number of executed JVM bytecode instructions as platform-independent measurement unit. Periodically, each thread aggregates the collected information concerning its CPU consumption within an account that is shared by all threads of a software component and executes scheduling code that may take actions in order to prevent the threads of a component from exceeding their granted CPU quota. In this way, the CPU accounting scheme of J-RAF2 does not rely on a dedicated scheduling thread, but the scheduling task is distributed among all threads in the system. Hence, the new approach does not rely on the underlying scheduling of the JVM.

This paper is structured as follows: In the next section we review the old CPU accounting scheme of J-RAF and show its limitations. Section 3 explains the details of our new approach for CPU accounting. Section 4 evaluates the performance of applications using our new CPU accounting scheme. Finally, the last section summarizes the benefits of J-RAF2 and concludes this paper.

2   The Old CPU Accounting Scheme and Its Limitations

In the old version of J-RAF [4] each thread accounts locally for the number of JVM bytecode instructions it has executed. A periodically executing high-priority scheduling thread accumulates that accounting information from all threads in the system, ag-

---

[1] http://www.jraf2.org/

gregates it for individual application components, and ensures that CPU quota are respected, e.g., by terminating components that exceed their allowed CPU shares[2] or by lowering the priorities of threads that are excessively consuming processing power.

Each thread has an associated `OldCPUAccount` object maintaining a `long` counter, which is updated by the owning thread[3]. Table 1 shows some parts of the `OldCPUAccount` implementation. Because the scheduler thread has to read the value of the `consumption` variable, it has to be declared as `volatile` in order to force the JVM to immediately propagate every update from the working memory of a thread to the master copy in the main memory [9, 11].

Table 1. The `OldCPUAccount` implementation in the old accounting scheme.

```
public final class OldCPUAccount {
  public volatile long consumption;

  ...
}
```

In general, updating the counter requires loading the `consumption` field of the `OldCPUAccount` object from memory (it is `volatile`), incrementing the loaded value accordingly, and storing the new value in the memory. The accounting instructions are inserted in the beginning of each accounting block. An accounting block is related to the concept of basic block of code with the difference that method and constructor invocations may occur at any place within an accounting block. Details concerning the definition of accounting blocks can be found in [4]. Table 3 shows how the examplary code fragment given in table 2 is transformed according to this rewriting scheme. In this rewriting example we assume that the accounting object is passed as an extra argument to the method. For the sake of easy readability, we show all transformations at the Java level, even though the implementation works at the JVM bytecode level.

The main problem with this accounting scheme is that it relies on the scheduler of the JVM to ensure that a high-priority scheduler thread executes periodically in order to make use of the local accounting information of the individual threads. Unfortunately, the semantics of thread priorities are not well defined in the Java specification [9] and in the JVM specification [11]. For instance, the Java specification states: "Every thread has

---

[2] Current standard Java runtime systems do not offer a clean way to force the termination of components [6]. In order to enable the safe termination of a Java component (reclaiming all its allocated resources and ensuring the consistency of the system), the runtime system has to provide strong isolation properties. For instance, J-SEAL2 [2] is a Java library which provides strong isolation properties by preventing components from sharing object references. More recently, JSR 121 [10] specifies a Java extension to isolate components.

[3] This association may be implemented by a thread-local variable, by extending the `Thread` class of the Java Development Kit (JDK) with a special field to store the thread's accounting object, or by extending the method signatures to pass the accounting object as an extra argument. However, these details are outside the scope of this paper, they can be found in [4] and more recently in [3].

Table 2. Exemplary method to be rewritten for CPU accounting.

```
void f() {
    X;
    while (true) {
        if (C) {
            Y;
        }
        Z;
    }
}
```

Table 3. Exemplary method rewritten according to the old CPU accounting scheme.

```
void f(OldCPUAccount cpu) {
    cpu.consumption += ...;
    X;
    while (true) {
        cpu.consumption += ...;
        if (C) {
            cpu.consumption += ...;
            Y;
        }
        cpu.consumption += ...;
        Z;
    }
}
```

a priority. When there is competition for processing resources, threads with higher priority are generally executed in preference to threads with lower priority. Such preference is not, however, a guarantee that the highest priority thread will always be running, and thread priorities cannot be used to reliably implement mutual exclusion." When testing certain scheduling strategies (to be periodically executed by a scheduling thread) we encountered very different behaviour on different JVMs. On some JVMs our scheduler worked as intended, whereas other JVMs seemed not to respect thread priorities at all. Hence, due to the vague specification of the semantics of thread priorities, it is not possible to write platform-independent scheduling code based on priority assignment.

Another problem with this approach is its inferior performance. Updating a `volatile long` variable in each accounting block causes excessive overhead on several recent state-of-the-art JVMs. Past performance evaluations, such as in [4, 3], did not show this problem, since in the settings of these measurements the `consumption` variable was a `volatile int`. However, on fast processors the whole range of `int` may be exhausted within a millisecond of accounted execution or less. As there are no guarantees that the scheduler would run frequently enough to detect all overflows, we had to revert to a `volatile long` counter in order not to lose accounting information.

3   The New CPU Accounting Scheme and Its Benefits

Our new scheme for CPU accounting solves all the problems mentioned in section 2. It does without a dedicated scheduler thread by distributing the scheduling task to all threads in the system. Periodically, each thread reports its locally collected accounting information to an account that is shared between all threads of a component and executes scheduling functionality in order to ensure that a given resource quota is not exceeded (e.g., the component may be terminated if there is a hard limit on the total amount of bytecode instructions it may execute, or the thread may be delayed in order to meet a restriction on its execution rate). We call this approach *self-accounting*.

3.1   Implementation of `ThreadCPUAccount`

Like in the old approach, each thread has its associated `ThreadCPUAccount` which is shown in table 4. During execution each thread updates the `consumption` counter of its `ThreadCPUAccount` as in the old accounting scheme. Now the `consumption` variable is an `int` and it is not `volatile`, because only a single thread accesses it and ensures that there is no overflow.

Each threads invokes the `consume()` method of its `ThreadCPUAccount`, when the local `consumption` counter exceeds a certain threshold defined by the `granularity` variable. In order to optimize the comparison whether the `consumption` counter exceeds the `granularity`, the counter runs from `-granularity` to zero, and when it equals or exceeds zero, the `consume()` method is called. In the JVM bytecode there are dedicated instructions for the comparison with zero. We use the `iflt` instruction in order to skip the invocation of `consume()` if `consumption` is below zero.

Normally, each `ThreadCPUAccount` refers to an implementation of `CPUManager` (see table 5), which is shared between all threads belonging to a component. The first constructor of `ThreadCPUAccount` requires a reference to a `CPUManager`. The second constructor, which takes a value for the accounting granularity, is used only during bootstrapping of the JVM (`manager == null`). If the JDK has been rewritten for CPU accounting, the initial bootstrapping thread requires an associated `ThreadCPUAccount` object for its proper execution. However, loading complex user-defined classes during the bootstrapping of the JVM is dangerous, as it may violate certain dependencies in the classloading sequence. For this reason, a `ThreadCPUAccount` object can be created without previous allocation of a `CPUManager` implementation so that only two classes are inserted into the initial classloading sequence of the JVM: `ThreadCPUAccount` and `CPUManager`. Both of them only depend on `java.lang.Object`. After the bootstrapping (e.g., when the `main(String[])` method of an application is invoked), the `setManager(CPUManager)` method is used to associate `ThreadCPUAccount` objects that have been allocated and collected (e.g., in an array) during the bootstrapping with a `CPUManager`. As the variable `manager` is `volatile`, the thread associated with the `ThreadCPUAccount` object will notice the presence of the `CPUManager` upon the following invocation of `consume()`.

Table 4. The `ThreadCPUAccount` implementation in the new accounting scheme.

```
public final class ThreadCPUAccount {
   public int consumption;
   private long aggregatedConsumption = 0;
   private int granularity;
   private boolean consumeInvoked = false;
   private volatile CPUManager manager;

   public ThreadCPUAccount (CPUManager m) {
      manager = m;
      granularity = manager.getGranularity();
      consumption = -granularity;
   }

   public ThreadCPUAccount(int g) {
      manager = null;
      granularity = g;
      consumption = -granularity;
   }

   public void setManager(CPUManager m) {
      manager = m;
   }

   public void consume() {
      long amountCons =
         (long)consumption + granularity;
      if (manager == null) {
         aggregatedConsumption += amountCons;
         consumption = -granularity;
      }
      else {
         granularity = manager.getGranularity();
         consumption = -granularity;
         if (consumeInvoked) {
            aggregatedConsumption += amountCons;
         }
         else {
            amountCons += aggregatedConsumption;
            aggregatedConsumption = 0;
            consumeInvoked = true;
            manager.consume(amountCons);
            consumeInvoked = false;
         }
      }
   }
}
   ...
}
```

Table 5. The (simplified) `CPUManager` interface.

```
public interface CPUManager {
    public int getGranularity();
    public void consume(long c);
}
```

After the bootstrapping the `granularity` variable in `ThreadCPUAccount` is updated during each invocation of the `consume()` method. Thus, the `CPUManager` implementation may allow to change the accounting granularity dynamically. However, the new granularity does not become active for a certain thread immediately, but only after this thread has called `consume()`.

The `consume()` method of `ThreadCPUAccount` passes the locally collected information concerning the number of executed bytecode instructions to the `consume(long)` method of the `CPUManager` which implements custom scheduling policies. As sometimes `consume(long)` may execute a large number of instructions and the code implementing this method may have been rewritten for CPU accounting as well, it is important to prevent a recursive invocation of `consume(long)`. We use the flag `consumeInvoked` for this purpose. If a thread invokes the `consume()` method of its associated `ThreadCPUAccount` while it is executing the `consume(long)` method of its `CPUManager`, it simply accumulates the information on CPU consumption within the `aggregatedConsumption` variable of its `ThreadCPUAccount`. After the `consume(long)` method has returned, the thread will continue normal execution and upon the subsequent invocation of `consume()` the `aggregatedConsumption` will be taken into account. During bootstrapping a similar mechanism ensures that information concerning the CPU consumption is aggregated internally within the `aggregatedConsumption` field, as a `CPUManager` may not yet be available.

Details concerning the management of `CPUManager` objects, the association of `ThreadCPUAccount` with `CPUManager` objects, and of threads with `ThreadCPUAccount` objects are not in the scope of this paper. If J-RAF2 is used to integrate CPU management features into a Servlet or EJB container, the management of `CPUManager` objects is under the control of the container.

3.2   Bytecode Transformation Scheme

In order to make use of the new CPU accounting scheme, methods are rewritten in the following way:

1. Insertion of conditionals in order to invoke the `consume()` method periodically. The rationale behind these rules is to minimize the number of checks whether `consume()` has to be invoked for performance reasons, but to make sure that malicious code cannot execute an unlimited number of bytecode instructions without invocation of `consume()`. The conditional "`if (cpu.consumption >= 0) cpu.consume();`" is inserted in the following locations (the variable `cpu` refers to the `ThreadCPUAccount` of the currently executing thread):

(a) In the beginning of each loop.
(b) In the beginning of each JVM subroutine. This ensures that the conditional is present in the execution of recursive JVM subroutines.
(c) In the beginning of each exception handler.
(d) In the beginning of each method/constructor. This ensures that the conditional is present in the execution of recursive methods. For performance reasons, the insertion in the beginning of methods may be omitted if each possible execution path terminates or passes by an already inserted conditional before any method/constructor invocation (invokeinterface, invokespecial, invokestatic, invokevirtual). For instance, this optimization applies to leaf methods.
(e) In each possible execution path after $MAXPATH$ bytecode instructions, where $MAXPATH$ is a global parameter passed to the bytecode rewriting tool. This means that the maximum number of instructions executed within one method before the conditional is being evaluated is limited to $MAXPATH$. In order to avoid an overflow of the consumption counter, $MAXPATH$ should not exceed 2^{15} (see section 3.5 for an explanation).

2. The run() method of each class that implements the Runnable interface is rewritten according to table 6 in order to invoke consume() before the thread terminates. After the thread has terminated, its ThreadCPUAccount becomes eligible for garbage collection.

3. Finally, the instructions that update the consumption counter are inserted at the beginning of each accounting block, like in the old CPU accounting scheme. In order to reduce the accounting overhead, the conditionals inserted before are not considered as separate accounting blocks. The number of bytecode instructions required for the evaluation of the conditional is added to the size of the accounting block they precede.

Table 6. The rewritten run() method.

```
public void run(ThreadCPUAccount cpu) {
    try {...}
    finally {cpu.consume();}
}
```

3.3   Rewriting Example

Table 7 illustrates how the exemplary method of table 2 is transformed using the new CPU accounting scheme. We assume that the code block X includes a method invocation, hence the conditional at the beginning of the method cannot be omitted.

3.4   Exemplary CPUManager Implementations

The following tables 8 and 9 show simplified examples how the accounting information of multiple threads may be aggregated and used. Both CPUAccounting and

Table 7. Exemplary method rewritten according to the new CPU accounting scheme.

```
void f(ThreadCPUAccount cpu) {
   cpu.consumption += ...;
   if (cpu.consumption >= 0) cpu.consume();
   X;
   while (true) {
       cpu.consumption += ...;
       if (cpu.consumption >= 0) cpu.consume();
       if (C) {
           cpu.consumption += ...;
           Y;
       }
       cpu.consumption += ...;
       Z;
   }
}
```

CPUControl implement CPUManager and provide specific implementations of the consume(long) method. CPUAccounting supports the dynamic adaptation of the accounting granularity. The variable granularity is volatile in order to ensure that the consume() method of ThreadCPUAccount alyways reads the up-to-date value.

Note that the consume(long) method is synchronized, as multiple threads may invoke it concurrently. The CPUAccounting implementation simply maintains the sum of all reported consumption information, whereas the CPUControl implementation enforces a strict limit and terminates a component when its threads exceed that limit. In this example we assume that the component whose CPU consumption shall be limited executes within a separate isolate. This is a notional example, as the isolation API [10] is missing in current standard JVMs. More sophisticated scheduling strategies could, for instance, delay the execution of threads when their execution rate exceeds a given threshold. However, attention has to be paid in order to prevent deadlocks and priority inversions.

3.5 Scheduling Delay

The delay until a thread invokes the scheduling code (as a custom implementation of the consume(long) method of CPUManager) is affected by the following factors:

1. The current accounting granularity for the thread. This value is bounded by Integer.MAX_VALUE, i.e., $2^{31} - 1$.
2. The number of bytecode instructions until the next conditional C is executed that checks whether the consumption variable has reached or exceeded zero. This value is bounded by the number of bytecode instructions on the longest execution path between two conditionals C. The worst case is a method M of maximum length that consists of a series of invocations of a leaf method L. We assume that

Table 8. Exemplary CPUManager implementation: CPU accounting without control.

```java
public class CPUAccounting implements CPUManager {
   protected long consumption = 0;
   protected volatile int granularity;

   public CPUAccounting(int g) {granularity = g;}

   public int getGranularity() {
      return granularity;
   }

   public void setGranularity(int g) {
      granularity = g;
   }

   public synchronized long getConsumption() {
      return consumption;
   }

   public synchronized void consume(long c) {
      consumption += c;
   }
}
```

Table 9. Exemplary CPUManager implementation: CPU control.

```java
public class CPUControl extends CPUAccounting {
   private Isolate isolate;
   private long limit;

   public CPUControl(int g, Isolate i, long l) {
      super(g);
      isolate = i;
      limit = l;
   }

   public synchronized void consume(long c) {
      super.consume(c);
      if (consumption > limit) isolate.halt();
   }
}
```

L has $MAXPATH - 1$ bytecode instructions, no JVM subroutines, no exception handlers, and no loops. M will have the conditional C in the beginning and after each segment of $MAXPATH$ instructions, whereas C does not occur in L. During the execution of M, C is reached every $MAXPATH * (MAXPATH - 1)$ instructions, i.e., before $MAXPATH^2$ instructions.

Considering these two factors, in the worst case the `consume()` method of `ThreadCPUAccount` (which in turn will invoke the `consume(long)` method of `CPUManager`) will be invoked after each $(2^{31} - 1)$ 2 executed bytecode instructions. If 2^{15}, the `int` counter `consumption` in `ThreadCPUAccount` will not overflow, because the initial counter value is `-granularity` and it will not exceed 2^{30}, well below `Integer.MAX_VALUE`). Using recent hardware and a state-of-the-art JVM, the execution of 2^{32} bytecode instructions may take only a fraction of a millisecond, of course depending on the complexity of the executed instructions.

For a component with   concurrent threads, in total less than bytecode instructions are executed before all its threads invoke the scheduling function. If the number of threads in a component can be high, the accounting granularity may be reduced in order to achieve a fine-grained scheduling. However, as the delay until an individual thread invokes the scheduling code is not only influenced by the accounting granularity, it may be necessary to use a smaller value for   during the rewriting.

3.6 Preventing Malicious Manipulations of `ThreadCPUAccount` Objects

As the accounting code is spread throughout the application classes and libraries, the `consumption` counter of `ThreadCPUAccount` has to be `public`. Therefore, malicious code could try to explicitly reset this counter in order to hide its CPU consumption.

To prevent this kind of attack, our bytecode rewriting tool includes a special verifier that is able to ensure that a class does not use features of `ThreadCPUAccount` before it is being transformed. The verifier is executed before rewriting untrusted code. If untrusted code tries to access `ThreadCPUAccount`, the verifier rejects it and the code shall not be loaded into the JVM. For trusted code, the verifier is not executed, as trusted code may need to access functions of `ThreadCPUAccount` for management purpose.

The verifier checks the constant pool [11] of untrusted classes in order to ensure that the `ThreadCPUAccount` class is not referenced. This technique of extended bytecode verification, which can be implemented very efficiently, has been successfully used in the JavaSeal [14] and J-SEAL2 [2] mobile object kernels. Moreover, if malicious code is allowed to use reflection, a simple check can be inserted in `java.lang.Class` during the rewriting of the JDK in order to prevent malicious code from accessing the accounting internals by reflection.

4   Evaluation

In this section we present a brief overview of the benchmarks we have executed to validate our new accounting scheme. We ran the SPEC JVM98 benchmark suite [13] on a Linux RedHat 9 computer (Intel Pentium 4, 2.6 GHz, 512 MB RAM). For all settings, the entire JVM98 benchmark was run 10 times, and the final results were obtained by calculating the geometric means of the median of each sub-test. Here we present the

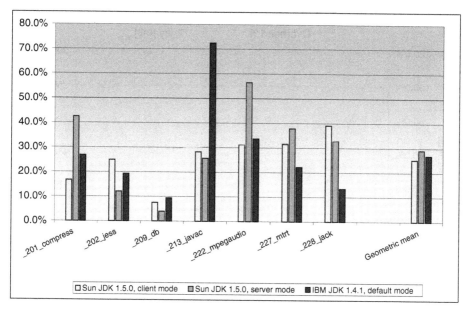

Fig. 1. Overheads due to CPU accounting in SPEC JVM98.

measurements made with the IBM JDK 1.4.1 platform in its default execution mode, as well as the Sun JDK 1.5.0 beta 1 platform in its 'client' and 'server' modes. In our test we used a single CPUManager with the most basic accounting policy, i.e., the one described in table 8, and with the highest possible granularity.

The most significant setting we measured was the performance of the rewritten JVM98 application on top of rewritten JDKs, and we found that the average overhead (execution time of modified code vs. execution time of unmodified code) was below 30% (see figure 1).

Another interesting measurement we made was to determine the impact of the choice of a granularity (see figure 2). The granularity has a direct influence on the responsiveness of the implementation w.r.t. the chosen management policy: the lower the granularity, the more frequently the management actions will take place. In our current implementation, and on the given computer, this interval is not measurable with granularities below 10,000,000 bytecode instructions. Another valuable lesson learned is that granularities of 100,000 and more exhibit practically the same level of overhead. The latter measurements were made exclusively on the 'compress' sub-benchmark of SPEC JVM98[4], hence the asymptotical values are slightly different from the above mentioned average overhead[5].

As a final remark, it should be emphasized that these results all correspond to a perfectly accurate accounting of executed bytecode instructions, which is a level of

---

[4] This was for simplicity, and 'compress' was chosen because it exhibits a performance which is usually closest to the overall average value.

[5] All performance measurements have an intrinsic imprecision of 2–3% depending on complex factors such as the load history of the test machine.

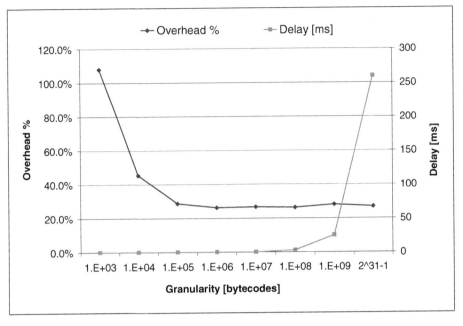

Fig. 2. Granularity versus overhead and delay.

precision not always necessary in practice. Currently, we are working on approximation schemes, which already enable us to reduce the overheads down to below 20%.

With the algorithms described here, the rewriting process takes only a very short time. For instance, rewriting the 20660 methods of the 2790 core classes of IBM JDK 1.4.1 takes less than one minute on our test machine. Each method is treated separately, but some algorithms could be enhanced with limited forms of interprocedural analysis. We do however not allow ourselves to do global analysis, as this might restrict the developer's freedom to extend classes gradually, and to load new sub-classes dynamically.

5   Conclusions

To summarize, the new CPU accounting scheme of J-RAF2 offers the following benefits, which make it an ideal candidate for enhancing Java server environments and mobile object systems with resource management features:

- Full portability. J-RAF2 is implemented in pure Java. In has been tested with several standard JVMs in different environments, including also the Java 2 Micro Edition [5].
- Platform-independent unit of accounting. A time-based measurement unit makes it hard to establish a contract concerning the resource usage between a client and a server, as the client does not exactly know how much workload can be completed within a given resource limit (since this depends on the hardware characteristics of the server). In contrast, using the number of executed bytecode instructions is

independent of system properties of the server environment. To improve accounting precision, various JVM bytecode instructions could be associated with different weights. At the moment, our implementation counts all instructions equally.

- Flexible accounting/controlling strategies. J-RAF2 allows custom implementations of the `CPUManager` interface.
- Fine-grained control of scheduling granularity. As described in section 3.5, the accounting delay can be adjusted; to some extend dynamically at runtime, to some extend during the rewriting process.
- Independence of JVM thread scheduling. The new CPU accounting scheme of J-RAF2 does not rely on thread priorities anymore.
- Moderate overhead. We have shown that the new CPU accounting scheme does not increase the overhead with respect to the old scheme. However, the new scheme brings many benefits, such as the independence of the JVM scheduling, or the prevention of overflows.

Concerning limitations, the major hurdle of our approach is that it cannot account for the execution of native code. We should also note that our evaluation was done without any optimizations to reduce the number of accounting sites. Work is in progress to provide a complete optimization framework, which allows to trade-off between accounting precision and overhead.

Acknowledgements

This work was partly financed by the Swiss National Science Foundation.

References

1. G. Back, W. Hsieh, and J. Lepreau. Processes in KaffeOS: Isolation, resource management, and sharing in Java. In *Proceedings of the Fourth Symposium on Operating Systems Design and Implementation (OSDI'2000)*, San Diego, CA, USA, Oct. 2000.
2. W. Binder. Design and implementation of the J-SEAL2 mobile agent kernel. In *The 2001 Symposium on Applications and the Internet (SAINT-2001)*, San Diego, CA, USA, Jan. 2001.
3. W. Binder and V. Calderon. Creating a resource-aware JDK. In *ECOOP 2002 Workshop on Resource Management for Safe Languages*, Malaga, Spain, June 2002. http://www.ovmj.org/workshops/resman/.
4. W. Binder, J. Hulaas, A. Villazón, and R. Vidal. Portable resource control in Java: The J-SEAL2 approach. In *ACM Conference on Object-Oriented Programming, Systems, Languages, and Applications (OOPSLA-2001)*, Tampa Bay, Florida, USA, Oct. 2001.
5. W. Binder and B. Lichtl. Using a secure mobile object kernel as operating system on embedded devices to support the dynamic upload of applications. *Lecture Notes in Computer Science*, 2535, 2002.
6. W. Binder and V. Roth. Secure mobile agent systems using Java: Where are we heading? In *Seventeenth ACM Symposium on Applied Computing (SAC-2002)*, Madrid, Spain, Mar. 2002.
7. G. Czajkowski and L. Daynes. Multitasking without compromise: A virtual machine evolution. In *ACM Conference on Object-Oriented Programming, Systems, Languages, and Applications (OOPSLA'01)*, Tampa Bay, Florida, Oct. 2001.

8. G. Czajkowski and T. von Eicken. JRes: A resource accounting interface for Java. In *Proceedings of the 13th Conference on Object-Oriented Programming, Systems, Languages, and Applications (OOPSLA-98)*, volume 33, 10 of *ACM SIGPLAN Notices*, pages 21–35, New York, USA, Oct. 18–22 1998. ACM Press.

9. J. Gosling, B. Joy, G. L. Steele, and G. Bracha. *The Java language specification*. Java series. Addison-Wesley, Reading, MA, USA, second edition, 2000.

10. Java Community Process. JSR 121 – Application Isolation API Specification. Web pages at http://jcp.org/jsr/detail/121.jsp.

11. T. Lindholm and F. Yellin. *The Java Virtual Machine Specification*. Addison-Wesley, Reading, MA, USA, second edition, 1999.

12. N. Suri, J. M. Bradshaw, M. R. Breedy, P. T. Groth, G. A. Hill, R. Jeffers, T. S. Mitrovich, B. R. Pouliot, and D. S. Smith. NOMADS: toward a strong and safe mobile agent system. In C. Sierra, G. Maria, and J. S. Rosenschein, editors, *Proceedings of the 4th International Conference on Autonomous Agents (AGENTS-00)*, pages 163–164, NY, June 3–7 2000. ACM Press.

13. The Standard Performance Evaluation Corporation. SPEC JVM98 Benchmarks. Web pages at http://www.spec.org/osg/jvm98/.

14. J. Vitek, C. Bryce, and W. Binder. Designing JavaSeal or how to make Java safe for agents. Technical report, University of Geneva, July 1998. http://cui.unige.ch/OSG/publications/OO-articles/ TechnicalReports/98/javaSeal.pdf.

Organizing Knowledge in a Semantic Web
for Pathology

Robert Tolksdorf and Elena Paslaru Bontas

Freie Universität Berlin, Institut für Informatik
AG Netzbasierte Informationssysteme, Takustr. 9, D-14195 Berlin, Germany
research@robert-tolksdorf.de, paslaru@inf.fu-berlin.de
http://www.robert-tolksdorf.de

Abstract. Digital pathology and telepathology allow for the extended
usage of electronic images for diagnostics, support or educational purposes in anatomical or clinical pathology. Current approaches have not
found wide acceptance in routine pathology, mainly due to limitations in
image retrieval. In this paper we propose a semantic retrieval system for
the pathology domain. The system combines text and image information and offers advanced content-based retrieval services for diagnosis,
differential diagnosis and teaching tasks. At the core of the system is a
Semantic Web gathering both ontological domain knowledge and rules
describing key tasks and processes in pathology.

1   Introduction

Digital pathology and telepathology intend to extend the usage of electronic
images for diagnostic support or educational purposes in anatomical or clinical pathology. The advantages of these approaches are generally accepted and
several applications are already available. Nevertheless, none of the available
applications has found wide acceptance for diagnostic tasks, mainly due to the
huge amount of data resulting from the digitalization process and the limitations
of image-based retrieval. In this paper we propose a *semantic* retrieval system
for the pathology domain. The system brings both text and image information
together and offers advanced content-based retrieval services for diagnosis, differential diagnosis and teaching tasks. At the core of the system there is a Semantic
Web-based knowledge base containing both ontological domain knowledge, and
rules describing key tasks and processes in pathology. The usage of *Semantic
Web* standards and domain ontologies facilitates the realization of a distributed
infrastructure for knowledge sharing and exchange.

The rest of this paper is organized as follows: The remaining introductory
sections present the setting of the project, telepathology (Section 1.1), and its
main ideas and features (Section 2). Section 3 provides an insight into the technical aspects of the retrieval system by enumerating the technical requirements
and the associated system architecture, followed by a detailed description of
the system components. At this point we will present our achievements and the
challenges we are currently confronted with in the realization of the main com-

M. Weske and P. Liggesmeyer (Eds.): NODe 2004, LNCS 3263, pp. 39–54, 2004.
© Springer-Verlag Berlin Heidelberg 2004

ponents. Section 4 delimits our approach from related research efforts in this domain, while Section 5 is dedicated to future work.

1.1 Telepathology

Telepathology is a key domain in telemedicine. By using telepathology approaches like virtual microscopy, pathologists analyze high quality digital images on a display screen instead of conventional glass slides with the common microscope. Such digital images are taken by a camera attached to the microscope and stored for retrieval and reuse (with or without textual annotations) in a database or directly in a patient record.

Health care information systems, which store and integrate information and coordinate actions among health care professionals, have been realized at various places in the last decades. New developments in telemedicine allow medical personnel to remotely deliver health care to the patient. At the Charité Institute of Pathology in Berlin, the first web-based virtual microscope allows histological information to be evaluated, transferred, and stored in digital format [16, 15]. This technique offers significant advantages compared to the classical approach, by supporting communication and exchange among professionals not sharing the same workplace location and improving quality assurance mechanisms. However, to realize a complete computer-based infrastructure for pathology, one needs not only advanced support in the management of digital images. There is a need for a more efficient integration of the medical reports, which are produced by pathologists to describe their observations from analyzing the slides at the microscope.

Common information systems in pathology restrict their retrieval capabilities to automatic picture analysis and ignore corresponding medical reports. Such analysis algorithms have the essential drawback that they operate exclusively on structural – or syntactical – parameters such as color, texture and basic geometrical forms while ignoring the real content and the actual meaning of the pictures. Medical reports, however, contain much more than that since they are textual representations of the picturally represented *content* of the slides. By that they capture *implicitly* the actual semantics of what the picture graphically represents, for example "a tumor" in contrast to "a red blob" or "a co-located set of red pixels". In the project described in this paper, we take the semantics aspects a step further: We interpret the reports as semantic high-quality image metadata prepared by human experts. We use ontology-based text processing algorithms to make the semantic content *explicit* and build a system that takes advantage of the explicitly represented knowledge.

2 A Semantic Web for Pathology

The project "Semantic Web for Pathology"[1] aims to realize a Semantic Web-based text and picture retrieval system for lung pathology. For this purpose we

[1] The project "Semantic Web in the Pathology" is funded by the Deutsche Forschungsgemeinschaft, as a cooperation among the Charité Institute of Pathology, the Institute for Computer Science at the FU Berlin and the Department of Linguistics at the University of Potsdam, Germany.

concentrate our efforts in three interrelated directions: 1) the construction of a *knowledge base*, 2) the development of *knowledge reuse algorithms* and of a 3) *semantic annotation schema* for medical reports and digital histological images.

The knowledge base contains domain ontologies, generic ontologies and rules. Domain ontologies are used for the machine-processable representation of pathological knowledge, while generic ontologies capture common sense knowledge that can be useful in knowledge-intensive tasks. Several very complex libraries of ontologies are already available for this purpose. While ontologies model the background knowledge of the pathologists, the rules are used to describe the decision processes using this knowledge: diagnostics, microscope analysis, observations etc. The acquisition of such rules, which play a crucial role for the retrieval, will be accomplished through intensive collaboration with domain experts. Further on, we analyze the textual data with text processing algorithms and annotate it with concepts from the knowledge base in order to improve precision and recall in retrieval operations. The annotation scheme is harmonized with the pathology knowledge base by using the corresponding medical ontologies as controlled vocabulary for the annotations.

2.1   Main Features

We foresee several valuable uses of the planned system in routine pathology. First, it may be used as an assistant tool for diagnosis tasks. Since knowledge is made explicit, it supports new query capabilities for diagnosis tasks: similarity or identity of cases based on semantic rules and medical ontologies, differential diagnosis, semantically precise statistical information about occurrences of certain distinguishing criteria in a diagnosis case. The provided information will be very valuable in diagnosis work especially for the under-diagnosed cases, since such situations require deeper investigation of the problem domain and a very strict control mechanism for the diagnosis quality [5]. Second, advanced retrieval capabilities may be used for educational purposes by teaching personnel and students. Currently, enormous amounts of knowledge are lost by being stored in data bases, which are behaving as real data sinks. They can and should be used for teaching, eg. for case-based medical education. The retrieval and reuse of the stored information is limited to string matching techniques and requires technical know-how of the underlying storage system (e.g. query language, relational scheme). Besides, the link between pathology reports and the corresponding digital slides is currently not available. Third, quality assurance and checking of diagnostic decisions can be assured more efficiently because the system uses axioms and rules to automatically check consistency and validity. Finally, explicit knowledge can be exchanged with external parties like other hospitals. The representation within the system is already the transfer format for information. Semantic Web technologies are by design open for the integration of knowledge that is relative to different ontologies and rules. Therefore we intend to use mainly such technologies for the realization of the retrieval system.

2.2   Use Cases and Technical Requirements

The technical analysis and design of the pathology retrieval system is closely related to typical usage scenarios, which are not necessarily related to routine pathology. The system will be used in all probability for under-diagnosed cases, where a second or third opinion is to be consulted or the specialist usually reverts to certified control sources, like the Internet or printed material. Such information sources have a significant drawback: they offer limited capabilities for a thematically focused search. Both manual search within printed materials and Internet search, based on common or even medicine-related search engines, is time-consuming and not specific enough to be integrated into everyday pathology. Instead, our system offers the possibility to search the archive of medical reports for similar cases or differential diagnoses (retrieve findings with similar symptoms but different diagnoses). It is improbable that the system will be consulted for routine cases, covering approximately 80 percent of the total archive, which are analyzed on the fly by the pathologists without the need for additional information sources.

The acceptance of the system is strictly related to its "minimal invasive" character: it should not imply any change to the current work flows[2] and should achieve good precision results. Recall is also important but since the two parameters are usually contradictory, we favor precision because of the predominant usage of the system for under-diagnosed cases within which every detail may play an important role for the final results. The minimal invasive feature will be reflected in a careful design of intuitive user interfaces and query language.

Another important setting is teaching: therefore, the system should be able to generate different reference materials and to retrieve information about typical pathology cases and their diagnosis. The key feature for the second scenario is the flexibility to generate and present domain information.

The network aspect is important for both settings. Pathologists use the system for cases where they need the remote collaboration of other specialists. The teaching scenario also assumes a distributed infrastructure, so that the resources can be accessed anytime, anywhere. The usage of Semantic Web technologies on one hand, and of standards like XML/OWL and the medical HL7/DICOM on the other, are conditions for the realization of this requirement.

Scalability and performance are critical factors for the acceptance of the retrieval system. In our application, the amount of image data is impressive. Every particular case contains up to 10 medical reports. Each of these are based on up to 50 digital histological images, each of them with a size of 4-5 GB. Our first prototypical implementation of the system deals with approximately 700 reports and a part of the corresponding digitised slides. The storage of images will still be subject to the use of specialized image databases. Our approach of resorting to the description of images contained in the reports and their processing in the system makes the requirements on scalability with the number and complexity of cases independent of the size of the image data. There is no image

---

[2] The system should be integrated into available digital pathology projects, like the Digital Virtual Microscope (see Section 1.1).

processing foreseen, instead we use the result of the image analysis performed by human experts, the pathologists. Remaining scalability and performance issues are affected by the quality of the underlying Semantic Web components and the complexity of models used and inferences drawn therein. Currently, there are strong efforts to produce Semantic Web components with industrial strength, such as inference engines that go beyond the poor performance of early research prototypes. Our system will benefit from this performance gain in the infrastructure. The complexity of models, rules and queries triggering inferences remains a critical issue. While we have a substantial basis of models with existing standards it is not yet clear , what heuristics should guide the selection of the granularity of models to be eventually used and of the details of rules to be applied when reporting "similar" cases. Therefore we restrict ourselves to small models and rulesets that generate sufficiently precise answers by the system with minimal inferencing effort. The precise methodology for doing so is presented in 3.2.

3   Engineering the System

Technically the system relies on Semantic Web technologies. The Semantic Web [1] aims to provide automated information access based on machine-processable semantics of data. The first steps in this direction have been made through the realization of appropriate representation languages for Web knowledge sources like RDF(S) and OWL and the increasing dissemination of ontologies, that provide a common basis for annotation and support automatic inferencing for knowledge generation.

Our approach makes use of these Semantic Web technologies in order to represent pathological knowledge explicitly and, consequently refine the retrieval algorithms on a semantic level: medical and generic ontologies are integrated into a pathology knowledge base, which serves also as an annotation vocabulary for medical reports and histological images. We use OWL/RDF(S) for the representation of the knowledge base and for the annotation of the information items and XML-based medical standards like HL7/CDA[3] for the reports.

In medicine and biology exhaustive domain ontologies have been developed and are constantly incorporating new pieces of knowledge. Ontologies like UMLS[4], GALEN[5], Gene Ontology [4] provide a good basis for the development of Semantic Web applications for medicine purposes. These ontologies are therefore used as the initial knowledge base of the semantical retrieval system for pathology. In addition, to put our goals into practice we still need to integrate the individual domain knowledge sources and to adapt them to the requirements of the Semantic Web, which means in the first place to formalize them in a Semantic Web representation language. We address the main issues w.r.t. available medical ontologies and the concrete formalization in detail in Section 3.2.

---

[3] HL7: http://www.hl7.org
[4] http://www.nlm.nih.gov/research/umls
[5] http://www.opengalen.org

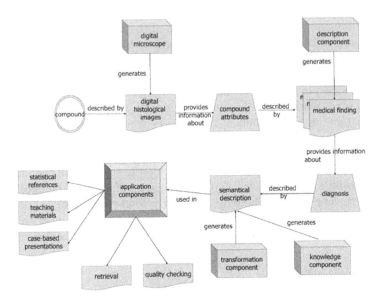

Fig. 1. System architecture "Semantic Web for Pathology"

3.1 System Architecture

The system architecture, which has arisen from the use cases and the corresponding technical requirements (Figure 1) consists of four main components: a description component, a knowledge component, a transformation component and application components.

The core of the system architecture is the knowledge component, which consists of domain and generic ontologies, as well as a rule engine. The description component allows the XML encoding of the textual and pictural data. Both the available pathology data base at the Charité hospital and data to be generated are described in XML in this manner. The transformation component takes the XML-structured data set, analyzes it linguistically and semantically and integrates it within the semantic network underlying the knowledge component. Due to the application-oriented character of the system, special attention in the architecture is paid to the application components, which implement the functionality of the system as presented in Section 2. The search component is used both by pathologists in order to retrieve information concerning diagnosis tasks or by teaching personnel and students. We plan also a component for the generation of statistical evaluations (e.g. related to the most frequent disease symptoms, relationships between patient data and disease evolution etc.) and for the generation of case-oriented teaching materials and presentations (see Figure 1). The quality checking service is intended to evaluate the consistency of medical reports.

3.2   Main Components

The Description Component. The description component is concerned with the basic formalization of medical reports and digital histological images. For this purpose it deals with two principal data sources: data, which is already available at the Institute of Pathology at the Charité hospital and future data. The goal of this process is to offer a homogeneous encoding of medical reports, on one side and picture annotations on the other side, both for existent and future material. The data should be first encoded in XML and subsequently analyzed using ontology-enhanced text analysis algorithms in order to be annotated with ontology concepts. For the generation of new XML-based information we developed an editor tool, which can be integrated in the actual version of the Digital Virtual Microscope [16, 15]. By means of this tool pathologists can analyze digitized histological images and simultaneously enter or update the corresponding medical report, which are subsequently stored in a XML data base. The second source of raw data was naturally the medical reports archive at the Charité. The medical reports of this type have been extracted from their primary text-oriented storage and transformed in XML.

We developed a HL7/CDA compatible XML scheme for the medical reports, which reflects the logical structure of the data. Such medical data is organized consequently more or less in four major parts:

- **macroscopy** describing physical properties and the appearance of the original compound.
- **microscopy** concerned with the detailed description of the slides analyzed at the microscope.
- **diagnosis** summarizing the conclusions and the diagnosis.
- **comments** usually presenting additional facts playing a role in the diagnosis argumentation (patient data, patient history etc.) or an alternative diagnosis for ambiguous cases.

Additionally, such a medical report contains information from the patient record and references to digital images. The connection to the digital images is fundamental for efficient retrieval, which should contain apart from the relevant textual information the corresponding image region the pathologist refers to in a certain portion of text. Since the size of such images is 4-5 GB, it is not sufficient to retrieve complete images to a certain user query, but the concrete image sector. For this purpose we use the functionality of the virtual digital microscope, which allows digital slides to be annotated with so-called "observation paths" on one hand, and register an additional "dictation path" on the other. The observation path contains image coordinates, image resolution and time stamps registered while the pathologist was analyzing a specific digital image. The dictation path sums up the same data, this time registered while the pathologist was typing the medical report. The complete path-related information flows into the "diagnosis path", which mirrors the way the diagnosis decision was accomplished. A fragment of a XML-encoded medical report is presented in Figure 2.

The proposed XML scheme reconstructs the structure of the real medical reports and is HL7-compatible. Though the compatibility restricts the format

```
<?xml version="1.0" encoding="ISO-8859-1" standalone="no" ?>
<levelone xmlns="urn::hl7-org/cda"
xmlns:sciphox="urn::sciphox-org/sciphox"
xmlns:xsi="http://www.w3.org/2001/XMLSchema-instance"
xsi:schemaLocation="urn::hl7-org/cda sciphox-cda.xsd"
xmlns:swpatho="urn::swpatho-org">
<clinical_document_header>
...
<local_header ignore="all" descriptor="swpatho">
<swpatho:swpatho-ssu type="Kostentraeger" country="de" version="v1">
<swpatho:Kostentraegerbezeichnung V="CHA"/></swpatho:swpatho-ssu>
<swpatho:swpatho-ssu type="Schreibkraft" country="de" version="v1">
<swpatho:Schreibkraftkuerzel V="SKFX"/></swpatho:swpatho-ssu>
<swpatho:swpatho-ssu type="E-Nummer" country="de" version="v1">
<swpatho:E-Nummer V="E01152-01"/></swpatho:swpatho-ssu>
</local_header>
...
</clinical_document_header>
<body>
 <section><caption>Befund</caption>
  <section><caption>Makroskopie</caption>
    <paragraph><content>Zwei Gewebszylinder von 15 und 4 mm Laenge.
    </content></paragraph>
  </section>
  <section><caption>Mikroskopie</caption>
    <coded_entry><coded_entry.value V="5" S="UID" /></coded_entry>
    <coded_entry><coded_entry.value V="6" S="PID" /></coded_entry>
    <coded_entry><coded_entry.value V="Feb 09 13:53:16 CET 2004"
    S="StartTime"/></coded_entry>
    <coded_entry><coded_entry.value V="Feb 09 13:53:18 CET 2004"
    S="StopTime"/></coded_entry>
    <paragraph><content>Stanzbiopsate aus Lungengewebe mit
    deutlicher Stoerung der alveolaren  Textur, soweit noch
    nachweisbar deutlich Verbreiterung der Alveolarsepten,
    stellenweise Nachweis von Bronchialepithelregeneraten.
    Restliche Alveolarlumina z.T. durch Fibroblastenproliferate
    verlegt...</content></paragraph>
  </section>
  <section><caption>Kritischer_Bericht</caption>
    <paragraph><content>Stanzbiopsate aus der Lunge mit Zeichen der
    organisierenden Pneumonie (klin. Mittellappen).</content></paragraph>
  </section>
  <section><caption>Kommentar</caption>
    <paragraph><content>...Im vorliegenden Material kein Anhalt
    fuer eine Lymphom-Manifestation. Kein Karzinom.</content></paragraph>
  </section>
 </section>
</body>
</levelone>
```

Fig. 2. Fragment of a medical report in XML

of the XML reports (the information must be encoded within "section", "paragraphs" and "coded_entry" tags, which is not necessarily the most straight forward manner of formalizing it), it is an important issue, especially for the distributed setting, for the exchange and reuse of information.

The Knowledge Component. The knowledge component includes the medical knowledge base and the algorithms for the realization of the applications. As initial input we used UMLS, as the most complex medical thesaurus currently available. UMLS as in the actual release contains over 1,5 million concepts from over 100 medical libraries and is permanently growing. New sources and actual versions of already integrated sources are permanently mapped to the UMLS knowledge format. Due to the complexity of the thesaurus and the limitations of current Semantic Web tools we need to customize the available medical collection w.r.t. to two important axes: the identification of relevant libraries and concepts corresponding to "lung pathology" from UMLS and their adaption to the particularities of language and vocabulary of the case report archive.

This two-phase approach is justified by the application-oriented character of the system. We do not intend to build a general Semantic Web knowledge base for pathology, or even lung pathology, but one, which is tailored for and can be efficiently used in our application setting. Despite standards and tools for the main technologies, building concrete Semantic Web applications, their potential and acceptance at a larger scale is still a challenging issue for the Semantic Web research community.

Identifying Relevant Knowledge in UMLS. The straight-forward method to address this issue is to use the UMLS Knowledge Server[6], which provides the MetamorphoSys tool and an additional API to tailor the thesaurus to specific application needs. However, both allow mainly syntactical filtering methods (e.g. exclude complete UMLS sources, exclude languages or term synonyms) and do not offer means to analyze the semantics of particular libraries or to use only relevant parts of them. We adopted two approaches to overcome this problem.

– *Top-down Approach.* The aim of the top-down approach was to restrict the huge amount of medical information from UMLS to the domain "pathology". For this purpose, we consulted a team of domain experts (pathologists), who identified potential relevant UMLS libraries. However, the complexity and content heterogeneity (most of the libraries contain concepts belonging to different medicine specialities) of the particular libraries made a manual identification difficult and inefficient. Approximately 50 percent of the UMLS libraries have been selected as possible relevant for lung pathology, containing more than 500000 concepts. Managing an ontology of such dimensions with Semantic Web technologies is related to unsolved issues w.r.t. to scalability and performance of the system. Besides, building the knowledge base implies also a subsequent adaptation of the content, performed by domain

---

[6] UMLS Knowledge Source Server: http://umlsks.nlm.nih.gov

experts, that should be able to evaluate and modify the ontology. Therefore, besides technical drawbacks, an ontology of such complexity can not be used efficiently by humans as well.

– *Bottom-up Approach.* In the second approach we used the case reports archive to identify concepts, which actually occur in medical reports (i.e. are really used by pathologists while putting down their observations and therefore will also occur as search parameters). For this purpose we used a retrieval engine mapping a lexicon representing the vocabulary of the reports archive to the content of the UMLS sources. The lexicon containing the most frequent nominal phrases was the result of the lexical analysis of the medical reports (in German). The lexicon was subsequently translated to English (due to the restricted set of German terms within UMLS: e.g. from 500000 concepts only 12000 have corresponding German translations in the actual version 2003AC of UMLS) and compared to UMLS. The result of this task was a list of 10 UMLS libraries, still containing approximately 350000 different concepts. The size of the concept set can be explained if we consider the fact that the UMLS knowledge is concentrated in several major libraries (e.g. MeSH[7], SNOMED98[8]), which cover important parts of the complete thesaurus and therefore contain most of the concepts in our lexicon. To differentiate among the derived libraries we mapped in a second step 10 central concepts in lung anatomy and extracted similar or related concepts from UMLS sources. A total of approximately 400 concepts describing the anatomy of the lung served as initial input for the domain ontology.

Adapting the Ontology to the Application Domain. The linguistic analysis of the patient report corpus proved the content-related limitations of UMLS. Comparing the results of the lexical analysis with the UMLS content, we recognize some possible extension directions for our ontology: properties like solid, colour, unary predicates and generic properties and concepts: length, diameter, space, spacial objects and their relations. Domain-specific extensions are also revealed through a comparison of the corpus-based lexicon and the generated ontology. For this purpose we modelled additional pathology-specific concepts, like the components and typical core content of a medical report, and integrate them in the available ontology.

OWL Representation. The next important issue after identifying an initial set of relevant concepts is the transformation of the raw UMLS data in a Semantic Web formalization, like RDF(S) or OWL. Our analysis in the application domain has revealed the necessity of a powerful representation language, which can capture most of the semantical features of the medical knowledge. For this purpose we will use mostly OWL instead of RDF(S) because of its expressiveness and inferencing capabilities.

Medicine ontologies, despite containing a huge amount of concepts or terms, have seldom been developed for machine processing but rather as controlled

---

[7] Medical Subject Headings: http://www.nlm.nih.gov/mesh/meshhome.html
[8] Snomed Information: http://www.snomed.org

vocabularies and taxonomies for specific tasks in medicine [14]. UMLS distinguishes between two data models, which are closely interrelated: The UMLS Semantic Network, containing generic medicine concepts ("semantic types") and relations ("semantic relations"), and the UMLS Metathesaurus. The last one incorporates libraries, like Gene Ontology, SNOMED or MeSH, and consists of "UMLS concepts" referencing semantic types and UMLS relations partially mapped to semantic relations. From a strict Semantic Web point of view UMLS proved to be deficiently designed and incomplete. Apart from the absence of an at least Semantic Web compatible representation language, it adopts an error-prone modeling style, which is characterized by few semantic relations among concepts and an ambiguous way to interpret such relations (e.g. concepts of the UMLS Metathesaurus are connected through relations like "related", "broader", "narrower", "similar", "other-related"). A typical example is the usage of the relation "is-a" for both instantiation and specialization/generalization, the usage of a unique "part-of" relation with different meanings ("functional part", "content", "component", "substance") or the usage of one of these relations instead of the other. Mathematical properties of the same semantical relation (e.g. transitivity) are not fulfilled for each pair of concepts connected by the relation and the "is-a" relation between two concepts does not always guarantee the inheritance of the properties of the parent concept to its children.

We generated a core domain ontology in OWL based on the original UMLS knowledge base. From a modelling perspective, we model each UMLS concept as an OWL class, save associated definitions and alternative concept names (so-called UMLS Terms and UMLS Strings) with language specification (German and English) and relate it to the corresponding UMLS sources. We also map UMLS relations with a specified meaning to range restrictions on the corresponding concepts and cumulate fuzzy relations like "synonyms", "related", "other-related" etc. to a generic "related_to" relationship. We leave additional details about the modelling primitives to another paper. This way the generated ontology is the result of a partial direct mapping from the UMLS thesaurus. The UMLS Semantic Network was also formalized in OWL since every UMLS concept is connected to it. After an automatic discovery of the (logical) inconsistencies of the model, we are currently working on a methodology for the semi-automatic adaptation of the OWL ontology in order to correct these errors and to include pathology-specific knowledge, like frequently-used concepts from texts not supported by UMLS.

The Transformation Component. The transformation component is closely related to the knowledge component and implements features required for the text-based processing of the medical reports and image descriptions [12]. For this purpose we are developing a noun phrasing module, which identifies domain-specific phrases from medical reports. The module incorporates a tokenizer, a tagger and a ontology-based phrase generator. The phrase generation process interacts with the knowledge base, since it uses medical ontologies to identify relevant (multi-word) phrases and in the same time puts together a lexicon, tailored for the particular application setting: the domain of lung pathology and the language used in the medical reports, which is German. The lexicon also provides indications of the usage limitations of an essentially English-oriented thesaurus like UMLS in our concrete setting. The case reports are annotated by means of text processing with concepts from the knowledge base/ontology. Therefore the linguistic component needs to recognize concepts and their characteristics, relations among concepts from text. The result of these procedure is an intermediate logical representation (see Figure 4 for an example representation of the XML fragment report from Figure 3). As a result of the phrasing module, the XML-encoded medical reports contain semantically relevant phrases, which can be referenced to concepts of the knowledge base.

```
<section><caption>Befund</caption>
 <section><caption>Makroskopie</caption>
  <paragraph><content>[1]Zwei Gewebszylinder von 15 und 4 mm Laenge[1].
  </content></paragraph>
 </section>
 <section><caption>Mikroskopie</caption>

  ...

  <paragraph><content>[2]Stanzbiopsate aus Lungengewebe mit
  deutlicher Stoerung der alveolaren  Textur, soweit noch
  nachweisbar deutlich Verbreiterung der Alveolarsepten,
  stellenweise Nachweis von Bronchialepithelregeneraten[2].
  [3]Restliche Alveolarlumina z.T. durch Fibroblastenproliferate
  verlegt[3]. [4]Im Interstitium ein gemischt entzuendliches
  Infiltrat, bestehend aus Plasmazellen und Lymphozyten[4].
  [5]Darunter relativ viele CD3-positive kleine und mittelgrosse
  T-Lymphozyten und CD68-positive Makrophagen[5].</content></paragraph>
 </section>
 <section><caption>Kritischer_Bericht</caption>
  <paragraph><content>[6]Stanzbiopsate aus der Lunge mit Zeichen der
  organisierenden Pneumonie (klin.Mittellappen)[6].</content></paragraph>
 </section>
 <section><caption>Kommentar</caption>...</section>
</section>
```

Fig. 3. Input of the transformation component

The logical forms produced by the parser are transformed into OWL-compliant representations. This process is fairly straightforward, as should be clear from comparing the intermediate representation in Figure 4 with the target representation in Figure 5[9]. The algorithms create unique identifiers for concept instances and takes into account plural entities by generating several separate instances of the same concept. Appropriateness conditions for properties are applied: if a property is not defined for a certain type of entity, the analysis is rejected.

---

[9] Every medical report will be formalized in OWL as instances. The corresponding concepts are modelled separately (as classes).

```
[1]card(x1, 2) AND cylinder(x1) AND length(x1, [15, 14])
[2]unspec_plur_det(x2) AND punch_biopsat(x2)
        AND from_rel(x2, x3) AND unspec_plur_det(x3) AND lung_tissue(x3)
        AND with_rel(x3, x4) AND def_det(x4) AND disturbance(x4, x5)
        AND def_det(x5) AND texture(x5) AND alveolar(x5)
    unspec_det(x6) AND extension(x6, x7) AND def_det_plur(x7)
        AND aleveolar_septum(x7) AND unspec_det(x8) AND evidence(x8, x9)
        AND indef_det(x9) AND epithelial(x9) AND bronchial(x9)
        AND regenerates(x9)
[3]def_det(x10) AND alveolarlumina(x10)
    unspec_det_plur(x11) AND fibrolastial_proliferate(x11)
[4]def_det(x12) AND interstitium(x12)
    indef_det(x13) AND inflammatory(x13) AND infiltrate(x13)
    AND consisting_of_rel(x13, x14) AND unspec_det_plur(x14)
    AND konj(x14, x15, x16) AND plasma_cell(x15) AND lymphocyte(x16)
[5]indef_det_plur(x17)  AND konj(x17, x18, x19) AND  t_lymphocyte(x18)
        AND cd68_positive(x19) AND macrophagus(x19)
[6]indef_det_plur(x20) AND punch_biopsate(x20) AND from_rel(x20, x21)
        AND def_det(x21) AND lung(x21) AND with_rel(x20, x22)
        AND evidence(x22, x23) AND def_det(x23) AND organising(x23)
        AND pneumonia(x23)
```

Fig. 4. Intermediate output of the transformation component

Application Components. The Semantic Web for Pathology will assist the following application components:

- **search component** will be used primarily for diagnosis tasks. It will allow not only the basic retrieval of text/image information items, but also support differential diagnosis tasks. The semantic retrieval is oriented towards several typical categories of queries:
  - **statistical queries** e.g. the probability/frequency of a particular carcinoma in a certain age group.
  - **matching queries** e.g. comparison of cases with common characteristics, text and image information to similar cases.
  - **image queries** e.g. cases containing images with certain content- or image-specific constraints.
  Additionally, the retrieval should be adapted to the characteristics of the pathology domain and involve issues like the diagnosis path. (see Section 3.2).
- **quality checking component** will be used in quality assurance and management of diagnosis processes. Quality criteria, diagnosis standards and their verification are expressed by means of rules.
- **statistical component** will generate statistical material related to the relative frequency or demographic distribution of diseases and their complications.
- **teaching component** will generate teaching materials, using features of the previous components (statistical studies, reference cases)

```
. . . .
<Lung_Tissue rdf:ID="lung_tissue_x3">
   <partOf>
     <Lung_C0024109 rdf:ID="lung1">
       <hasSource rdf:resource="umlssources.owl#UWDA"/>
       ... properties of the lung ...
     </Lung_C0024109>
   </partOf>
 </Lung_Tissue>
 <Punch_biopsat rdf:ID="punch_biopsat_x2">
   <from rdf:resource="#lung_tissue_x3"/>
 </Punch_biopsat>
 <alveola rdf:ID="alveola_x5">
  <hasTexture rdf:datatype="http:/.../XMLSchema#string">disturbed</hasTexture>
  <relatedTo rdf:resource="#lung1"/>
 </alveola>
 <Cylinder rdf:ID="cylinder_x1">
    <length rdf:datatype="http://www.w3.org/2001/XMLSchema#float">15.0</length>
    <formOf rdf:resource="#punch_biopsat_x2">
 </Cylinder>
 <Cylinder rdf:ID="cylinder_x2">
    <length rdf:datatype="http://www.w3.org/2001/XMLSchema#float">14.0</length>
    <formOf rdf:resource="#punch_biopsat_x2">
 </Cylinder>
. . . .
```

Fig. 5. Fragment of the OWL output of the transformation component

4   Related Work

Medicine is one of the best examples of application domains where ontologies have already been deployed on a large scale and have already demonstrated their utility. Most of these domain ontologies (including UMLS) are based on different design requirements in comparison to computerized or more specific Semantic Web applications. They are actually huge collections of medical terms, organized in hierarchies and cannot be used directly in Semantic Web applications. This issue has been addressed in project GALEN, where the authors developed a special representation language, tailored for the particularities of the (English) medical vocabulary. However, the usage of a proprietary representation makes the ontological knowledge difficult to be extended by third parties or exchanged in a Semantic Web. The usage of ontologies for building knowledge bases for medicine has already been subject of several research projects [2, 13, 8, 3, 9]. The most important representatives are the ONIONS [8] and MEDSYNDIKATE [13] projects. In ONIONS the authors aim to develop a generic framework for ontology merging and use UMLS as an example to apply their methodology. Therefore they need a detailed analysis of the ontological properties of UMLS, using a Loom formalization. MEDSYNDIKATE is also confronted with the ontological commitment beyond UMLS in order to use it in text processing algorithms for knowledge discovery. UMLS serves in this case as an annotation vocabulary for medical texts. Both projects offer valuable experiences and facts concerning UMLS and medical ontologies generally, but they do not use Semantic Web technologies to facilitate knowledge share and reuse, which is the crucial feature of ontologies.

As outlined in Section 1 several systems for digital pathology and telepathology have been developed to extend the usage of digital images and networked systems in everyday pathology. Available retrieval systems basically rely on automatic image classification [6] and on algorithms concerning structural image characteristics e.g. colour, texture, patterns [6, 11, 17, 10]. Therefore they are able to retrieve similar images, but their content is not further considered. Some approaches also consider meta data annotations for images, which could be aligned to the UMLS standard [7]. However there is no available system or methodology for the development of a pathology-relevant retrieval system, which takes into account both textual and image information from a semantic perspective. The system we proposed in this paper will be able to represent the real meaning of the digital histological slides by correlating them with medical reports formalized in OWL.

5   Conclusions and Future Work

In this paper we presented our work towards a Semantic Web based retrieval system for pathology. The system is based on a comprehensive knowledge base, which formalizes pathology-relevant knowledge explicitly by integrating available medicine ontologies like UMLS and rules describing diagnostic guidelines. It is intended to provide both retrieval and knowledge management functionalities. In order to achieve these goals we adopted XML-based schemes for the uniform representation of medical reports and digital images and generated a prototype ontology for lung pathology based on UMLS knowledge sources and the lexical analysis of an archive of pathology medical reports. Current work includes the specification of algorithms for the semantical annotation of the medical reports, for the incremental enrichment of the core ontology and for the acquisition of domain-specific rules.

References

1. T. Berners-Lee, J. Hendler, and O. Lassila. The semantic web. *Scientific American*, 284(5):34–43, 5 2001.
2. A. Burgun and O.Bodenreider. Mapping the UMLS semantic network into general ontologies. In *Proc. of the AMIA Symposium*, 2001.
3. G. Carenini and J. Moore. Using the UMLS semantic network as a basis for constructing a terminological knowledge base: A preliminary report. In *Proceedings of 17th Symposium on Computer Applications in Medical Care (SCAMC '93)*, 1993.
4. The Gene Ontology Consortium. Gene ontology: tool for the unification of biology. *Nature Genetics*, 25:25–30, 2000.
5. F. Demichellis, V. Della Mea, S. Forti, P. Dalla Palma, and C.A. Beltrami. Digital storage of glass slide for quality assurance in histopathology and cytopathology. *Telemed Telecare*, 8(3):138–42, 2002.

6. E.A. El-Kwae, H. Xu, and M.R. Kabuka. Content-based retrieval in picture archiving and communication systems. *Journal of Digital Imaging*, 13(2):70–81, 2000.
7. T. Frankewitsch and U. Prokosch. Navigation in medical internet image databases. *Med Inform Internet Med*, 26(1):1–15, 2001.
8. A. Gangemi, D. M. Pisanelli, and G. Steve. An overview of the ONIONS project: Applying ontologies to the integration of medical terminologies. *Data Knowledge Engineering*, 31(2):183–220, 1999.
9. H. Gu, Y. Perl, J. Geller, M. Halper, L. Liu, and J. Cimino. Representing the UMLS as an OODB: Modeling issues and advantages, 2000.
10. M.E. Mattie, L. Staib, E. Stratman, H.D. Tagare, J. Duncan, and P.L. Miller. Pathmaster: Content-based cell image retrieval using automated feature extraction. *Journal of the AMIA*, 7(4):404–15, 2000.
11. H. Qi and W.E. Snyder. Content-based image retrieval in picture archiving and communications systems. *Journal of Digital Imaging*, 12(2 Suppl 1):81–3, 1999.
12. D. Schlangen, M. Stede, and E. Paslaru Bontas. Feeding OWL: Extracting and representing the content of pathology reports. In *to appear in Proc. NLPXML 2004*, 2004.
13. S. Schulz and U. Hahn. Medical knowledge reengineering - converting major portions of the UMLS into a terminological knowledge base. *International Journal of Medical Informatics*, 2001.
14. S. Schulz, M. Romacker, and U. Hahn. Knowledge engineering the UMLS. *Stud Health Technol Inform*, 77:701–5, 2000.
15. Patentanmeldung: Slide Scanner – Vorrichtung und Verfahren, 2002. Aktenzeichen 102 36 417.6 des DPMA vom 5.8.2002.
16. Patentanmeldung: Virtuelles Mikroskop – Vorrichtung und Verfahren, 2002. Aktenzeichen 102 25 174.6 des DPMA vom 31.05.2002.
17. James Z. Wang. Pathfinder: Multiresolution region-based Searching of Pathology Images using IRM. *Proc. of the AMIA Symp*, pages 883–7, 2000.

Listening to Agents – Transparent Representation and Presentation of Agent Communication in Mobile Systems

Matthias Jöst, Matthias Merdes, and Rainer Malaka

European Media Laboratory
Schloss-Wolfsbrunnenweg 31c
69118 Heidelberg
{Matthias.Joest,Matthias.Merdes,
Rainer.Malaka}@eml-d.villa-bosch.de

Abstract. In the research domain agent-based systems are widely used for mobile and distributed information systems. Their underlying paradigm provides
excellent mechanisms to isolate tasks in independent modules that can be reused and combined in multiple ways. In order to facilitate the communication
between such agents a common domain-knowledge needs to be collected and
stored in an ontology. This paper introduces an XML-based ontology representation for mobile multi-agent systems. A uniform XSLT-based mechanism that
allows for transforming agent communication into a format readable by human
users is presented. We show how the resulting combination of domain representation and presentation allows highly flexible agent systems where users interface agents can feed information from any service agent to the user or vice
versa and how this approach can be easily extended to take user- or context-
adaptive presentation strategies into account. Additionally, we describe how
these mechanisms are integrated into a prototypical mobile multi-modal tourist
information system and we present some evaluation results.

1 Introduction

As mobile computers and networks are getting more powerful, new and complex
multi-modal information systems enter the scene. Such information systems allow
users to interact naturally with many services in a flexible way and through a variety
of interface devices. A number of research initiatives such as the DARPA Communi-
cator in the US or European consortia aim at building systems that allow agent-based
access to a broad range of heterogeneous data and at providing multi-modal user interfaces [8][25]. These systems must be realized as distributed systems for two reasons. On the one hand, services are located on various hosts and, on the other hand,
components for advanced multi-modal systems such as language recognizers and
multi-modal presentation managers are too large to run on a mobile device. Moreover,
in order to allow for flexible systems, where new modalities or new services can easily be added, the architecture must be extensible.

Especially in the academic domain, agent-based technologies have been proposed
for these distributed systems. Software agents represent building blocks and encapsulate functionalities of software components. There are many aspects of agent-based

M. Weske and P. Liggesmeyer (Eds.): NODe 2004, LNCS 3263, pp. 55–68, 2004.
© Springer-Verlag Berlin Heidelberg 2004

systems such as social behavior or mobile code. However, here we want to focus on the aspect of service encapsulation and agent-human communication [12][17][22]. The agent-based software design is more flexible than other distributed architectures because of the ad-hoc integration of agents [13]. Agents are realized as independent entities that communicate with others in order to solve a problem. A knowledge representation, namely the respective agent ontology, is used as a structured model of the world knowledge necessary to communicate requests to and answers from agents [5][9]. The problem arises how this complex representation of world knowledge and agent interaction can be transformed into a suitable presentation for human users in a general and flexible way. This mapping from knowledge representation to content presentation is essentially a special question of computer-human interaction. In recent years information exchange in distributed systems based on the processing of XML documents has become a widely used mechanism. However, XML alone is only part of the solution for transparent representation and presentation of information in mobile, distributed multi-modal systems. In this paper we present a uniform mechanism, which represents complex agent communication using ontologies, and which transfers this information into user-perceivable forms. The created output can include various formats ranging from simple XHTML representations to more sophisticated formats, such as Scalable Vector Graphics – SVG or Extensible 3D Graphics – X3D. These formats can, in turn, be rendered appropriately in a standards-based Web-browsing engine.

We employed this mechanism within an application in the tourism domain. Tourism information systems pose high demands to a system with respect to information content, delivery, and presentation. Precursors in this domain were approaches in the CyberGuide [1] and Guide [3] projects but in contrast to their rather static system design with a fixed set of components and functionalities, we followed an agent approach. Especially multi-modal and mobile systems require a considerable number of different agents and a sophisticated communication language in order to allow for location-based services that use advanced interaction metaphors including natural language interaction. We integrated our representation and presentation mechanisms into an existing prototypical research system that realizes a mobile tourist information system for a famous historical city in Germany [16][17][27]. We could thus demonstrate that through this mechanism of XML-based processing throughout all layers of the system – from a user interface input and output to database query mechanisms – agent communication can be transformed into multi-modal information that is intelligible for humans.

In the following, we will first briefly present the underlying agent platform. After a more detailed description of the agent communication and its ontology as well as the XML-based representation formalism, we will then focus on the proposed paradigm for representing agent messages for agent-human interaction and its implementation in a content processing and presentation mechanism.

2   Agent Platform, Ontology, and Interaction

2.1   Agent Architecture

A number of agent platforms has been developed and proposed for mobile and distributed information systems. Among the most popular standards is the FIPA multi-agent standard (Foundation for Intelligent Physical Agents – http://www.fipa.org.). For our system, we use the agent platform RAJA [5] that is based upon FIPA OS and extends it with features of resource-adaptivity [4][7]. The architecture follows well-known multi-layer approaches with several levels of abstraction which can be found in a number of systems in similar ways [9][23][26]. All software components within the system are realized as software agents that reside on one of the three layers. Figure 1 gives a schematic overview of the overall system. The input and output layers on top are in charge of handling the interaction with the user by capturing the user input (either via pointing gesture or speech) and processing the system output. In the middle the planning layer with the Dialog Manager as main component is responsible for dispatching user requests to various service agents. Service agents in the bottom service layer are the foundation of the architecture and form the last link in the processing chain from the user request to database queries. The databases or information repositories themselves are wrapped by some service agents.

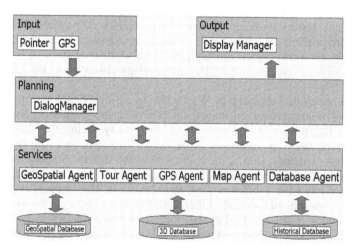

Fig. 1. Simplified system architecture. The software agents can be allocated to three schematic layers (In-/Output, Planning and Service).

The advantage of this very generic agent architecture is that it can be customized to various purposes and, depending on the particular task, some service agents can be integrated or left out and depending on a particular interaction paradigm, input and output agents can support the needed multi-modal forms of interaction.

Some typical agents used for location-based applications are the GeoSpatial Agent, the Tour Agent, the GPS agent, the Map Agent, and the Sights Agent. The GeoSpatial Agent handles all spatial requests, for example identifying objects in a certain region. The Tour Agent calculates sightseeing tours from a weighted network topology in which the edges and nodes are associated with preference values resulting from user profiles [10][14]. The GPS Agent locates the user based on coordinates received from GPS satellites, the Map Agent generates dynamic maps and the Sights Agent delivers textual description of sights and related images.

This small community of agents is a basis for a location-based service infrastructure in one city and can easily be extended by adding new agents that either specialize on the same sort of content but cover a different area, e.g., a GeoSpatial Agent for another city, or by new agents that bring in new content types such as cinema information. Brokers in the planning layer can then integrate information and negotiate with competing agents. In order to facilitate multi-modal interaction, other agents are specialized in processing natural language (NLP), i.e. analysis and generation.

2.2 Ontology as Means for Agent Communication

In general, agents communicate via a shared communication language. The most popular ones are the Knowledge Query and Messaging Language - KQML [9] resulting from the Knowledge Sharing Effort - KSE and the FIPA Agent Communication Language (ACL) [15]. Our system employs the FIPA – ACL that consist of several attributes like sender, receiver, communication type, and a content slot as the generic container for the message itself. The message content is expressed in terms of a system-wide ontology corresponding to the structural part of the world knowledge of the tourist and city history domains. It therefore comprises all real world objects and topics that are possible discourse topics of the agent community and the user. Moreover, not only the world objects are modeled, but also the operations on them and the resulting objects can be expressed. Thus the ontology covers all of the agents' capabilities.

One can classify this approach by Wache [26] as a Single Ontology Approach with the benefit of a straightforward implementation of agents supporting the ontology. Additionally it provides less/no semantic heterogeneity during the communication between agents. Its major drawback is the need for adaptation of the agents if the global ontology changes. Due to the restriction to the tourism domain it is not very difficult to find the minimal ontology commitment [11] even if the different components/agents might have a different view on the domain. The ontology is represented in an XML Schema and extends other formalizations such as the Geographical Markup Language (GML) defined by the OpenGIS Consortium (www.opengis.org) as well as the X3D (www.web3d.org) definition. It also contains the domain model and all actions and corresponding replies that can be handled by the different agents (as shown in Fig. 2). A single element in this repository is called Domain Model Object – DMO. Within the system the data-binding framework Castor (www.castor.org) is used to map XML representations to Java objects and vice versa.

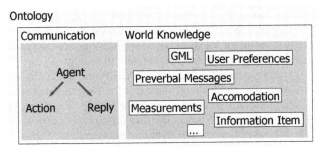

Fig. 2. Elements of the system ontology consisting of the agent communication and interaction and of the overall world knowledge of the system.

This relieves agent developers from low-level handling of XML parsing and generation and allows the direct programmatic manipulation of XML structures as Java objects. Furthermore it reduces the drawback of the single ontology approach. The fact that not only real world entities but also requests to agents such as database queries are modeled in the ontology is also advantageous in terms of flexibility and interoperability. The following example demonstrates these advantages using a database query DMO and the respective Database Agent.

Figure 3 illustrates a request action for a Database Agent. This agent can handle requests for specific objects, e.g. historic events or sights information, stored in the database whereas the XML-representation (shown as XML schema in Fig. 3) of such database requests is stored in the ontology. This representation can be transformed into a Java Class (Fig. 3 shown as UML notation) and be instantiated for a particular request with an Object ID or the name of the requested object and the type of information that should be delivered, for example images or textual descriptions. This flexibility is achieved by modeling the high-level concept of an information query in the ontology at the appropriate level of granularity, that is, without using unsuitable details specific for the database type used.

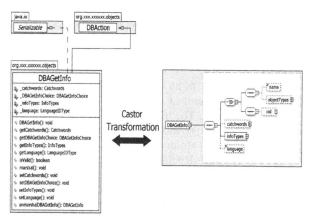

Fig. 3. Example of a DMO database request: As Java class (left) and XML schema (right).

The database DMO is essentially an abstract representation of a general database query. The Database Agent can map this abstract query to a concrete query suitable for a certain kind of persistence mechanism, in this case to a relational database system. As the ontological representation of the query abstracts from the type of the underlying database management system, it can easily support other kinds of database systems such as OODBMS or XML databases. This would only require replacing the Database Agent without the need to change the clients of the agent or the architecture of the system.

2.3   An Example of Agent Interaction: Location-Based Database Requests

We can now illustrate agent interaction on the basis of the introduced ontology. Fig. 2 presents an example of a sequence of agent actions incorporating the agents intro-

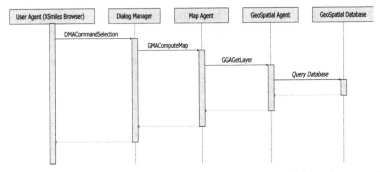

Fig. 4. Sequence diagram of internal system behavior. Communication between different agents.

duced above. The user clicks with a pointing device (such as a pen on PDAs) on a command button on her mobile device.

The GUI agent creates a *DMACommandSelection* DMO and sends it to the Dialog Manager. This agent transforms this DMO to a *GMAComputeMap* DMO that asks the Map Agent to render a map. Additionally, these DMOs contain the current position of the user in order to adapt the map extent to it. The Map Agent requests the map layers from the GeoSpatial Agent via the DMO *GGAGetLayer,* and finally the GeoSpatial Agent queries the spatial database.

The Map Agent renders the map as an image, encapsulates it into a DMO including further attributes like the map extent or highlighted locations, and returns it via the Dialog Manager to the GUI agent. The use of position information in the query is an example of a location-based query, or more general, a context-aware query. Note that all actions and content information are modeled as instances of the ontology.

This enables a flexible and high-level integration of agents into a complex system. In a larger system, broker agents would also be involved in order to negotiate service offers from competing agents and agents could also act independently in order to provide pro-active services. Moreover, in the following we will describe how the system can provide a means for context-sensitive (and other kinds of dynamic) adaptation of content.

3   Content Processing, Adaptation, and Presentation

The previous paragraphs introduced the mechanism of content and service representation. We now want to introduce the aspect of content presentation based on the ontology representation. The flexible representation of any object in the ontology is well suited for a mobile scenario. In the following, we introduce a mechanism that allows for displaying any agent communication on a user interface managed by a user interface agent running on a mobile client.

3.1   Content and Content Processing

An important issue for a mobile tourist information system is the provision of interesting content in a suitable way. Such a system should therefore exploit the full potential of mobile computers and make use of multimedia presentations in order to enhance the static content of travel books. Multimedia and multi-modal presentations incorporating images, maps, text, video, language etc. can be of great use in particular in mobile scenarios where users have more time constraints and need to capture information ad hoc and under distractive environmental conditions. Moreover, depending on the situation, some channels for information delivery might be useless or even harmful and alternative ways of information delivery must be used. A user who drives a car, for instance, must not read a text while driving but should use audible system output.

The content incorporated in our system covers multi-dimensional information of the city with her rich history including various different content types ranging from geographical/spatial information, images, and text components to three-dimensional views or animations of the ancient town. The geographical information, stored in a geo-spatial database (GIS), covers multiple information layers, from the street network to the more than 35 000 buildings of the city. Events and persons play a role in the city's past or even present, build an extensive network of relations. These are represented in a database covering over 2000 persons and more than 4000 descriptions. Naturally, this information has a strong relation to its spatial dimension stored in the geo-spatial database. Additionally, the historical database contains various image types ranging from current views of the city to historic copper engravings or paintings. Furthermore, there are animations available showing three-dimensional reconstructions of buildings no longer existing in today's townscape and producing a vivid impression of the ancient town.

All these various information sources can be combined to multi-modal presentations and, depending on the communicative goal, more or less media can be incorporated in a particular situation. The diversity of content ranging from simple images to complex 3D-models requires appropriate mechanisms to customize it according to various situations, clients, user contexts, etc. This is the task of a user interface agent that presents the content to the user on the mobile system. It has to forward requests to agents such as database queries by capturing pointing device user input and to deliver the results in an appropriate way. The agent makes heavy use of a GUI framework that was developed for this purpose.

The idea of this GUI framework is to provide an extensible Web-browsing framework, which supports many multimedia content types and allows content adaptation. It is based on the open-source XSmiles (www.xsmiles.org) multimedia browser frame-work [20][24]. This is a generic browser that supports a number of XML-based multimedia content types such as Extensible Hypertext Markup Language (XHTML), Synchronized Multimedia Integration Language (SMIL), Scalable Vector Graphics (SVG), Extensible 3D Graphics (X3D) and others. XSmiles supports a number of predefined user interface types for, e.g., desktop, PDA, TV, and future smart phone environments. As none of the predefined GUI components matches the requirements for our system perfectly, we developed a new one. The XSmiles framework allows an elegant integration of such a custom GUI via configuration files. It is possible to develop a new GUI without modifying the original XSmiles sources. This minimizes the efforts necessary for updates and will therefore facilitate future maintenance of the system and can easily be used in other applications in an analogous way.

The GUI component itself is designed as a plug-in container for so-called 'appearance plug-ins'. These appearance plug-ins are small and simple components, possibly even single classes that exist within the GUI component. They encapsulate the Look-

and-Feel of an application and make use of the browser functionality of the surrounding component. Our aim was to clearly separate the application-specific code such as controls for map manipulation from the generic support for browsing hyperlinked documents and rendering multimedia content.

Building the GUI framework on top of a standards-based browser framework not only minimizes the development efforts but also implies all the advantages of these standards such as openness, interoperability, and extensibility.

3.2 Flexible Content Presentation

The agent paradigm used here for a mobile system was chosen because of its flexibility and its extensibility. We introduced an XML-based ontology in order to represent all content and service functionality on a semantic level that abstracts from the implementation of services. Depending on the actual configuration of the agent system, agents can either be directly fed by the user with requests or be activated by other agents and agent output can be delivered to the user directly or through multiple further processing steps. Therefore, the goal of our paradigm of content representation and presentation is to allow for direct human-agent communication on any level of the system. Thus the user can 'listen' to the agents' conversation and all agent communication is completely transparent to a human witness. It should be noted that the paradigm of 'listening to agents' is to be understood on a conceptual rather than a physical level. In the actual configuration most agent interaction will not be piped through to the tourists, because details of the internal agent communication are only of interest for system debugging purpose. Rather agents act as autonomous entities that carry out their tasks according to their desires or intentions regardless of whether or not a user might be 'listening' and only at the end of the processing chain the result is transformed into a perceivable format.

The objects and services modeled in the ontology are rendered for humans using a translation entity that is associated with each concept in the ontology. All agent communication and its content in the ontology, i.e. the DMOs, are XML-based, which is not only beneficial in terms of openness and interoperability but also implies possibilities for further processing of this content using suitable tools for these standardized technologies.

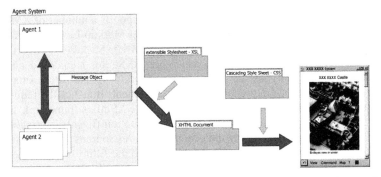

Fig. 5. Processing pipeline of the system content, from the agent message to the user interface via two steps.

In our GUI framework we employ the XSLT standard for transforming from one XML language into another in order to visualize the contents of agent messages. For the actual design of the presentation layer, a flexible, powerful, and maintainable solution is necessary that allows for easy extension of the system and allows adaptation strategies for various mobile scenarios. The software design strategy of separation of concerns (SOC) is a good means to define distinct responsibilities, clearly separate these, and finally map the detected responsibilities to entities such as components, engines, technologies, etc that solve the respective tasks.

In our case the relevant concerns are:

- Definition of content data
- Further selection/adaptation and layout of the content
- Definition of the rendering style comprising colors, font size, etc.

The definition of content data is the result of a database query and possibly further content-specific processing (such as rendering maps from spatial layers). It is contained in the content slot of an incoming message. The selection, ordering, and layout of the data are achieved by an XSLT style sheet transformation. Finally, the rendering style is encapsulated in a Cascading Style Sheet (CSS). This processing pipeline for multimedia content is illustrated in Figure 5. Note that this is the generic process for all types of query results, and more specifically that any media-specific processing of database query results (such as rendering of layers of spatial information as maps) is not shown. One of the benefits of this approach is the fact that content-adaptation and presentation of the different types of database results can be treated in a uniform way, independently of the type of content and type of underlying data source.

Currently, each possible DMO – such as results of historical content database queries or post-processed spatial database queries (computed maps or planned tours) – is associated with its own XSLT style sheet. These style sheets, however, are static, i.e. they only depend on the type of DMO and not on context, dialog state, or other dynamic information. In future versions, a presentation planner could create XSLT and even CSS style sheets on the fly. It would then be possible to dynamically decide both *what* to present to the user (suppressing data or enriching it with additional information), and *how*, i.e. which media to employ and which style properties to use with this kind of media (colors, fonts for graphics, volume for sound, resolution for video, etc.) Although not currently implemented, this possibility should be easily supported within the existing architecture.

4 Implementation

The prototype system in the current implementation is deployed on a laptop that communicates through a wireless peer-to-peer LAN connection with a PDA. In order to facilitate user interaction a GUI agent runs on the agent platform. Its display is exported via a VNC server to the PDA. An alternative architecture would be to split the GUI agent into two parts, one for the server side running on the laptop, and one running as HTTP client on its own agent platform on the handheld device. As the development of lightweight agent platforms for small devices [21] is an active research area this issue currently cannot be settled conclusively. We have implemented, deployed, and evaluated the system on multiple machines under various laboratory conditions with respect to different in- and output devices (e.g. PDA, head-mounted displays, 3D pointer). Additionally, the system was evaluated with various agent settings.

5 Evaluation

Recently we conducted an initial field trial for the agent system including the proposed user-agent communication processing by use of XML technologies. The general focus was on user interaction issues and the overall system stability and performance. The trial was performed in a German city at different major sights with university students as evaluators and naïve users, mainly tourists as test persons. Each test person was given two tasks, which can be categorized as typical for location-based services:

1. Select a major sight of the city from the given list and try to get some information about this sight.
2. Request the system to show the selected sight on the map and try to find some further sights nearby. Obtain information about these sights.

Fig. 6. Evaluation under real world conditions.

A single evaluation procedure including the system test and an extensive questionnaire afterwards took about 15 minutes. Overall we had 21 test persons, mostly German tourists but there were also other nationalities represented although the information content of the system was in German. If a foreign tourist evaluated the system, the evaluator had to translate the different contents, by means of textual descriptions, into English. In the following we present some of the relevant evaluation results.

First, the test persons had to rate the overall appearance of the system and the presented textual information. As shown in Figure 7 the user interface gained quite a satisfying rating. It was specially tailored to the handheld use, with a pen as pointing device [see Fig. 5 as an example].

The interaction possibilities on the user interface framework level were quite limited in order to support the ease-of-learning paradigm suggested by Nielson [19]. Regarding the information content (e.g. textual descriptions of sights, images etc.), its presentation and the relations between the different content entities, one can recognize that the total acceptance was also convincing but the variation in the user ratings increased. The appearance of the map was considered worse than that of conventional maps. Here the limitations on mobile clients like PDAs with there limited screen size, display brightness and coloring come into play due to the fact that the graphical entities of maps are less structured than textual descriptions and therefore harder to view. This effect might also be amplified by the influence of the outdoor evaluation (e.g. different sunlight levels during the day etc.).

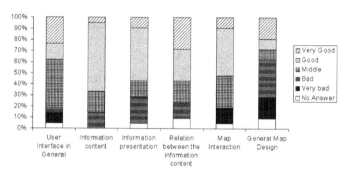

Fig. 7. User acceptance ratings for the user interface in general as well as the different content types and their representation.

Regarding the user rating for the overall system performance there is room for improvements of the agent system. More than half of the participants rated the system as too slow. This assessment might be grounded on the one hand in high user expectations and on the other hand in technical issues.

Concerning the user expectations one can assert that those users who had internet access at home which they use frequently (approx. 70 % of the participants) rated the system more often as slow than users who do not use the internet. In order to qualify this result from the technical perspective we have to cite that the evaluated system was running on a Pentium III 800 MHz with 256 RAM and that the agent system itself is very processor power consuming. A significant measure is the fact that the agent system creates over 230 threads only at startup.

Another issue that causes the unsatisfying system speed is the agent communication itself, be means of large content objects that have to be handled by the system and processed to a human perceivable output format. The size of such a single message object can exceed the 300 KB limit (as XML file).

To summarize both described aspects, the user acceptance for the content presentation and the overall system performance, one can conclude that both are tightly associated. In order to fulfill the different user demands in an even more satisfying way, the system has to take the user's preferences into account. Of course, there is also a need to address the issue of system performance on the single agent level, for example, with usage of profiling tools in order to identify bottlenecks.

6 Conclusion and Future Work

Mobile multi-modal systems allowing a high level of flexibility cannot be built as monolithic software systems. Successful architectures integrate many components in

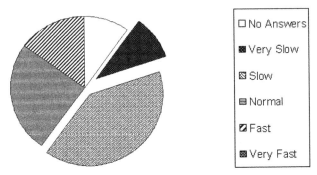

Fig. 8. User ratings for the general response time.

an open infrastructure where both service and user-interface components can be replaced, removed or added in order to customize the system for a specific application
domain or a specific combination of input and output devices. Moreover, the system
architecture must be based on a distributed platform since some components may be
too large for the mobile device and some services may reside on servers and must be
accessed through a (wireless) network. Software agents are one of the answers to
these challenges. Multi agent systems are in particular well suited for mobile information systems and some systems even allow for resource-aware computations in mobile
and distributed environments [6][7][8][17]. However, software agents are still software components and the agent platform leaves the agent interaction and representation of communication entities to the developers, who have to encode these objects in
some ontology.

In this paper we presented a uniform framework for representing such an ontology
for data querying, retrieving, post-processing, adaptation, and presentation. We apply
this framework within a mobile tourist information system for a historical European
city. Additionally, we could successfully realize the system that provides location-
based services and multimedia information retrieval on mobile devices. Furthermore,
we have evaluated the system in an initial trial under real world conditions.

In our approach, we represent all agent communication in an XML-based ontology.
This allows for making use of the full power and flexibility of XML technologies
such as XML data binding and XSLT transformations. The round-trip XML processing pipeline allows for an easy integration of new data sources, new functionalities
(encapsulated in agents) and a flexible output processing and rendering of various
media types.

As a result of the evaluation we have shown that this generic mechanism is suitable
for mobile information system but needs some further improvements by adapting
the processed content to the users. In our architecture on can identify several positions
where such a customization might be addressed:

- The content agents (e.g. the DBAgent) might customize their acquisition methods
  to the user needs for example tailors their queries.
- Additional user or context agents can filter the content according to the user preferences or some contextual information.
- A User centered agent message processing mechanism might customize the content presentation to the user's needs and the situational context by generating dynamic XSL files.

Right now we are enhancing our architecture by a user agent that tries to extract user preference by observing the user interaction.

In general the work presented is a good basis for a more general framework that takes such user and contextual information into account and provides content and service adaptation beyond simple location-based information retrieval by applying methods and techniques of adaptive hypermedia evolved in the WWW context [2]. Likewise this mechanism can also be used to enhance and adapt the user interface framework itself [18].

The proposed way of representing and presenting information in mobile systems helps to design systems and components that can be extended and re-used in a more productive way than in many systems today.

Acknowledgements

This work has been funded by the Klaus Tschira Foundation (KTS) and the German Ministry of Education and Research within the SmartKom (01IL905C) and GEIST (01IRA12C) projects.

References

1. Abowd, G. D., Atkeson, C. G., Hong, J., Long, S., Kooper R., and Pinkerton, M.: Cyberguide: A mobile context-aware tour guide. In ACM Wireless Networks, 3:421–433, 1997.
2. Brusilovsky, P. (1996) Methods and techniques of adaptive hypermedia. User Modeling and User-Adapted Interaction 6 (2-3), 87-129.
3. Cheverst, K., Mitchell, K., Davies, N. (1998): Design of an Object Model for a Context Sensitive Tourist GUIDE. In Proceedings of the International Workshop on Interactive Applications of Mobile Computing (IMC98).
4. Baus J, Ding Y, Kray, C, Walther U.: Towards adaptive location-aware mobile assistants. In Proceedings. of the Workshop on Artificial Intelligence in Mobile Systems (AIMS2001). Seattle, Washington, August 5, pp. 1-6, 2001.
5. Bayardo, R. et.al.: Infosleuth: Agent-based semantic integration of information in open and dynamic environments. In Proceedings of the 97 ACM SIGMOD International Conference on Management of Data, pages 195–206, Tuson-Arizona, June 1997.
6. Ding, Y., Kray, C., Malaka, R. and Schillo, M.: RAJA-A Resource-Adaptive Java Agent Infrastructure. In Proceedings of the 5th International Conference on Autonomous Agents 2001, ACM Press, Montreal, p. 332–339
7. Ding Y. Malaka R., Pfisterer D.: An open framework for load balanced multi-agent systems, In: Proceedings of Workshop on Ubiquitous Agents on embedded, wearable, and mobile devices, held in conjunction with First International Joint Conference on Autonomous Agents and Multi-Agent Systems (AAMAS 2002), Bologna, Italy, 2002.
8. Elting Ch, Möhler G: Modeling Output in the EMBASSI Multimodal Dialog System. In Proceedings of the 4th IEEE International Conference on Multimodal Interfaces 2002; Oct. 14th-16th - Pittsburgh, USA.
9. Finin, T. et.al.: KQML as an Agent Communication Language, In 3rd International Conference on Information and Knowledge Management (CIKM94), ACM Press, December 1994.
10. Fink, J., Kobsa A.(2002): User Modeling in Personalized City Tours. In Artificial Intelligence Review 18(1), 33-74.
11. Gruber, T.R. (1995). Toward Principles for the Design of Ontologies Used for Knowledge Sharing, In Int. Journal of Human-Computer Studies, Vol. 43, pp.907-928.

12. Jennings, N., Wooldridge, M.: Intelligents Agents: Theory and Practice. In The Knowledge Engineering Review, 10(2), 1999.
13. Jenning, N.: An Agent-based approach for building complex software systems, In Communications of the ACM, Vol. 44, No. 4, April 2001.
14. Joest M., Stille W.: A user-aware tour proposal framework using a hybrid optimization approach, In Proceedings of the tenth ACM international symposium on Advances in geographic information systems, Mc Lean,USA, 2002
15. Labrou, Y., Finn, T. and Y. Peng (1999): Agent Communication Languages: the Current Landscape, IEEE Intelligent Systems, 14 (2), 45-52
16. Malaka, R. and Zipf, A.: DEEP MAP - Challenging IT research in the framework of a tourist information system. In: Fesenmaier, D. Klein, S. and Buhalis, D. (Eds.): Information and Communication Technologies in Tourism 2000. In Proceedings of ENTER 2000, 7th. International Congress on Tourism and Communications Technologies in Tourism. Barcelona. Spain. Springer Computer Science, Wien, New York. p. 15-27.
17. Malaka, R., Porzel, R., Zipf, A. and Chandrasekhara, V.: Integration of smart components for building your personal mobile guide. In: Proceedings of AIMS 2000. Workshop on Artificial Intelligence in mobile Systems.Workshop at ECAI 2000 (European Conference on Artificial Intelligence). Berlin.
18. Moran, D., Cheyer, A., Julia, L., and Park, S. Multimodal user interfaces in the Open Agent Architecture. In Proceedings of IUI-97. Orlando, Jan. 1997. 61-68.
19. Nielson, J. (1999): Designing Web Usability: The Practice of Simplicity, New Riders, 1ed.
20. Pihkala, K., Honkala, M. and Vuorimaa, P., A Browser Framework for Hybrid XML Documents, In Proceedings of the 6th IASTED International Conference, Internet and Multimedia Systems, and Applications, (IMSA 2002), August 12-14, 2002, Kauai, Hawaii, USA.
21. Sasu Tarkoma and Mikko Laukkanen, Supporting software agents on small devices. In Proceedings of the first international joint conference on Autonomous agents and multi-agent systems, 2002, Bologna, Italy, p. 565–566.
22. Singh, M. P., Rao, A. S. and Wooldridge, M. editors: Intelligent Agents IV, Springer-Verlag Lecture Notes in AI Volume 1365, February 1998.
23. Stone, P., Veloso; M.: Multiagent systems: A survey from a machine learning perspective. Submitted to Journal of Artificial Intelligence Research (JAIR), February 1997.
24. Vuorimaa, P., Ropponen, T., and Knorring, T.: X-Smiles XML browser, In The 2nd International Workshop on Networked Appliances, IWNA'2000, New Brunswick, NJ, USA, Nov. 30 – Dec. 1, 2000.
25. Wahlster, W., Reithinger, N. and Blocher, A.: SmartKom: Multimodal Communication with a Life-Like Character, In: Proceedings of Eurospeech2001, Aalborg (Dänemark), 2001.
26. Wache, H.; Vogele, T.; Visser, U.; Stuckenschmidt, H.; Schuster, G.; Neumann, H.; and Hubner, S. 2001. Ontology-based integration of information - a survey of existing approaches. In Stuckenschmidt, H., ed., IJCAI-01 Workshop: Ontologies and Information Sharing, 108–117.
27. Zipf A.,Malaka, R.: Developing "Location Based Services" (LBS) For Tourism - The Service Provider's View. In: Sheldon, P., Wöber, K. and Fesenmaier D. (Eds.): Information and Communication Technologies in Tourism 2001. Proceedings of ENTER 2001, 8th International Conference. Montreal. Springer Computer Science. Wien, New York. 83-92

Co-operative and Distributed Configuration

Ander Altuna, Alvaro Cabrerizo, Iñaki Laresgoiti, Nieves Peña, and Daniel Sastre

LABEIN Technological Center, Zamudio, Bizkaia, Spain
{aaltuna,acabrerizo,ilares,npena,dsastre}@labein.es

Abstract. Configuration problem solving is a topic that drove a lot of interest within the AI community. The World Wide Web has appeared as the vehicle to share information and facilitate businesses like the provision of simple configuration capabilities to users. Ontologies have gained acceptance within the research community as the way to make applications interoperable and drive the next intelligent generation of the World Wide Web known as the Semantic Web that many consider as a future enabler of future advance forms of collaborative e-business. It is just this consideration what has motivated the OBELIX[1] consortium to do research on multi-component product configuration, since collaborative design scenarios over the (Semantic) Web will become a future reality, but have not been researched in depth yet. This paper describes the efforts done and the results obtained in that direction.

Keywords: Collaborative Configuration, Multi-component Configuration, Services Composition, Semantic Web Technologies, Configuration.

1 Introduction

Configuration has been recognized as a topic of research since late 1980s. Most definitions of a configuration task found in the literature are a slight variant of the first generic definition given by Mittal and Frayman in 1989 [1], *"design activity of assembling an artifact that is made of a fixed set of well defined component types where components can interact only in predefined ways"*. Further research was made by Schwezfeger et al., 1991 [2], Günter, 1992 [3], Heinrich, 1991 [4], M. Kopisch and A. Günter, 1992 [5], Schwanke and Bernert, 1990 [6], Schweiger, 1992 [7], Tank, 1992 [8].

In this paper we will capture the different notions of configuration that appear in the literature to conform and explain the description of the Configuration Ontology developed in the OBELIX European project that will serve as the basis for the development of a Configuration Tool.

The need for "right –the –first –time" product configuration has never been greater [...] Companies lose 2-3% of revenue in rework and penalty costs due to errors made in the initial product configuration.

PC AI, January-February, 1996

---

[1] This work has been partially supported by the European Commission, as project No. IST-2001-33144 OBELIX (Ontology-Based Electronic Integration of compleX products and value chains) whose consortium is composed by LABEIN, VUA, ONTOPRISE, SINTEF, PTSS, TRØNDERENERGI, SENA.

M. Weske and P. Liggesmeyer (Eds.): NODe 2004, LNCS 3263, pp. 69–80, 2004.
© Springer-Verlag Berlin Heidelberg 2004

A Boeing 747 is made up of over 6 million parts, and a customer can choose among hundreds of options [...] Every option the customer chooses affects the availability of other options, and changes the planes price. It takes the sales agent days or weeks working with company engineers to make sure all the chosen pieces fit together, renegotiating the price at every step.

[...] customers sometimes received servers without room for the required disk drives, or without connecting cables, or with the wrong kind of preinstalled software. Fixing these mistakes costs [...] money, time and customer loyalty.

Frobes, June 3, 1996

After reading these citations we can imagine the importance of the configuration task in a company. Not only when a company wants to develop a new product, but also when it wants to sell it and lets the customer configure the final product.

Therefore configuration allows the change of industry orientation from mass production to mass customization. Meeting the demand for the increased needs for customization lead to product configuration.

During the last years, the Web has evolved from being an information-sharing place to a sale or advertising site. Nowadays, even small enterprises have a portal to announce themselves to the outside.

Within this context different classes of systems have been developed to meet company and future customer needs. Going from the most simple ones, where just complete and fixed products are offered to the customer from a products' catalog, to the more complex ones, where AI techniques are used and meeting customer's profiles and needs is taken into consideration.

Nowadays, some industrial markets have started the development of ontologies to define their products and services but still there is a great lack of these. But even taking as granted the existence of domain ontologies, off-line multi-product configuration tools based on them are still under development. It is just that lack what has motivated in the OBELIX project the development of an on-line multi-product configuration tool to allow a co-operative and distributed configuration of products and services.

The contribution of this paper is presenting and explaining the on-line multi-product configuration tool together with the generic Configuration Ontology in which it is based.

2   Configuration Ontology

We can view an ontology as a provider of a common vocabulary of an area together with the meaning of the terms and the relations between them [9].

In order to come to a generic Configuration Ontology, firstly it was important to understand the meaning of configuration. The most commonly used definition of the Configuration Task was given by Mittal & Frayman [1].

*"**Given**: Given: (A) a fixed, pre-defined set of components, where a component is described by a set of properties, ports for connecting it to other components, constraints at each port that describe the components that can be connected at that port, and other structural constraints; (B) some description of the desired configuration; and (C) possibly some criteria for making optimal selections."*

*"**Build**: One or more configurations that satisfy all the requirements, where a configuration is a set of components and a description of the connections between the components in the set, or, detect inconsistencies in the requirements."*

From the above definition and splitting it out, we have that configuration is:

a) A set of **components** (products/services), such that, these components can be described by a set of **properties** and **ports** connecting them to other components.

b) **Constraints** at each port that describe the components that can be connected at that port and other structural constraints.

c) **User requirements** with the description of the desired configuration; and possibly some criteria for optimizing the solution.

Therefore the main concepts that seem to be the candidates to appear in the Configuration Ontology are: **components, ports, connections, properties or attributes, constraints, user requirements...**

The ontology has been subdivided in three sub-ontologies that represent different aspects of the knowledge that is necessary for the specification of well-formed configuration problems.

– The **Configuration Components Ontology** is the ontology that contains all the static information and therefore provides the basic taxonomy definitions to define configuration problems: components, attributes, relations, etc...

– The **Configuration Constraint Ontology** is the ontology that contains the information to describe constraints. These constraints can apply to the components or to the desired configuration the Requirements Ontology and are associated to the Components Ontology and the Requirements Ontology respectively.

– The **Configuration Requirements Ontology** is the ontology that contains the information about how to solve the desired configuration, i.e. provides the taxonomies for describing the user requirements specification. This is the input/output description of a system that performs a configuration task.

All the above, aims to be an introduction to the following sub-sections where a top-level description of the **Configuration Ontology** is done based on the above sub-ontologies.

2.1   Top-Level Viewpoint of the Components Ontology

Before describing the concepts of this component ontology, it is important to clarify that the Configuration Ontology covers two types of configuration problems: *high-level configuration problems* and *detail-level configuration problems.* The former implies a parametric constraint satisfaction and therefore the components are grouped or associated, while the latter involves arrangement such that the components are connected through their ports.

Both types of configuration problems can be solved for tangible objects (e.g. personal computer), called *products,* or for intangible objects (e.g. the buying of energy) called *services*.

Component: A Component can be a primitive module (SimpleComponent) or an assembly of primitive modules (ConfiguredComponent) that participate in a configuration design. Components can be physical things (products) or may also represent functional and behavioral abstractions (services).

SimpleComponent: A Simple Component is the most basic component that participates in a configuration design. As subclass of Component, it inherits all the properties of Component.

ConfiguredComponent: A Configured Component is an assembly of Components (SimpleComponents or/and ConfiguredComponents) that can be linked via *Associations* (High level Configuration) or via *Connections* (Detail level Configuration).

Therefore a ConfiguredComponent is the solution of a performed configuration problem, but can play a role as Component to be configured in a new configuration problem.

As described in the configuration literature [10] [11] components have constraints, parameters and ports. As such, we can identify those concepts in the Components Ontology.

Structural Parameter: A Parameter is a unary function from Components to Parameter values, which are either scalar quantities or strings. These parameters will play an important role when performing *High Level Configuration* (configuration design involving parametric constraint satisfaction).

Port: Ports constitute the interface of the Components to the external world, i.e. the ports specify how they can be connected. These ports will play an important role when performing *Detail Level Configuration* (configuration design involving *arrangement*).

The ontology defines three sub-concepts of port in order to distinguish the ports that receive something from others and ports that give something to others. The former are called InputPort and the latter OutputPort. The term InputOutputPort is reserved for the Ports that can at the same give and receive something.

Resource: This concept stores the knowledge about what the ports are exchanging. The connectivity between ports can vary from zero to one when exchanging discrete resources or from zero to many when exchanging continuous resources. Usually the first case is for product configuration and the later for services. The Resource stores also information about how the port to which it belongs can be interconnected to others.

Connection: This concept indicates the degree of connectivity between two ports. The Connection concept arises as reification of the connection relationship between two ports (*hasConnection*). The Connection is related to ports and therefore to the Detail Level Configuration problem type.

Association: This concept indicates that a Component is member of a Configured Component. The Association concept arises as reification of the connection relationship between two Components (*hasAssociation*). The Association is related to Components and therefore to the High Level Configuration problem type.

Supplier: This concept is created in the ontology to achieve the collaborative configuration of products and services. The idea is allowing an on-line registration of new companies (suppliers) offering services or products. Therefore, this concept stores the supplier's knowledge about a particular domain which is represented by constraints.

Then, the collaboration is achieved in the following way: Once an expert defines the domain components ontology based on the components ontology schema, this ontology is loaded in an Ontology Server to make it public and accessible to different suppliers in the world. A supplier can register to provide configured components by creating a domain constraint ontology file applicable over the previously defined domain and by adding his reference in the domain components ontology through the supplier concept.

The following diagram summarizes the set of terms and relations of the Components Ontology.

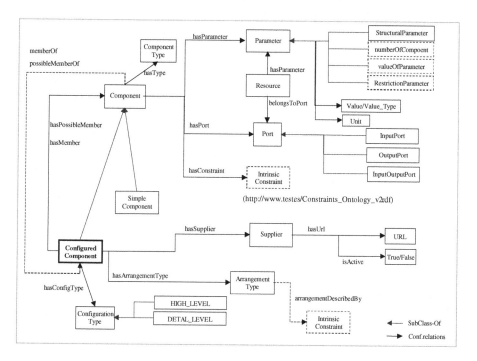

Fig. 1. Configuration Components Ontology.

The Components can also have Constraints but this will be described in the Constraint Ontology.

2.2   Top-Level Viewpoint of the Constraints Ontology

This ontology contains the information regarding the constraints applicable over the domain. The constraints come always from the specific domain knowledge, and therefore will be applied over the instances of the specification domain.

Intrinsic Constraints: This concept indicates the constraints that are applicable to the Components Ontology. Such constraints belong to the domain forever and will be applied no matter the User Requirements. Once these constraints have been applied a set of "valid solutions" is returned. (See Fig. 2)

Problem Specification Constraint: This concept indicates the constraints that come from the Requirements Ontology. These constraints are the transformation of the user requirements into well-specified constraints that describe the kind of solution requested by him. These constraints restrict the set of valid solutions to the set of all "suitable configurations". (See Fig. 2)

Optimal Criteria: This concept indicates the constraints that come from the Requirements Ontology. These constraints are the transformation from optimal criteria to well-specified constraints that describe the best solution to be found. Therefore these constraints restrict the set of suitable configurations to the set of "optimal configurations". (See Fig. 2)

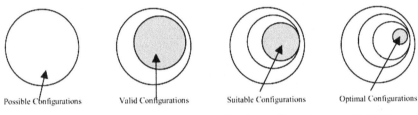

Possible Configurations   Valid Configurations   Suitable Configurations   Optimal Configurations

Fig. 2. Configuration understood as restricting the configuration space [13][15].

This ontology is linked to the Components Ontology and Requirements Ontology through the establishment of symmetric relations that have to be inferred by the configuration tool at run-time.

Moreover, a classification of constraints by type has been done in the following terms:

Unary Constraints: Constraints that prune the possible values of a ConfiguredComponent member.

Binary Symmetric Constraints: Constraints that are applicable to two Components in the same way, which means that no main actor, is involved in the Constraint (*e.g. A=B*).

Binary No-Symmetric Constraints: Constraints that are applicable to two Components but they don't act in the same way. There is a Component that acts as main actor and the other as secondary (*e.g. if A then B*).

Incremental constraints: Constraints that are incrementally applicable to a ConfiguredComponent, as a whole, when some of its members have assigned a concrete value.

Global Constraints: Constraints that are applicable to a ConfiguredComponent once the rest of the constraints have been satisfied, and all of its members have assigned a concrete value.

The following diagram shows the whole Constraint Ontology,

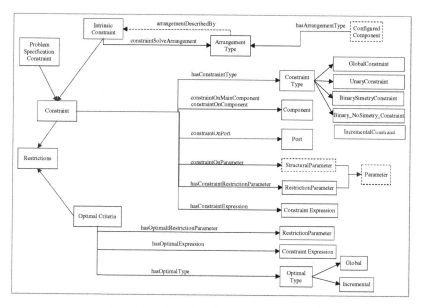

Fig. 3. Configuration Constraint Ontology.

2.3   Top-Level Viewpoint of the Requirements Ontology

This ontology contains the concepts and relations necessary to describe the desired configuration and some possibly criteria for optimizing the solution.

The concepts that are described are:

Customer Requirements: The Customer Requirements specify the characteristics of the configured component that the user wants to obtain. These requirements must be transformed by the designer with knowledge of the domain in a well-defined problem specification, i.e. in Problem Specification Constraints. The relation *describedByConstraints* manages this configuration knowledge.

As well as defining the constraints given by the user, the Customer Requirements must express the final Configured Component to be configured, to accomplish this goal the relation *describedByComponent* is used.

Restriction Parameter: The objective of this parameter is to parameterize the Problem Specification Constraints previously defined in the Constraint Ontology.

NumberOfComponents: Parameter created to customize at run-time the number of components involved in the configuration. The SimpleComponents in the Components Ontology can be created with a number that identifies the number of real instances that should take part in the configuration. But the customer can change this value.

ValueOfParamter: Parameters created to customize at run-time the customer requirements regarding the value of some Structural Parameters of the domain components.

The following diagram shows the model:

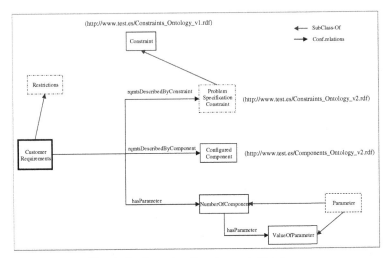

Fig. 4. Configuration Requirements Ontology.

3   Obelix Configuration Tool

The Configuration Tool uses the previously explained Configuration Ontology, to support collaborative configuration of products and services.

As explained before, the ontology allows each supplier to describe the constraints that are applicable to a specific domain. Therefore, the configuration problem solving process has been designed as a layer architecture of configuration tools that use a goal directed approach, both for the distribution of configuration problems to suppliers and for the composition of solutions.

The developed Configuration Tool is able to export and import RDF ontology files, and provides the basic integration mechanisms to be used as a module by other tools and applications. These integration mechanisms are based on four different client interfaces:

Problem Specification Interface: to facilitate the creation of domain Requirements by customers.

Constraint Specification Interface: to facilitate the creation of the constraints ontology files by constraint developers. Moreover a graphical user interface based on this interface has also been developed.

Configuration Execution Interface: to facilitate the execution of the Configuration Tool by theapplication .

Configuration Solution Interface: to facilitate the interpretation of solutions, given by the Configuration Tool, by the domain application.

3.1   Architecture

The Configuration Tool architecture is based on the following modules that are also shown in the Fig. 5.

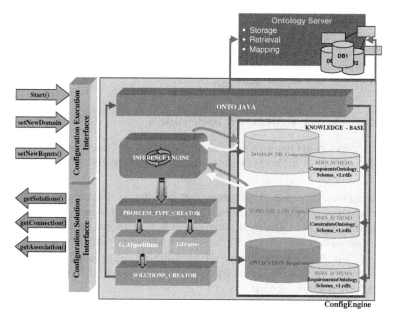

Fig. 5. Configuration Tool Architecture.

Knowledge Base Module

This module is in charge of managing the domain configuration knowledge based on the Configuration Ontology schema (RDFS). Therefore it detects any conflict in the domain, requirement or constraint ontology file and informs about them to the client application. This module acts as a knowledge repository with inference capabilities that allows intelligent queries over the configuration process [12], [17].

Once the configuration problem is solved, the solutions are also stored in this repository to make them accessible to the client application through the queries performed by the Configuration Solution Interface.

Problem Types Creator

This module is in charge of creating the configuration space for the two types of problems distinguished in the ontology: high-level and detail-level. It also distinguishes whether a product or service configuration has to be performed. And therefore redirects the problem to the adequate generic algorithm to solve the problem.

CSP Generic Algorithms

The resolution of the configuration problems is based on generic constrain satisfaction algorithms implemented in Java. This module contains a set of generic algorithms that are used to solve a configuration problem [15], [19], [19].

Constraint Library

This module contains two parts: a set of generic Java implemented constraints for both the detail-level configuration problems and high-level configuration problems, that can be instantiated into specific domains and specific domain constraints implemented by each supplier. These constraints will be later on loaded to be executed.

Solution Creator

As the Configuration Tool can solve the same configuration problem for different suppliers and all the solutions are stored in the knowledge base, this module is in charge of serializing each of the solutions in a different RDF solution ontology file and exporting it to an external Ontology Server.

4 Validation over Different Case Studies

Both the Configuration Ontology and the configuration tool have been validated along several applications in different sectors, using for that the following OBELIX case studies:

- *On-line design of events Application* that consists in a Furniture Configuration problem, where a fixed set of tables needs to be configured in a given arrangement and in an *Equipment Configuration problem*, where a fixed set of services need to be configured to achieve a specific set of compatible resources.
- *Demand Side Bidding Application* that consists in aggregating loads (electricity consumed at a certain time) sold by a fixed set of customers to manage consumption peaks at a minimum cost.
- *Energy Services Bundling Application* that consists in configuring a set of energy service elements to get all the feasible combinations that satisfy the specific user requirements.

In the first case, the configuration task has been performed over *tangible products*. A set of *tables, person, equipment, etc...* with different characteristics (size, quality, prize...) and ports to allow interconnectivity between them have been described using the *Components Ontology* described in section 2.1. Afterwards, one or more suppliers can describe the constraints that restrict the type of connections or associations that can be established between those products, the valid parameter values, etc... using the *Constraint Ontology* described in section 2.2. And finally, the customer demands and some, possible, optimizing criteria are specified using the *Requirements Ontology* described in section 2.3 to guide the search for a final solution suitable for that customer.

The second case has also implied a tangible product configuration but the third case, is the one that has served us to test the suitability of the Configuration Ontology to describe *service* configuration problems. Similar to the product case, the three sub-ontologies are used to map the knowledge that is necessary to describe the configuration task for this *energy service domain* in terms of the Configuration Ontology to later on be solved by the configuration tool. The Energy Services Bundling Application uses the Obelix configuration tool to offer a service-bundle, formed by a set of inter-connected service elements, suitable for some specified customer needs. This case has involved the integration of the Configuration Ontology with the Service Ontology developed by VUA and it has been more detailed explained in a recent published paper at the *IEEE Intelligent Systems* Journal [18].

5 Conclusions and Future Work

This paper shows that using ontologies and Semantic Web languages give a range of possibilities for collaboration in Internet for solving configuration problems. Multi-

product component configuration increases the distribution of the configuration problem solving-process involving successive actors. Moreover, thanks to the ontologies
the domains can be reused and combined to created new configuration domains.

The already tested case studies show that the configuration tool developed within
the Obelix project is very useful for the configuration of both tangible products (tables, person, etc...) and services (energy services). Moreover, the flexibility of the
developed architecture and the ontology make the tool widely applicable to various
configuration problems that can be found in different business areas. Therefore, the
next steps in this direction will be to carry on with this validation along real-life case
studies to continue its validation and evolution.

At this stage, the Configuration Ontology allows the definition of a configuration
problem to be solved by different suppliers, but right now this is only possible within
one supplier using the current tool. Therefore, the next steps will be in the direction of
allowing the participation of different suppliers in configuring a multi-product and in
describing the interactions through Web Services.

Moreover, the fact of having developed a generic ontology to describe configuration problems has allowed the used of it in different ontology based application and
tools based on ontology alignment or mapping techniques [18], which has demonstrate the *integrability* of both Configuration Ontology and Configuration Tool and
will serve as the basis for future integration in other domains.

References

1. S.Mittal & F- Frayman, Towards a generic model of configuration Tasks, IJCAI, Vol. 1,
   1989.
2. C. Schwenzfeger, H. Dörner, H. Schädler, K. Schädler, "Chemisches konfigurieren," *Workshop Planen und Konfigurieren*, 1992.
3. A. Günter, "Flexible Kontolle in Expertensystem zur Plannung und Konfigurierung in
   technischen Domänen", volume 3 of *DISKI*, 1992.
4. Heinrich "Ressourcen-orientierte modellierung als basis modularer technischer systeme",
   1991.
5. M. Kopisch, A. Günter, "Configuration of a Passenger Aircraft Cabin based on Conceptual
   Hierarchy, Constraints and flexible Control", *IEA/AIE 1992*: 421-430.
6. A. Schwanke, J. P. Bernert. Ressourcenorientierte Konfigurierung von Kommunikations-
   systemen. In 4. *Workshop Planen und Konfigurieren*, FAW-B-90008, pp.157–170, 1990.
7. J. Schweiger, "Generating Configuration Expert Systems from Conceptual Specifications
   of the Expert Knowledge", *EKAW 1992*: 191-210.
8. W. Tank, "Modellierung von Expertise über Konfigurationsaufgaben", *Infix*, Sankt Augustin, Germany, 1992.
9. T. R. Gruber. A translation approach to portable ontology specifications. Knowledge Acquisition 5:199-220, 1993.
10. B.J. Wielinga, A.TH. Schreiber, Configuration design problem solving. University of Am-
    sterdam, Department of Social Science Informatics.
11. Knowledge Systems Laboratory, Stanford University, Web Site.
12. Mark Stefik, Introduction to Knowledge Systems, *CA: Morgan Kaufmann Publishers, Inc.*,
    1995, San Francisco.
13. Expertise Model Document Part II: The CommonKADS Library. (Chapter 10, Christiane
    Löckenhoff and Tilo Messer)
14. Chandrasekaran, B., "Design problem solving: A task analysis", *AI Magazine*, 11:59--71,
    1990.

15. Löckenhoff, C. & Messer, T. Configuration. In: Breuker, J. & Van de Velde, W., "CommonKADS Library for Expertise Modelling", *Amsterdam: IOS Press*, pp 197-212, 1994.
16. Maher, M.L., "Process Models for Design Synthesis", *AI. Magazine,* winter 90, pp. 49-58
17. Pupple, F. (1993). Systems Introduction to Expert System. Berlin
18. H. Akkermans, Z. Baida, J. Gordijn, N. Peña, A. Altuna, I. Laresgoiti, "Value Webs: Ontology-Based Bundling of Real-World Services," *IEEE Intelligent Systems,* Vol. 19, No. 4, July/August 2004, (Special issue on Semantic Web Services)
19. T. Soininen, E. Gelle, "Dynamic Constraint Satisfaction in Configuration" In: Faltings B, Freuder EC, Friedrich EG, Felfernig A, editors. Configuration Papers from AAAI Workshop, AAAI; 1999. p. 95-106
20. D. Sabin, E.C. Freuder, "Configuration as Composite Constraint Satisfaction". In: Proc. Artificial Intelligence and Manufacturing Research Planning Workshop, AAA] Technical Report FS-96-03, 1996, pp. 28-36.

Micro-measurements
for Dynamic Aspect-Oriented Systems

Michael Haupt and Mira Mezini

Software Technology Group, Darmstadt University of Technology
{haupt,mezini}@informatik.tu-darmstadt.de

Abstract. The benefits of aspect-oriented programming (AOP) with respect to software design are getting more and more accepted, and measurements have shown that AOP does not necessarily introduce severe performance penalties. A benchmark suite for measuring the performance of AspectJ software is being developed. However, general benchmarks are missing for the emerging field of dynamic AOP, even though major J2EE application server vendors begin to employ dynamic aspects in their systems. Instead, work on dynamic AOP frequently comprises varying measurements. To be eventually able to classify such systems along their performance qualities, it is important to develop a benchmark suite for dynamic AOP. In this paper, we present a first building block for such a benchmark suite in the form of micro-measurements. We also present and discuss results gained by running the measurements in several dynamic AOP systems. A discussion of requirements for dynamic AOP benchmarks finishes the paper.

1 Introduction

Aspect-oriented software development is recently gaining more relevance. IBM has announced strong support for AOP [34], and dynamic aspects are used to implement cross-cutting concerns in complex middleware systems, namely J2EE application servers like JBoss [22, 23] and Bea WebLogic [6, 3, 9].

While the increasing acceptance of aspects is encouraging, simply relying on their conceptual influence on software development is not enough. As it is becoming more and more clear that software structure benefits from the adoption of aspect-oriented techniques, their impact on software performance must be regarded as well. Since the first versions of AspectJ [26, 2], the performance overhead introduced by using aspects instead of traditional object-oriented design has frequently been subject to consideration, and such measurements have shown that adopting aspect-oriented techniques does not harm performance [12, 41, 14, 19]. To be able to reason about the performance of AOP implementations, benchmarking tools or suites are needed that specifically measure the performance of aspect-oriented mechanisms. This holds not only for languages like AspectJ, but also for the field of dynamic aspects where there are many different tools and systems whose implementation approaches differ significantly.

M. Weske and P. Liggesmeyer (Eds.): NODe 2004, LNCS 3263, pp. 81–96, 2004.
© Springer-Verlag Berlin Heidelberg 2004

There exists a variety of established and accepted benchmarks for comparatively measuring the performance of Java virtual machine implementations, spanning several domains from typical Java applications of various kinds [37, 21] to server-side applications [36]. For AspectJ, the work of Dufour et al. [15] is the first to propose a suite of aspect-oriented benchmark applications covering most of AspectJ's language features. Still, there is no effort in the field of dynamic AOP that measures the performances of the multiple existing systems with dynamic weaving support. The recent adoption of different dynamic AOP tools in middleware implementations however calls for comparative measurements for two reasons: firstly, it is interesting to know what the performance impact of dynamic AOP systems is when compared to that of systems like AspectJ, and secondly, the different approaches need to be compared with each other to classify their respective impacts and qualities.

Since the main differences between the various dynamic AOP implementations lie in their specific ways to address dynamic weaving, providing measurements for the costs of basic operations in these systems is a reasonable first step towards a full-fledged benchmark suite. Operations like method invocations or member accesses are typical join point shadows [28] that are frequently decorated with invocations of advice functionality in aspect-oriented programming. Thus, the impact of different dynamic AOP implementations can well be reasoned about in terms of these operations' performance when they are unaffected or affected by aspects.

This paper makes three contributions, the first of which, an analysis of existing approaches to measuring AOP performance, is to be found in Sec. 2. In that section, we look at measurements that have been made to evaluate the general overhead of using aspects instead of traditional object-orientation, and measurements from the introductions of dynamic AOP implementations. We also discuss work that aims at providing a general benchmark for AspectJ applications. In Sec. 3, we present, as the second contribution, a collection of micro-measurement benchmarks widely applicable to dynamic AOP systems. The third contribution is made in Sec. 4, where we discuss the work presented so far and formulate requirements for dynamic AOP benchmark suites. Sec. 5 concludes and outlines ongoing and future work.

2   Performance Measurements for Aspect-Oriented Software

The work presented in this section can be classified in three categories. Work in the first serves to show that employing aspect orientation does not lead to severe performance penalties. These measurements have mostly been made for AspectJ. They usually take the approach of measuring the execution time of a "traditional" object-oriented system that has been refactored using aspects. In the second category, we group measurements made in conjunction with introducing systems supporting dynamic AOP. These measurements frequently compare the new systems' performance to that of equivalent implementations using AspectJ. The third category is made up of the work on dynamic metrics for aspect-oriented software by Dufour et al. [15].

2.1 Measuring AOP Overhead

To measure the overhead of using aspects instead of plain object-orientation, various measurements have been made, of which we present three typical examples. In all cases, aspect overheads are measured in systems of sufficient complexity, wherein aspects are used in three ways: they are just added to an existing system without having been relevant at design-time, or they are explicitly used to design the system from the start, or an existing system is refactored with aspects.

Díaz Pace and Campo [12] have implemented a control engineering system (TCS, *temperature control system*) in four different ways, using (a) traditional object-orientation, (b) AspectJ, (c) a reflection-based AOP system named TaxonomyAOP and (d) an event-based system named Bubble. For measurements, metrics were applied to the resulting source code, and the different implementations' response time was measured. This work actually contains a comparative performance study of AspectJ, TaxonomyAOP and Bubble, but for the latter two no further information is available.

Zhang and Jacobsen [41] have refactored an entire ORB implementation [29], realising several production aspects in AspectJ that were identified using aspect mining techniques. Performance was evaluated by collecting static metrics, measuring response time for remote invocations, and collecting performance data by inserting measurement points into the ORB's execution stack. The original ORB's performance was compared to that of the AspectJ version.

Hilsdale and Hugunin, in their work on advice weaving in AspectJ [19], have extended the Xalan XSLT processor [39] with tracing functionality. This aspect was introduced both hand-coded and with AspectJ. To collect performance data, the XSLTMark benchmark [40] was used.

2.2 Measurements for Dynamic AOP Systems

We group dynamic AOP systems according to their approaches to weaving:

Weaving class loaders: Systems in this group use an extended class loader to modify classes as they are loaded into the VM. Basically, each of the systems decorates join point shadows [28] with hooks or wrappers that branch execution to advice if necessary. The set of advice associated with a particular join point shadow can be extended and reduced at run-time.

Interception: Systems regarding a running application as a series of events reifying join points [17] often utilise the Java VM's debugger [25], assigning breakpoints to join point shadows. When a breakpoint is reached, the debugger is used to invoke advice functionality. A different approach is to modify a virtual machine's execution logic to signal join points when needed.

Run-time weaving: This category comprises systems that actually weave aspect code into the application code at run-time. This involves modification and recompilation of methods, which can be achieved through HotSwap [13], or through purposeful modification of a JVM implementation.

We will now give an overview of some dynamic AOP implementations for which measurement descriptions were available and depict how their authors have gathered performance data. In describing the particular systems, we refrain to assigning them to the above categories and give details only where necessary. We do not claim the list of discussed systems to be complete.

JAC. [30,20] belongs to the category of systems with weaving class loaders. To gather performance data, the authors have run a benchmark program that creates an object and calls an empty method on it. The benchmark was run in three versions: (a) with no modifications, (b) with an aspect introducing ten wrappers to the object to measure the wrapping overhead, and (c) with the same aspect exploiting JAC's feature of caching classes that have once been modified to disk to avoid load-time weaving. The time consumed by class loading – and, therefore, weaving – was also measured.

HandiWrap. [5] also employs a weaving class loader. The authors have used SPECjvm98 to measure the overhead due to adding hooks to methods. For more detailed measurements, the `mayac` compiler [4] was traced to obtain the time needed to invoke a frequently called single method looking up and returning values, which may be optimised by caching results. Caching was implemented as an aspect in HandiWrap and AspectJ, and the compiler was run in three versions for each implementation: (a) unmodified, (b) with shared caching (all target instances of the call sharing a cache), (c) with one cache per instance (using `pertarget` in AspectJ), and (d) with a cache for one particular call target (using the `if` pointcut designator in AspectJ).

PROSE. [31–33] is interception-based and exists in two versions, for each of which measurements were made. For the first version that uses debugger break-points to intercept execution [31], the JVM was used to run a benchmark [7] in normal and debug mode to measure debug mode overhead. Moreover, a printer spooler named Jspool was used that was decorated with an aspect executing an empty void method for every incoming service request. For method invocations, micro-measurements were made by calling an empty method decorated with an empty advice that was implemented in three ways: (a) advice functionality was hard-coded, (b) it was called through PROSE's interception mechanism, (c) it was called with parameters reified from the join point context.

The second version of PROSE [32] was implemented by extending IBM's Jikes Research Virtual Machine [1,24]. The VM's JIT compiler is modified to insert calls to an AOP infrastructure at all potential join point shadows. To measure the extensions' overhead, the JavaGrande [21] and SPECjvm98 [37] benchmarks were run on both the Jikes RVM and on PROSE. Micro-measurements were made for calls to empty methods and field set and get operations in three ways: (a) for join point shadows with no attached advice, (b) for activated locked join point shadows[1], and (c) for activated unlocked join point shadows with a subsequent call to an empty advice. Additional measurements were made to relate PROSE to JAC and HandiWrap.

Steamloom. [18, 8] belongs to the category of systems weaving at run-time. Like PROSE 2, it is an extension of the Jikes RVM, but it follows an entirely different approach by modifying method bytecodes and recompiling the methods to insert aspect code. SPECjvm98 was run on an unmodified build of Jikes and on Steamloom to measure the basic overhead. Micro-measurements were made for plain method invocations, and for the same methods decorated with empty advice. The total JIT compilation time for the SPECjvm98 benchmarks was measured as well. For measuring the performance of more complex aspect-oriented concepts, a simple application recursively computing Fibonacci numbers was run in three versions, each implemented in both Steamloom and AspectJ: (a) with no aspect, (b) with an aspect counting all invocations of the `fib()` method, and (c) with an aspect counting these invocations only when they occurred within a specific control flow (in AspectJ, this was implemented using `cflow`). In each case, the time needed to execute a call to `fib()` was measured. A single benchmark from SPECjvm98 (`_209_db`) was decorated with an aspect counting method invocations, where the set of methods to be counted was determined at run-time.

Wool. [35] is a hybrid approach using both interception through the JVM's debugger and run-time weaving through HotSwap. Join point shadows are intercepted using breakpoints until they have been invoked often enough; then, advice invocations are directly woven into the code using HotSwap. The authors have measured the debug mode overhead using SPECjvm98. To compare the performance of interception and run-time weaving, they have measured the time needed to invoke an empty method decorated with an empty advice both by intercepting through the debugger and by weaving through HotSwap. The SPEC `_202_jess` benchmark was decorated with an aspect introducing an empty advice to all public methods in the benchmark. Execution time was measured for (a) a hard-coded implementation of the aspect, (b) run-time weaving through HotSwap only, (c) interception through breakpoints only, and (d) hybrid Wool.

AspectWerkz. [9] employs load-time weaving through HotSwap and is therefore to be assigned to the "weaving class loader" category. Micro-measurements were made, where times for invoking empty advice and empty regular and introduced methods were recorded.

2.3   Dynamic Metrics for AspectJ Software

In their work on dynamic metrics for Java and AspectJ [14, 15], Dufour et al. have introduced *J [38], a toolkit that can be used to compute metrics from

---

[1] In this version of PROSE, join point shadows are locked when they occur in the context of advice execution to avoid aspect recursion.

previously generated traces of program executions. The AspectJ-related work based on *J is twofold: AspectJ-specific metrics were introduced, and a collection of benchmark applications was proposed. The different metrics are, e. g., used to compute the amount of bytecodes an AspectJ program executes to run the base application, advice code and aspect management, to measure the amount of aspect management bytecodes, or to measure how much code is executed in or on behalf of the AspectJ libraries. Other metrics are responsible for measuring dynamic properties of advice execution and join point shadow "hotness".

Based on the dynamic metrics, Dufour et al. have proposed eight benchmarks for AspectJ programs, some of which are based on applications originally designed and written using AspectJ, while in other cases, aspects were merely added to existing code. The benchmarks span all of AspectJ's language features. For some of them, hand-coded implementations were compared to AspectJ code.

The *DCM*, *NullCheck* and *LoD* benchmarks are based on the Certrevsim benchmark [11], an application for measuring the performance of certificate revocation schemes written in plain Java. DCM applies a third-party dynamic metric implemented in AspectJ to Certrevsim. NullCheck adds advice checking for illegal (`null`) method return values. The LoD benchmark is actually an application implemented in AspectJ that checks if another application (in this case, Certrevsim) conforms to the law of Demeter.

The *ProdLine* benchmark measures the performance of inter-type declarations and introductions. It is from the field of product-line engineering. *Bean* is taken from the AspectJ web page and uses aspects to turn ordinary classes into JavaBeans. The *Figure* benchmark originates from the same source and is here used as an implementation of the Observer design pattern. *Tetris* is an aspect-oriented implementation of the well-known game. *J Pool*, the last of the benchmarks, is intended to introduce a performance improvement to the *J tool by applying object pooling as an aspect.

2.4   Summary

A summary of the above can be found in Tabs. 1 and 2. Tab. 1 contains information on work focusing on AspectJ or the overhead of using aspects. In Tab. 2, results from work measuring dynamic AOP implementations are collected.

Production aspects are complex ones that have been carefully analysed and designed and that play an important role in an application – no "toy examples". They were only used in directly AspectJ-related works, but not when introducing dynamic AOP systems. The opposite approach is to *just add aspects*, without them being integral parts of the application's design. This approach was mostly taken in the dynamic AOP measurements.

Unlike the aspect overhead measurements, dynamic AOP measurements have made heavy use of more or less detailed *micro-measurements* to quantify the impact of aspect-oriented mechanisms on single operations. Occasionally, micro-measurements occurred paired with the hand-coded (tangled) implementation of advice whose performance was then compared to an equivalent aspect-oriented implementation (*hand-coded vs. AO*). *Weaving cost* was measured only for some

Table 1. Overview of AspectJ-related measurements.

	Díaz/Campo	Hilsdale/Hugunin	Zhang/Jacobsen	Dufour et al.
production aspects	✓	—	✓	✓
just add aspects	—	✓	—	✓
hand-coded vs. AO	✓	✓	—	✓
existing benchmarks	—	✓	—	✓
(dynamic) metrics	✓	—	✓	✓
advanced AOP	(✓)	—	(✓)	✓

Table 2. Overview of dynamic AOP system measurements.

	JAC	HandiWrap	PROSE	Steamloom	Wool	AspectWerkz
just add aspects	—	✓	✓	✓	✓	—
hand-coded vs. AO	—	—	✓	—	✓	—
existing benchmarks	—	✓	✓	✓	✓	—
micro-measurements	✓	✓	✓	✓	✓	✓
weaving cost	—	✓	—	✓	—	—
advanced AOP	—	✓	—	✓	—	—
compared to others	—	✓	✓	✓	—	—

of the dynamic AOP systems. For *advanced AOP* features like AspectJ's `cflow`, `pertarget`, etc. and their counterparts in dynamic AOP tools, we cannot clearly say that they have been used in the overhead measurements, but we believe that the examples of Diaz/Campo and Zhang/Jacobsen are sufficiently complex to have been realised using advanced concepts.

About half of the measurements were done using *existing benchmarks* like SPECjvm98 [37], JavaGrande [21] or XSLTMark [40]. In some cases, single benchmark applications were decorated with aspects to measure the cost of specific dynamic AO features. The use of JVM benchmarks is restricted to dynamic AOP system measurements. As for the comparison of different AOP implementations, some of the dynamic systems' authors have compared the performance of their approach to that of static weaving in AspectJ. The authors of PROSE have even drawn comparisons to JAC and HandiWrap.

3 Micro-measurements for Dynamic AOP

The presentation of related work in the previous section has shown that there is no unified approach to measuring the performance of dynamic AOP implementations. Instead, the authors of every single system introduce and use their own set of measurements, mostly micro-measurements that are however still too diverse. As dynamic AOP is recently gaining more relevance, a general suite of benchmarks is needed to be able to qualify dynamic AOP implementations. In this section, we will propose a collection of generally applicable micro-measurements that are intended to serve as a first step towards a complete benchmark.

3.1 Micro-measurements Catalogue

We identify the following micro-measurements:

1. *Cost of dynamic (un)weaving.* A crucial feature of dynamic AOP implementations is that aspects can be selectively deployed and undeployed. The cost

of this operation for a single aspect is in focus here. Some dynamic AOP implementations allow for deploying aspects on single instances and in single threads only, the cost of which has to be measured, too.

2. *Cost of executing a join point shadow.* Code at join point shadows (i. e., method invocations, member access, instantiation, etc.) can be subject to decoration with advice functionality. It is interesting to measure the cost of the mechanisms employed in different dynamic AOP systems to invoke advice, since measurement results gained thereby form a good foundation for reasoning about the different approaches' efficiency.
3. *Cost of reification of join point context information.* This includes, for example, binding advised methods' parameters and passing them to an advice.

The join point shadow measurements have to be done in the following contexts:

1. *Unadvised,* i. e., without any aspect addressing the join point shadow.
2. *Advised,* where every possible kind of advice (before, after, around) is to be applied and where the advice has to exist both without parameters and with a parameter that has to be bound from the join point context.
3. *With advanced features* such as the counterparts of AspectJ's cflow, perthis, perthread etc. Some systems support other advanced features like instance-local aspect deployment that have to be measured as well. Advanced features also have to be measured in advised and unadvised contexts.

With this catalogue of micro-measurements we hope to preposition a collection of building blocks for a widely acceptable dynamic AOP benchmark. Some of the measurements are not easily applicable to some of the existing dynamic AOP implementations (e. g., Steamloom currently does not support around advice). Moreover, some of them even address features that are not directly supported by other implementations and may thus lead to "bad" results for such systems (e. g., Steamloom directly supports instance-local aspect deployment, which has to be emulated in other implementations). Nevertheless, the wide range of dynamic AOP features needs to be covered.

3.2   Experimental Results

We have applied the *join point shadow execution* and *join point context reification* subset of the above micro-measurements to AspectWerkz 0.10 RC2 [3], JBoss AOP 1.0 Beta 2 [23], PROSE 1.2.1 [33], and Steamloom [8]. Each of these four systems represents a typical dynamic AOP implementation approach (cf. Sec. 2.2). The only operations for which we have made measurements were method invocations. We have restricted ourselves to this subset of the micro-measurement catalogue because it represents the least common denominator of the four systems' functionalities: AspectWerkz currently does not support dynamic (un)deployment, and Steamloom only works on method execution join points. All experiments were made on a Dual Xeon (3 GHz each) with 2 GB of memory, running Linux. JBoss AOP, PROSE and AspectWerkz were run on

Sun's standard VM (version 1.4.2_01) in client mode. The version of Steamloom we have used is based on version 2.2.1 of the Jikes RVM.

We have built our micro-measurement suite using the JavaGrande benchmark framework [10]. This framework defines three "sections" of benchmark applications, where section 1 comprises micro-measurements (expressing results in operations per second), and sections 2 and 3 contain implementations of core algorithms and complex applications, respectively. Each section provides an infrastructure for building specific benchmark applications. The framework has enabled us to implement, based on the section 1 interfaces, a set of core measurement applications equal for all dynamic AOP systems. For each particular dynamic AOP system, we only had to provide implementations for the aspects and a small application to set up and deploy them before starting the actual measurement process.

All measurements were made with no aspects, and with the aspects deployed. In addition, we measured the performance under `cflow`: the advice were to be executed only if their respective join points were reached from within the control flow of a given method. We have measured the performance of the advice both for the join points being reached outside and inside that control flow, to measure `cflow` management overhead. The advice applied to all join points were empty in the standard case. However, when the join point allowed for reifying some information from its context (such as a passed parameter or return value), the advice did so.

Measurement results are shown in Figs. 1-4. We have used an abbreviation scheme to describe the methods using three letters. The first letter denotes whether the method was **static** or **virtual**. The second defines the method's return type, namely **void** or **Object** (**v/o**). The third encodes if the method takes an **Object** parameter or none (**o/n**). On the left hand sides of the figures, measurement results for unadvised and advised method invocations are displayed. On the right hand sides, results for the same method invocations in the presence of `cflow` are given. The y axes all have a logarithmic scale and their unit is "method calls per second".

Let us first take a look at the cost of the different advice types in the four systems. In most cases, introducing advice to method invocations imposes some cost on the operations. There is no significant difference between the cost of before and after advice in any of the systems. However, around advice are special, which can be seen from the AspectWerkz and JBoss AOP measurements. AspectWerkz, being the only system supporting all three kinds of advice, exhibits a significantly higher cost for around advice than for before and after advice. JBoss AOP, due to its wrapper approach, only supports around advice, and the overhead introduced is about the same as with AspectWerkz.

Part of the observed overheads in the case of advice attached to join point shadows is of course due to the additional advice method invocation, but still there are large differences between the four observed systems: PROSE exhibits a performance drop of about four decimal powers in the best case, while Steamloom's performance loss is always less than one decimal power. AspectWerkz and

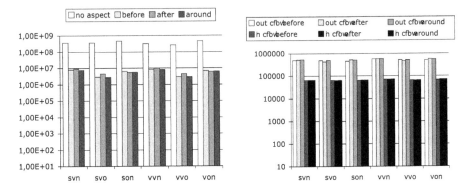

Fig. 1. AspectWerkz normal and `cflow` invocations.

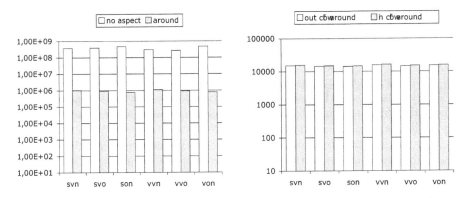

Fig. 2. JBoss AOP normal and `cflow` invocations.

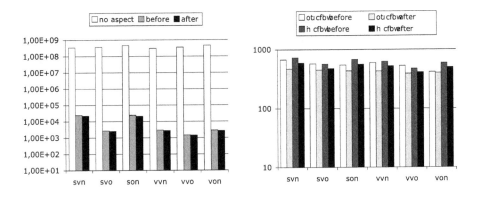

Fig. 3. PROSE normal and `cflow` invocations.

JBoss AOP range in between the two extremes. PROSE's approach to interception through the debugger infrastructure inflicts large performance penalties on decorated method invocations, while Steamloom does not suffer significantly

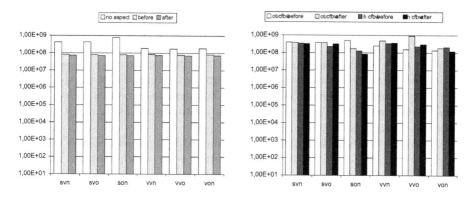

Fig. 4. Steamloom normal and `cflow` invocations.

from its minimalistic approach of just weaving in a method invocation and re-compiling the affected method.

The cost of reifying join point context information is generally low as compared to non-reifying method invocations. Most of the environments per default reify context information at join point shadows and simply provide APIs for accessing it. Steamloom does not do so, but this does not make a difference. Only AspectWerkz and PROSE exhibit a noteworthy performance loss when they have to reify a parameter from a method call.

With `cflow`, JBoss AOP and PROSE both make invocations of affected methods significantly more expensive, regardless of the methods being invoked inside the control flow or outside it. For PROSE, the cost is not much higher than in the absence of `cflow`, but JBoss AOP's `cflow` management appears to be rather expensive, causing a performance drop of another two decimal powers as compared to its performance of advised method invocations without `cflow`.

AspectWerkz and Steamloom both have a low cost if a method subject to `cflow` is called from outside the control flow. In Steamloom's case, the performance loss is extremely low, due to the `cflow` implementation using programmatic deployment [8]: a *cflow helper* aspect is deployed that decorates the control flow with a before/after advice pair which are responsible for deploying and undeploying the actual aspect whenever the control flow is entered or left.

To summarise, for the observed operation – method invocations – it has become clear that an approach to dynamic AOP based on debugger-supported interception is not the ideal solution. Albeit applications in PROSE run at almost no performance loss as long as no aspects are deployed, the performance of method invocations suffers significantly from the expensive mechanism PROSE employs. Since method invocations occur frequently in object-oriented software, this is a considerable drawback. AspectWerkz and JBoss AOP, using hooks and wrappers, perform better but still suffer from the default overhead introduced by performing *two* additional method invocations at decorated join point shadows: the first to the AOP infrastructure, and the second to the advice method. Steamloom clearly benefits from its straightforward approach of modifying method bytecodes only where explicitly needed and dynamically recompiling them.

4 Discussion

We will now first formulate some requirements for benchmarks in general, and for dynamic AOP benchmarks in particular. Most of the requirements are somewhat obvious and straightforwardly deducible from common sense, but their application to dynamic AOP reveals significant difficulties in some cases. After having formulated them, we will discuss the work presented in the previous sections with respect to these requirements.

Generally, benchmarks ought to be *widely applicable*, meaning that they can be run without modification on various platforms for which they are intended to yield performance data. All benchmarks targeting Java virtual machines – be they JVM (SPECjvm98, JavaGrande) or middleware (SPECjbb2000) benchmarks – have no problems in fulfilling this requirement since the underlying platform they run on is standardised [27]. Unfortunately, this is not true for dynamic AOP implementations, since there is no single dominant language or tool in this growing field. Instead, various implementation approaches each bring their own aspect, join point and dynamic deployment model, leading to a variety of APIs. As benchmarks also have to be *fair* with respect to their applicability to different platforms, there will have to be one implementation of a benchmark for every given dynamic AOP system, each of which needs to make use of the respective system's capabilities as efficiently as possible so that no single implementation is favoured.

Ideally, a benchmark application is a real-world application that is built using the features whose performance is to be measured. The major JVM benchmarks fulfil this requirement for Java virtual machines, and the proposed benchmark suite for AspectJ by Dufour et al. [15] (cf. Sec. 2.3) contains some applications in whose design and implementation aspects have played a significant role. The wide range of APIs and implementation approaches in the different dynamic AOP systems inflicts an extension to this requirement: it is not only interesting to measure the performance of applications of great complexity, but also that of basic operations and standard situations that frequently occur in such systems. Therefore, a benchmark suite for dynamic AOP ought to exhibit a *wide coverage of measurement granularity*.

It is also important that the used aspects be *production aspects* and not simple ones that do not improve the application's structure. Unfortunately, there is currently no complete application built using dynamic aspects. Nevertheless, first efforts to identify applications of dynamic aspects are being made [16] from which, in the long run, an appropriate set of applications will be extractable. It is imaginable that recent applications of dynamic aspects in middleware platforms will form the germ cells of dynamic AOP benchmarks.

Benchmarks must yield *comparable results*. However, the different dynamic AOP implementations are implemented on various platforms; e.g., PROSE is implemented using the standard JVM's debugger infrastructure, while Steamloom is implemented using a different VM with different performance characterics. Thus, simply expressing dynamic AOP benchmark results in units such as milliseconds or operations per second is not fully appropriate. Instead, benchmark results should be expressed using a *score* that abstracts, for dynamic AOP systems, from the performance of the underlying JVM.

Lastly, for a dynamic AOP benchmark suite, it is crucial that it covers more than only those mechanisms present in one specific dynamic AOP system. A benchmark should be applicable to as many dynamic AOP systems and should cover as many features thereof as possible. To achieve this, it needs to be based on abstractions that can be found in more or less every dynamic AOP language or toolkit. A *wide range of dynamic AOP features* needs to be covered. This of course raises the problem of incompatibilities between dynamic AOP systems again. Any feature from the measurements catalogue that is not offered by a particular system should be emulated as closely as possible in the benchmark implementation for that system.

Table 3. Summary of requirements for dynamic AOP benchmarks.

R1: wide applicability
R2: fairness
R3: wide coverage of measurement granularity
R4: production aspects
R5: comparable results (score)
R6: wide coverage of dynamic AOP features

We have summarised the requirements in Tab. 3. When we look at the work discussed and presented in the preceding sections, we ascertain that the measurements made for dynamic AOP systems so far fulfil only very few of the requirements (for an overview, see Tab. 4). We will now first discuss the fulfilment to be found in related work. PROSE, as the only system whose authors have compared its performance to that of other dynamic AOP implementations using one "standard benchmark", is marked as partially fulfilling R1 and R2. R5 was also marked because the comparison to other systems at least delivered comparable timing data, albeit no abstracted score. For both HandiWrap and PROSE, micro-measurements as well as complex applications were used, so R3 is marked in both cases. The only system that used an aspect that can be considered a production aspect was HandiWrap which introduced caching. A true wide coverage of dynamic AOP features was to be found in no work, but some authors measured the performance of advanced features. The sparse requirement coverage of the measurements in related work is quite natural, as most likely none of the authors had a *full* comparison of their work to other dynamic AOP implementations or even a general benchmark in mind.

Looking at our own micro-measurement suite, we can clearly claim to fulfil R1 and R2 since the measurement applications use the same core for all systems. R3 and R4 are clearly not fulfilled, which was not to be expected by a suite of micro-measurements. Our work also covers only the decoration of basic operations like method invocations and member accesses; the only advanced feature for which we have measurement support is `cflow`, so R6 is marked as partially fulfilled.

A benchmark suite fulfilling all of the requirements currently does not exist. However, the increasing use of dynamic aspects in production environments

Table 4. Fulfilment of dynamic AOP requirements by existing measurements.

	JAC	HandiWrap	PROSE	Steamloom	Wool	AspectWerkz	own work
R1	—	—	(√)	—	—	—	√
R2	—	—	(√)	—	—	—	√
R3	—	√	√	—	—	—	—
R4	—	(√)	—	—	—	—	—
R5	—	—	(√)	—	—	—	—
R6	—	(√)	—	(√)	—	—	(√)

clearly calls for generally applicable performance measurements in this field. We envision a benchmark suite along the line of the JavaGrande suite [21, 10] that covers basic operations as well as standard situations/algorithms and complex applications equally well. Our micro-measurements already form the first part of such a suite.

5 Conclusion

We have analysed measurements made both for rating the overhead of using aspects over object-orientation and for evaluating the performance of single dynamic AOP implementations. From the analysis, we can conclude that the set of properties to be taken into account for measuring performance is unifiable. All of the approaches to measuring the performance of particular dynamic AOP implementations have to a certain degree utilised *micro-measurements* to reason about the cost inflicted on specific single operations in application execution. From this observation we have collected a set of micro-measurements and formulated rules for their application to dynamic AOP implementations. To test their usability, we have applied a subset of the measurements to four systems that each follow a different strategy to achieve dynamic AOP support.

Since micro-measurements can only point out the performance of basic operations, we have formulated a set of requirements which we hold to be essential for a future full-fledged benchmark suite for dynamic AOP. None of the existing work fulfils all of the requirements, which was to be expected given that there have been no efforts so far to introduce a generally applicable benchmark suite for dynamic AOP. Our own work itself, being aimed at providing a unified set of micro-measurements, also does not fulfil all of the requirements, but clearly satisfies two of them. However, the measurement results have already, for the subset that was in the scope of this paper, revealed mechanisms that need to be paid special attention to when implementing a full benchmark suite.

In our ongoing work in this area, we aim at providing a benchmark suite covering the performance of all kinds of applications ranging from basic operations to complex applications. In doing so, we use the JavaGrande benchmark framework to implement the various benchmark applications. From measuring the low-level performance of existing dynamic AOP implementations using our micro-measurements presented in this paper, we will be able to identify more "points of interest" that are relevant for a dynamic AOP benchmark, and based on which we will identify and implement applications of sufficient size that may be built using dynamic aspects and that satisfy the requirements mentioned above. Apart from that, we are developing specific metrics for dynamic AOP and employ tools like *J to evaluate them. Results from metric computations will also be good indicators for the aforementioned points of interest.

Acknowledgements

The authors wish to thank the anonymous reviewers for their valuable comments that were of great help in improving this paper.

References

1. B. Alpern and et al. The Jalapeño Virtual Machine. *IBM System Journal*, 39(1):211–238, February 2000.
2. AspectJ Home Page. http://www.eclipse.org/aspectj/.
3. AspectWerkz Home Page. http://aspectwerkz.codehaus.org/.
4. J. Baker and W. C. Hsieh. Maya: Multiple-Dispatch Syntax Extension in Java. In J. Knoop and L. J. Hendren, editors, *Proc. PLDI 2002*, pages 270–281. ACM Press, 2002.
5. J. Baker and W. C. Hsieh. Runtime Aspect Weaving Through Metaprogramming. In G. Kiczales, editor, *Proc. AOSD 2002*, pages 86–95. ACM Press, 2002.
6. Bea WebLogic Home Page. http://www.bea.com/framework.jsp?CNT=index.htm&FP=/content/products/server.
7. D. Bell. Make Java Fast: Optimize! http://www.javaworld.com/javaworld/jw-04-1997/jw-04-optimize.html, 1997.
8. C. Bockisch, M. Haupt, M. Mezini, and K. Ostermann. Virtual Machine Support for Dynamic Join Points. In *Proc. AOSD 2004*. ACM Press, 2004.
9. J. Bonér. What Are the Key Issues for Commercial AOP Use: how Does AspectWerkz Address Them? In *Proc. AOSD 2004*, pages 5–6. ACM Press, 2004.
10. J. M. Bull, L. A. Smith, M. D. Westhead, D. S. Henty, and R. A. Davey. A Benchmark Suite for High Performance Java. *Concurrency: Practice and Experience*, 12(6):375–388, 2000.
11. Certrevsim Home Page. http://www.pvv.ntnu.no/~andrearn/certrev/sim.html.
12. J. A. Díaz Pace and M. R. Campo. Analyzing the Role of Aspects in Software Design. *Communications of the ACM*, 44(10):66–73, 2001.
13. M. Dmitriev. Towards Flexible and Safe Technology for Runtime Evolution of Java Language Applications. In *Workshop on Engineering Complex Object-Oriented Systems for Evolution, Proceedings (at OOPSLA 2001)*, 2001.
14. B. Dufour, K. Driesen, L. Hendren, and C. Verbrugge. Dynamic Metrics for Java. In *Proc. OOPSLA 2003*, pages 149–168. ACM Press, 2003.
15. B. Dufour, C. Goard, L. Hendren, C. Verbrugge, O. de Moor, and G. Sittampalam. Measuring the Dynamic Behaviour of AspectJ Programs. In *Proc. OOPSLA 2004*, 2004. to appear.
16. R. E. Filman, M. Haupt, K. Mehner, and M. Mezini (eds.). Proceedings of the 2003 Dynamic Aspects Workshop. Technical Report RIACS Technical Report No. 04.01, RIACS, 2004.

17. R. E. Filman and K. Havelund. Source-Code Instrumentation and Quantification of Events. In G. T. Leavens and R. Cytron, editors, *FOAL 2002 Workshop (at AOSD 2002)*, pages 45–49, 2002.
18. M. Haupt, C. Bockisch, M. Mezini, and K. Ostermann. Towards Aspect-Aware Execution Models. Technical Report TUD-ST-2003-01, Software Technology Group, Darmstadt University of Technology, 2003.
19. E. Hilsdale and J. Hugunin. Advice Weaving in AspectJ. In *Proc. AOSD 2004*. ACM Press, 2004.
20. JAC Home Page. `http://jac.aopsys.com/`.
21. JavaGrande Benchmarks Home Page. `http://www.dhpc.adelaide.edu.au/projects/javagrande/benchmarks/`.
22. JBoss Home Page. `http://www.jboss.org/`.
23. JBoss AOP Home Page. `http://www.jboss.org/developers/projects/jboss/aop.jsp`.
24. The Jikes Research Virtual Machine. `http://www-124.ibm.com/developerworks/oss/jikesrvm/`.
25. Java Platform Debugger Architecture Home Page. `http://java.sun.com/j2se/1.4.1/docs/guide/jpda/index.html`.
26. G. Kiczales, E. Hilsdale, J. Hugunin, M. Kersten, J. Palm, and W. G. Griswold. An Overview of AspectJ. In J. Lindskov Knudsen, editor, *Proc. ECOOP 2001*, volume 2072 of *LNCS*, pages 327–353. Springer, 2001.
27. T. Lindholm and F. Yellin. *The Java Virtual Machine Specification*. Addison-Wesley, 2nd edition, 1999.
28. H. Masuhara, G. Kiczales, and C. Dutchyn. A Compilation and Optimization Model for Aspect-Oriented Programs. In G. Hedin, editor, *Proc. CC 2003*, volume 2622 of *LNCS*, pages 46–60. Springer, 2003.
29. ORBacus Home Page. `http://www.orbacus.com/`.
30. R. Pawlak, L. Seinturier, L. Duchien, and G. Florin. JAC: A Flexible Solution for Aspect-Oriented Programming in Java. In A. Yonezawa and S. Matsuoka, editors, *Proc. Reflection 2001*, volume 2192 of *LNCS*, pages 1–24. Springer, 2001.
31. A. Popovici, T. Gross, and G. Alonso. Dynamic Weaving for Aspect-Oriented Programming. In G. Kiczales, editor, *Proc. AOSD 2002*. ACM Press, 2002.
32. A. Popovici, T. Gross, and G. Alonso. Just-in-Time Aspects. In *Proc. AOSD 2003*. ACM Press, 2003.
33. PROSE Home Page. `http://ikplab11.inf.ethz.ch:9000/prose/`.
34. D. Sabbah. Aspects: from Promise to Reality. In *Proc. AOSD 2004*, pages 1–2. ACM Press, 2004.
35. Y. Sato, S. Chiba, and M. Tatsubori. A Selective, Just-in-Time Aspect Weaver. In F. Pfenning and Y. Smaragdakis, editors, *Proc. GPCE 2003*, volume 2830 of *LNCS*, pages 189–208. Springer, 2003.
36. SPECjbb2000 Home Page. `http://www.specbench.org/osg/jbb2000/`.
37. SPECjvm98 Home Page. `http://www.spec.org/osg/jvm98/`.
38. *J Home Page. `http://www.sable.mcgill.ca/~bdufou1/starj/`.
39. Xalan Home Page. `http://xml.apache.org/xalan-j/`.
40. XSLTMark Home Page. `http://www.datapower.com/xmldev/xsltmark.html`.
41. C. Zhang and H.-A. Jacobsen. Quantifying Aspects in Middleware Platforms. In *Proc. AOSD 2003*, pages 130–139. ACM Press, 2003.

Testing of Service-Oriented Architectures –
A Practical Approach

Schahram Dustdar[1] and Stephan Haslinger[2]

[1] Distributed Systems Group, Vienna University of Technology
dustdar@infosys.tuwien.ac.at
[2] UCS GmbH, Vienna, Austria
stephan.haslinger@ucs.at

Abstract. Service-Oriented Architectures (SOAs) have recently emerged as a new promising paradigm for supporting distributed computing. Testing SOAs is very challenging and automated test tools can help to reduce the development costs enormously. In this paper we will propose an approach as to how automatic testing for SOAs can be done. We will introduce a Meta language in XML, which allows defining test cases for services. This paper focuses on a real life prototype implementation called SITT (Service Integration Test Tool). It has the possibility to test and monitor if certain workflows between multiple service endpoints really behave as described with the XML Meta language. This paper shows how SITT is designed and we will present its features by introducing a real-world application scenario from the domain of Telecommunications providers, namely "Mobile Number Portability".

Keywords: Service-Oriented Architecture, Automatic Testing, Web services.

1 Introduction

Service-Oriented Architectures (SOAs) have recently emerged as a promising paradigm for supporting distributed computing. SOAs are often used in intra-enterprise-integration, such as Message Oriented Messaging systems, as well as in inter-enterprise-integration, where Web services are utilized. As the systems are often asynchronous, testing can be very challenging. Testing of such systems therefore, often goes hand in hand with setting up test systems performing some message exchanges and to analyse the results. This is very time consuming and inefficient, as manual intervention is needed. An ideal state would be if such tests could be performed automatically by just pressing a button of a test system and getting back a report of the performed tests and results. This would help to advance the quality and reliability of the system and would help to find errors in the system earlier in the development phase. It is obvious that such a test system always has the need for adapting it to special test scenarios. In this paper we present one approach how a deployment of such a test system could look like. The contribution of this paper is a description of a test system for SOAs (SITT), as well as a Meta language in XML, which is used to describe the test cases for SITT. The goal is to give the implementer a powerful tool, so that testing can be done in early stages of the development cycle. The concept will be designed in a way that the test system can be also used for monitoring the system once it is deployed. The reconfiguration from the test system to a

M. Weske and P. Liggesmeyer (Eds.): NODe 2004, LNCS 3263, pp. 97–109, 2004.

monitoring system should be as easy as possible. The advantage of this concept is that the test system can function as a monitoring system just by doing little reconfiguration. As our discussion with developers working in the field of EAI showed, many of them argued that it is not always possible for them to set up an efficient monitoring tool once the product is deployed, as the development cycles in some areas is very low. Time for setting up monitoring is often not planned. If we think about telecom companies, the development cycles are sometimes just a few weeks for launching a new product to the market. We can imagine that in some cases time for testing and monitoring has not the highest priority in the project plan. With an automated testing tool it is obvious that such disadvantages can get corrected.

2   The Need for Testing

This section provides an introduction to current integration techniques and testing. It helps to understand which decisions led us to the investigation of testing for SOAs. The production of a high quality software product requires application of both defect prevention and defect detection techniques. A common defect detection strategy is to subject the product to several phases of testing such as unit, integration and system testing. These testing phases consume significant project resources and cycle time. As software companies continue to search for ways for reducing cycle time and development costs while increasing quality, software-testing processes emerge as a prime target for investigation [15]. In average software testing needs from 40% to 85% of the whole development life cycle [15, 10]. Even if testing is very cost intensive, surveys showed that testing in every stage of the development cycle reduces the whole cost for a system. Testing can help to find errors in the system at an early stage and therefore time and cost intensive rectification of defects can get reduced. An experiment showed that developers are much more efficient when using automated test. Here a short abstract of a survey:

> The experiment indicates that the tool has a statistically significant effect on developer success in completing a programming task, without affecting time worked. Developers using continuous testing were three times more likely to complete the task before the deadline than those without. Most participants found continuous testing to be useful and believed that it helped them write better code faster and 90% would recommend the tool to others. The participants were more resilient to distraction than we had feared and intuitively developed ways of incorporating the feedback into their workflow [16].

In some areas automated testing of software parts is much more efficient and easier than manual testing, even if we like to point out that this is not always the case. Sometimes the configuration for automated tests needs more time than a manual test would do. The current state in software development is that testing is widely recognised as a key success factor, but that automated tests are rarely used. The problem often is that tools for automated testing are seldom integrated in software development IDE´s. JUnit integrated with the Eclipse-IDE is one of the creditable exceptions. As our research showed, there are tools for automated testing on the market but most of them focus on unit and regression testing. There is less research on how distributed objects, spread around several different machines can be tested. When we work in the area of SOA we face the problem that testing can be sometimes very crucial, extremely time consuming, and error-prone. Sometimes it needs more time to set up a test environment and to analyse the results than to write the source code itself. Whenever a change in one of the source code parts arises a new test has to be done and very often there is no stable test environment. This then leads to the problem of setting up the whole test environment for every single change. In such cases the investment for testing can explode. There are no reliable surveys which provide information on how much was invested in integration technique in the last years, but IDC [17] predicted that in 2003 50 billion dollars will be invested into software covering integration and there is an upward forecast for the next years. We assume that a large proportion of this investment was due to manual testing the components. If testing can be automated in a desirable way this would be a big economy of time and money without decreasing the quality of the software. The approach we are presenting in the following sections tries to show how a test tool could be designed to automate tests for SOAs. This paper is structured as follows. In Section 3 we will present an example, which shows the complexity of testing in the field of SOAs. In Section 4 we will then present the design concept of the tool. Section 5 gives an overview what can be tested. The XML Meta language can be found in the appendix [21].

3   Example – Mobile Number Portability

To highlight the challenge of testing SOAs we will first present an example and will then describe how a test suite could assist in testing such a system. For this we are using an example out of the telecom world, namely "Mobile Number Portability". Mobile Number Portability (MNP) is enforced by the European Union on its member states. Every Telco in Europe has to give his customers the possibility to change the service provider without losing his current telephone number [19]. Telecom companies have to set up a very flexible and reliable system when exchanging customer data for MNP. We presented an approach for this real world scenario in [19]. Assume Telco A has to port out a customer and therefore has to sent a request (portCustomer_Request()) to every one of its national partners, which we assume are four. To fulfil a successful "port out" each of these four partners has to acknowledge (portCustomer_Response()) the request within a certain timeframe, assumed to be three hours. After the successful receipt of the four acknowledgements the business process of Telco A proposes that the 'port out'-request has to be published (Customer_successfully_ported()) to the internal messaging bus and that at least the SAP system has to receive it within 2 hours after acknowledgement. Figure 1 provides a graphical overview of this example. If we assume to test such a scenario manually, then it is obvious that a person would have to check some kind of log entries if the test succeeded or not. This can be very time consuming and besides this it is imaginable that such a test may not be done during the day, as it is likely that developers are working on the system. This scenario is a good example for showing the need of testing workflows. Here a lot of endpoints are working together to fulfil a certain goal. SITT assists the tester to test such workflows effectively. Tests familiar to these are needed very often in the set up phase of such a particular system and besides this often other project relevant problems are putting pressure on the test and development team. To set up such a scenario with the tool we will present in this paper requires some time and specific knowledge of the test person, but only consumes a little percentage of time and money as continuous manual tests would do. Once the workflow

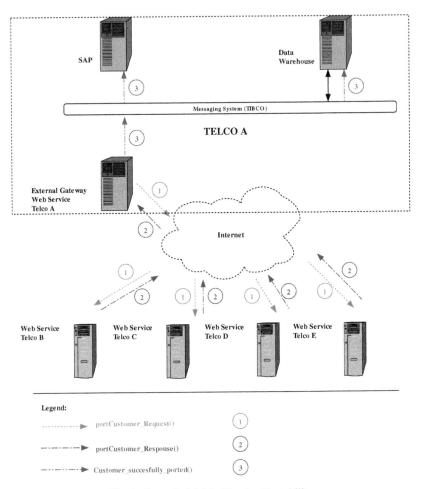

Fig. 1. Example Mobile Number Portability.

is set up properly the test can be done automatically and the results will be presented in a report. The tests can also be done scheduled over the night, therefore not disturbing daily work.

4 Design Concept

In this section we present the overall design for our test tool, called SITT. SITT is an acronym for "Service Integration Test Tool". The service endpoints can be Web services as well as adaptors to any kind of messaging product, such as "Tibco Rendezvous". Hence, whenever we talk about a service, we are not just talking about one service endpoint, instead, we refer to a set of service endpoints working together to fulfil a certain goal. This concept is also known as "Service Orchestration". The idea behind SITT is to test services and their workflow by analysing the message flows. To fetch every message a service endpoint receives or sends, the message has to be written to a log file in a standardized manner. In the paper we will always refer to messages which get exchanged between service endpoints, but of course also function calls are eligible to test. The input of the log files is then read by a so-called "Test Agent" (TA) and is then sent to the "Master Agent" (MA). We refer to software as agents, but like to point out that we do not refer to any agent paradigm. After a certain time span it is possible to analyse if every message and their replies where in the right order and fulfilled conditions like "response time" and so on. With this analysis a deep insight of the messaging system can be achieved. It is also possible to analyse if a messaging system is working properly to a Service Level Agreement (SLA). Sometimes such SLAs include conditions like "a certain message has to be answered by the receiver within x seconds". All test scenarios will be stored in a database for later retrieval and traceability. In the next subsections we will explain in detail the design of SITT. The test suite in the first phase uses 2 different kinds of XML sources. One XML source is used to hold configuration data for the MA and the TAs. The other XML source holds information about the test strategy used by the test daemon. The Appendix [21] gives detailed information about the Meta language and also provides sample XML files for configuration and testing by focusing on the MNP example from Section 3.

4.1 Idea and Configuration

Figure 2 shows a graphical overview of SITT. Every service endpoint involved writes the appropriate information to a log file. The information is read by the TA and is then sent to the MA over a socket connection. Figure 2 shows that on Host1 two service endpoints are running. Both are writing to the same log file. This is not necessary. If the service endpoints would use different log files then two TAs would have to run on Host1, one for every specific log file. If we think about a test suite for SOAs maybe one idea could be that the test suite itself sends messages, which are stored before. This would of course enhance the features of the test suite dramatically. But how could this be solved? One way could be to store messages in a file, or in the database and the test suite would have control of a certain service endpoint to distribute the messages. This testing of workflows could be tested much easier, as we will show later. We thought about a solution where SITT takes control over a certain service endpoint, which would function as an initiator for test cases, but after some design studies we found out that it is not practicable to create a common test suite with such a feature. Nevertheless, SITT can assist testers efficiently. It also has the possibility of recording test cases. This means that once a test case is executed and all the information from the TAs is received, such a test case can function as a template. Whenever the same test is run again the results can be matched to the appropriate template and SITT analyses if the test succeeded or failed. Recording of tests has one drawback, namely that tests matching to a template have to provide exactly the same results in every field the TAs collect from the log file. Just the timestamp can vary. In Figure 2 all TAs connect independently to the MA, which follows a point-to-point structure. If we would have to test a system with a huge amount of services, for instance 1000, then this could lead to a performance problem. For the first phase of SITT, where we will use to suite to gather information about the usefulness of such a

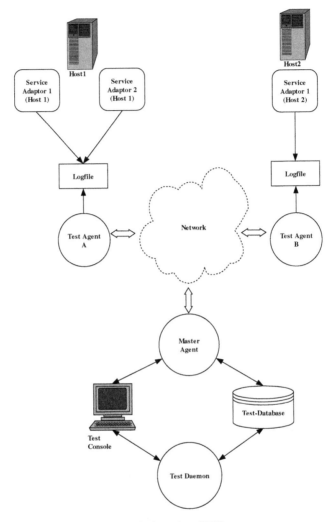

Fig. 2. Overview SITT.

tool, this is acceptable. In a future enhancement this problem may be solved by re-placing the point-to-point connections with a bus structure.

4.2   Test Agents

Test agents (TA) are programs, which run on the same machine as a service endpoint. Their purpose is to parse the log files the service endpoints are producing and to send this information to the Master agent (MA). The MA then stores the messages into the test database. In certain time intervals (normally every few seconds) messages from the test database are analysed from the test daemon against the predefined test behaviour described with the XML Meta language. After the TAs are started, an initialisation is done, which means that the TA connects to the MA via a socket over a certain port. The port is of course configurable. Afterwards the TA sends an initialisation-message to the MA, which makes it possible for the MA to know which TA is online and which not. The initialisation-message contains the name of the TA which is unique. With this information the MA retrieves configuration information for the TA from the configuration repository, which is an XML-File. We will present the structure of this XML-file in the appendix [21]. The MA then sends back the configuration information for the TA. After the TA acknowledges the configuration, the TA is online and configured for the test. This has to be done for every TA, which is involved in testing. It is obvious that the TA can be written in any programming language as long as the TA keeps with the protocol the MA expects. This makes the design very flexible as new TAs can be written in any preferable programming language.

4.3 Online Testing

Online testing means that testing is done in real-time with TAs. The test daemon frequently analyses the information the TAs send back to the MA and which are stored in the database. This testing mode can be used if every TA is able to open a connection to the MA. In some scenarios it is possible that the TA is not able to open a connection to the MA, e.g., due to the security policy or when the machine where the service is located, is not in the scope of the same department or company. In such cases online testing alone is not suitable enough. To eliminate this drawback SITT also has a possibility of Batch Testing.

4.4 Batch Testing

In certain cases it is not possible to test all involved service endpoints online via a direct connection of the TAs to the MA. In such cases SITT has the possibility to transfer the log files directly (via ftp, rcp, and so on) to the machine where the MA is running or to any other machine from where a connection to the MA can be opened. Then a TA is started. This extracts the important messages from the log file and sends them to the MA. In order the MA stores the information equivalent to the normal message exchange, in the test database. Afterwards the test daemon starts to analyse the test output. Batch testing is very powerful in inter-enterprise integration. In Section 3 we presented an example where batch testing is needed, as the Telco B, C, D, and E do not use SITT. Batch testing is a very powerful method to debug and trace system behaviour when an external system seems to have an error and the error cannot be analysed with the reply messages from the external system. One precondition is that the log files have a well-known structure. In few instances this will be true when working with external partners. In such cases, a special tool has to clear the exchanged log files to the fixed structure.

4.5 Test Daemon

Every test possibility which will be introduced in section 5 can be tested with SITT. The information for the tests are collected by the TAs and sent to the MA, which then inserts the information into the test database. The design of the database will be not covered in this paper. After the collection of all information the test daemon runs and analyses if the test succeeded or failed according to the test description in XML. Statistical information like performance and reliability can be retrieved by the user whenever needed. There will be a possibility to retrieve the information with simple group functions, such as "getting the count of all messages sent by service endpoint A for one particular day".

4.6 Log Files

SITT relies on log files with a fixed structure. The developer of the service endpoint has to take care that the service is producing valid log files according to the structure presented in this section. We assume that for every message exchanged, which means for every retrieved or sent message, one entry in the log file can be found. Every entry has to include the following:

Table 1. Log File Structure.

Field Name	Short Value Field Name[1]	Value Description	Mandatory/ Optional
Unique Pattern	UP	'SITT-MESSAGE:'	M
MessageID	MID	A unique ID for the message. In the first phase SITT needs a fixed MessageID for every message; in a future enhancement this drawback will be solved by introducing algebraic functions for calculating MessageIDs.	M
Timestamp	TS	Format: YYYY-MM-DD HH24:MI:SS The timestamp has to be in Greenwich Mean Time (GMT).	M
ServiceName	SN	A unique name of the service endpoint.	M
MessageString	MS	The message itself as ascii-string 'NA' if no MessageString is available.	O
DirectionIndicator	DI	'S': if the service was sending a message 'R': if the service was retrieving a message.	M
MessagePriority	MP	A valid priority index for the service if available: E.g.: JMS provides a 10 level priority (0-9), where 9 is the highest priority and 0 the lowest. 'NA' if there is no MessagePriority or the priority is not known.	O
Retrieved from	RF	Service name of the sender if available and DirectionIndicator is R. When using a publish-subscribe service the value is fixed 'PS'. 'NA' if the ServiceName of the sender is not known and it is no publish-subscribe service.	M
Sent to	ST	Service name of the recipient if available and DirectionIndicator is S. When using publish-subscribe service the value is fixed 'PS'. 'NA' if the ServiceName of the receiver is not known and it is no publish-subscribe service.	M
MessageSubject	MS	Subject of the message. 'NA' if no subject is available. The subject is important for publish-subscribe services.	O

[1] The Short Value will be used by the 'Message Exchange Protocol' between the TA and the MA.

Table 1 shows a structured log file for SITT. SITT should function as a generic test tool suitable for a wide range of SOAs, e.g., for Web services, adaptors for messaging systems and so on. The log file structure was designed in a way to cover most of the aspects needed in testing workflows for such services. If a value is mandatory it is marked with an "M" in the column "Mandatory/Optional", if it is obligatory it is marked with an "O". Not every service can provide a meaningful value for every field and therefore not every possible test scenario can be run for every service. We would like to point out that the structure was chosen to have the possibility to test as many features of SOAs as possible, even if the structure is not exhaustive. There might be cases where additional attributes seem to be suitable.

5   Test Facilities and Test Strategy

Before we come to the XML Meta language used by SITT, we will discuss the test strategy of SITT, mainly which functions can be tested. SITT shows our first attempt of what can be tested in SOAs, but is not exhaustive. The design is built to plug in new test possibilities easily. The main focus in the first release is to test workflows. We provide a detailed description showing which test cases, nearly useful for every SOA, can be tested, their meaning and their relevance.

5.1   Predetermined Workflow

The most powerful test possibility is to test if predetermined workflows are processed in the right way as determined by the designer or tester of the system. This feature will be used to extend SITT as a monitoring tool for messaging systems. This is a research project and the results will be released soon. SITT will have the possibility to test simple workflows between service endpoints. Our work showed that this is the most challenging part of a test suite for messaging systems and we believe that test systems in the future have to focus on this stronger to be successful on the market. The XML files covering the example from section 3 can be found in the appendix [21]. At the first sight it looks complicated to build such a XML file but we would like to point out that this drawback will be solved by introducing a GUI for setting up such test cases. In future our research will also cover if and how orchestration languages, such as BPEL, could be extended to be used by SITT.

5.2   Message Ordering

Messages sent by a message producer with the same message priority and delivery mode and on the same topic in the case of pub/sub messaging style, must be delivered in the same order as it was sent [2].

Figure 3 shows different messages sent from a publisher / sender to a subscriber / receiver. Even we would suppose Msg to be delivered before Msg' this is not the case, as Msg has a lower priority than Msg'. In the first implementation of SITT we will not provide a possibility to test messaging order if the messages have different priorities. In such a case SITT will fail. Our research is focusing on how the impact of message priority can be tested and there are some ideas which can be implemented, but nevertheless, the setup in the XML Meta language for those scenarios would be very challenging for the tester and we think that the usability of the test tool would decrease.

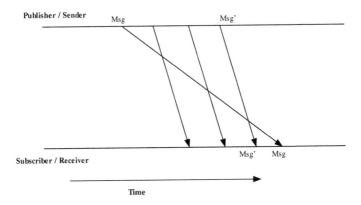

Fig. 3. Message Ordering.

5.3 Message Delivery

Many messaging systems are built in a way that they guarantee message delivery, e.g., using a messaging bus. Even if this is guaranteed it makes sense to test if a message really got delivered to certain recipients. If the messaging system does not support reliable message exchange, e.g. a Web service, this test case is even more relevant, as there is no mechanism for reliable message delivery. If the designer likes to test if every service actually received certain messages this information has to be provided in the XML Source for test scenarios. It can test if a service endpoint really sent or retrieved every single message. We will provide the possibility to indicate a timeframe in which the message has to be sent or received. Every message occurring after the timeframe will be not indicated as sent or received.

5.4 Performance / Throughput

Performance is used very often in software development without explaining the meaning of it and leaving the user just with a clue. In SITT performance covers following aspects:

– Messages sent by service endpoint / Timeframe:
  Number of messages a service endpoint sent in a specified timeframe
– Messages received by service endpoint / Timeframe:
  Number of messages a service endpoint received in a specified timeframe.
– Messages sent by a group of service endpoints / Timeframe:
  Any preferred endpoints can be grouped by a service name to a particular group. The number will function as an indicator. This indicator makes sense if some service endpoints are designed to function in standby mode, where one service endpoint can take over the work of the other in case of any failure.

– Messages received by a group of service endpoints / Timeframe:
  Similar to "Messages sent by a group of service endpoints", this time indicating received messages.

These measures can be used to test if SOAs adhere to certain SLAs.

5.5 Reliability

Reliability gives an indicator how stable the system works through predetermined workflows. Reliability is defined as following:

Successful workflows / #of all tested workflows

Every workflow is equitable, which means that the system makes no distinction in the importance of a workflow.

Example:
20 times "Workflow 1" and 25 times "Workflow 2" are tested. Workflow 1 ends successfully 13 times and Workflow 2 ends successfully 4 times. The reliability indicator in this case would be: 17 / 45 = 0.37. This means that 37% of all tested workflows ended successfully. In this example Workflow 2 seems to be a complicated workflow, which fails more often. Maybe this behaviour is something the test person knows and which cannot be changed easily. In such a test environment the reliability of the whole system would be very low, even if it the system is quite stable and just one service endpoint is not functioning properly. To give the tester a better granularity for this indicator the reliability indicator could be introduced for every single workflow or for groups of workflows. This will be a future enhancement of SITT.

6 Related Work

There is some research in the field of testing services, which is mainly focusing on testing Web services. AWSST (Automatic Web Services Testing Tool) [24] is a framework, which has the possibility to make load/stress testing and authorization testing. Coyote [22] tests services in a way that test scenarios are generated from the WSDL description of the Web service. The idea behind these concepts is more or less to invoke the services and to test the behaviour. In [23] a concept is presented how WSDL could be extended to perform black box testing. In [25] a new compile-time analysis that enables a testing methodology for white-box coverage testing of error recovery code (i.e., exception handlers) in Java web services, using compiler directed fault injection, is presented. These concepts can help to reduce the complexity of testing Web services very much and lead to a better deployment and robustness of services. In contrast SITT can be used to test if certain workflows are executed in the right order and has the advantage that the service endpoint can be any type of service adaptor, not just a Web service.

7 Conclusions

In this paper we presented an approach for automated testing of Service-Oriented Architectures. The test strategy of the tool mainly focuses on testing workflows between differend service endpoints. To show the effectiveness of such an automatization, we develop a tool called SITT and expect to have a stable version until end of 2004. Nevertheless, our research showed that highly complex services are very hard to test and that testing consumes a lot of money and time. By automatizing these manual and repetitive tests a tool can assist the test team in a highly effective way. Automatic testing does not mean that there is no work for setting up tests and that testing can then be seen just as a simple process at the end of development. In fact setting up the test cases for a tool consumes also some time and needs experience of the test team, but once the test cases are in place they can be repeated whenever needed and the test results are much easier to interpret as they are in contrast to manual testing. As SITT is still in development there may be some slight changes in the XML Meta language, as we may find that some attributes are failing or that some elements do not provide the reasonable information needed.

8 Future Work

The next steps in our work are to finalize and stabilize our current prototype implementation of SITT and to investigate how such a tool increases the effectiveness of a development cycle and how it is accepted by a test team. Furthermore we will concentrate on setting up a monitoring system for SOAs based on SITT. Additionally, we are researching how message ordering with messages of different priority can be tested reasonably. We are also working on how analysing the message itself can increase the usefulness of the test suite and we will introduce a feature finding messages belonging together by introducing algebraic functions to calculate a further MessageID on base of a still known MessageID. Besides this, we are focusing on generating valuable test cases easier, as this is now done manually by the test persons. Further we will introduce a GUI for creating test cases more comfortably. In our further research we will investigate if orchestration languages, such as BPEL, could be utilized for describing test scenarios for SITT. Besides this we will extend SITT with proxy functionality, so that testing for Web services can be done by analysing the messages, which are exchanged between the service endpoints.

References

1. http://expect.nist.gov/
2. Dean Kuo, Doug Palmer: "Automated Analysis of Java Message Service Providers". Middleware 2001 : IFIP/ACM International Conference on Distributed Systems Platforms Heidelberg, Germany, November 12-16, 2001.
3. Karim Baina; Boualem Benatallah; Fabio Casati; Farouk Toumani: "Model-Driven Web Service Development". Procs of CAiSE 2004. Riga, Latvia. June 2004.
4. Daniela Grigori, Fabio Casati, Malu Castellanos, Umesh Dayal, Ming-Chien Shan, Mehmet Sayal. Business Process Intelligence. Computers in Industry to appear.
5. Boualem Benatallah, Fabio Casati, Farouk Toumani, Rachid Hamadi. Conceptual Modeling of Web Service Conversations. Procs of CAiSE 2003. June 2003.
6. Tevfik Bultan, Xiang Fu, Richard Hull, Jianwen Su: „Conversation Specification: A New Approach to Design and Analysis of E-Service Composition". The Twelfth International World Wide Web Conference. Budapest, Hungary. 20-24 May 2003.
7. James E. Hanson, Prabir Nandi, Santosh Kumaran: "Conversation Support for Business Process Integration". Sixth International ENTERPRISE DISTRIBUTED OBJECT COMPUTING Conference (EDOC´02). Lausanne, Switzerland. September 17 - 20, 2002.

8. Olaf Henninger; Miao Lu; Hasan Ural: "Automatic Generation of Test Purposes for Testing Distributed Systems". Formal Approaches to Software Testing: Third International Workshop, FATES 2003. Montreal, Quebec, Canada. October 6th, 2003.
9. Vladimír Mařík, Luboš Král, Radek Mařík: "Software Testing & Diagnostics: Theory & Practice". SOFSEM 2000: Theory and Practice of Informatics: 27th Conference on Current Trends in Theory and Practice of Informatics. Milovy, Czech Republic. November/December 2000.
10. Vinod Suvarna, Mahesh Chandra: "Estimation Technique for Automated Testing". IBM Whitepaper.
11. James B. Michael, Bernard J. Bossuyt, Byron B. Snyder: "Metrics for Measuring the Effectiveness of Software-Testing Tools". 13th International Symposium on Software Reliability Engineering (ISSRE´02). Annapolis, Maryland. November 12-15,2002.
12. McKinsey & Company: "EAI – elementarer Treiber der künftigen Wettbewerbsposition". Management & Consulting 1 / 2001. online at: http://bto.mckinsey.de
13. Meta Group Deutschland GmbH: "e-business und Enterprise Application Integration: Der Schlüssel zum e-Erfolg". online at: http://www.metagroup.de
14. Jessica Chen: „On Using Static Analysis in Distributed System Testing".Engineering Distributed Objects: Second International Workshop, EDO 2000. Davis, CA, USA. November 2000.
15. James S. Collofello, Zhen Yang, Derek Merrill, Ioana Rus, and John D. Tvedt: "Modeling Software Testing Processes". submitted to the International Phoenix Conference on Computers and Communications(IPCCC'96), 1996.
16. David Saff, Michael D. Ernst: "An experimental evaluation of continous testing during development". In ISSTA 2004, Proceedings of the 2004 International Symposium on Software Testing and Analysis, (Boston, MA, USA), July 12-14, 2004.
17. http://www.idc.com
18. Antonia Bertolino, Paola Inverardi, Henry Muccini: "Formal Methods in Testing Software Architecture". Formal Methods for Software Architectures: Third International School on Formal Methods for the Design of Computer, Communication and Software Systems: Software Architectures, SFM 2003, Bertinoro, Italy, September 22-27, 2003.
19. Schahram Dustdar, Stephan Haslinger: "Service-oriented Modeling with UML – A Case Study". Submitted to International Journal of Cooperative Information Systems (IJCIS) – "Special issue on Service Oriented Modeling", 2004.
20. Martin Fowler: "Patterns of Enterprise Application Architecture". Addison Wesley, 2003.
21. http://www.infosys.tuwien.ac.at/staff/sd/NODE_Appendix_for_SITT_V1.0.pdf
22. W. T. Tsai, Ray Paul, Weiwei Song, Zhibin Cao: "Coyote: An XML-Based Framework for Web Services Testing". 7th IEEE International Symposium on High Assurance Systems Engineering (HASE'02). Tokyo, Japan. October 23-25, 2002.
23. W. T. Tsai, Ray Paul, Yamin Wang, Chun Fan, Dong Wang: "Extending WSDL to Facilitate Web Services Testing". 7th IEEE International Symposium on High Assurance Systems Engineering (HASE'02). Tokyo, Japan. October 23-25, 2002.
24. Ying Li, Minglu Li, Jiadi Yu: "Web Services Testing, the Methodology, and the Implementation of the Automation-Testing Tool". Grid and Cooperative Computing: Second International Workshop, GCC 2003. Shanghai, China. December 7-10. 2003.
25. Chen Fu, Barbara Ryder, Ana Milanova, and David Wannacott: "Testing of Java Web Services for Robustness". To appear in Proceedings of the International Symposium on Software Testing and Analysis (ISSTA 2004), July, 2004.

A UML Profile for GUI Layout

Kai Blankenhorn and Mario Jeckle

University of Applied Sciences Furtwangen, 78120 Furtwangen, Germany

Abstract. The Unified Modeling Language (UML) is a visual language
for modeling complex systems in an object oriented manner. Although
various structural and behavioral aspects of the system under development can be modeled, a description mechanism for graphical user interfaces (GUIs) still lacks.
Since UML 2.0 offers profiling mechanisms for extending the existing
modeling language by the user, new diagram types which reside on the
existing language's metamodel can be added in a lightweight manner.
Therefore we propose a UML profile for expressing GUI layout information which allows for modeling the static representation of graphical
user interfaces. In contrast to earlier approaches, the profile can be used
to create an abstract representation of a GUI based on a notation commonly used by graphics designers. All layout information is added using
the recently published UML 2.0 diagram interchange specification.

1 Introduction

Graphical user interfaces (GUIs) are currently the dominant species of user interfaces. Due to system diversity GUIs are common in various flavors. Starting
from Web-based user interfaces offering a rich set of presentation elements whose
degree of standardization is limited, ranging to elaborate graphical designs such
as supported by common windowing toolkits (e. g. GTK+, Java Swing).

Creating the layout of a GUI, i. e. selecting appropriate widgets for a user
task as well as positioning and dimensioning them on a screen, cannot be done
in an ad-hoc manner efficiently. Therefore, designers make use of modeling by
creating sketches of various aspects of a system [10]. Among other things, graphics designers create wireframes to roughly describe the layout of a screen before
elaborating it in a graphics editing application. These wireframes are also used
by project managers and customers to illustrate their ideas and propose them
to the designer. By using a graphical representation of their ideas they avoid
common misconceptions that appear when describing their ideas verbally.

On the other hand, modeling is a well-established concept of software engineering. In recent years, the UNIFIED MODELING LANGUAGE (UML)[13] has
matured to the leading language for creating object oriented models. It can be
applied to any software project no matter of its domain. Aspects modeled range
from high-level interaction like use cases to fine-grained class and activity specifications. Modeling all important aspects of a system reduces the risk of making
design errors that are difficult to correct afterwards, and is highly desirable. User

M. Weske and P. Liggesmeyer (Eds.): NODe 2004, LNCS 3263, pp. 110–121, 2004.
© Springer-Verlag Berlin Heidelberg 2004

Interfaces *are* an important aspect of software systems: They have a huge impact on overall cost and productivity [9], and for websites they are a critical factor for success [17]. Correcting errors in user interface design can be extremely costly, as UI code makes up about 50% of application code.[18] Therefore, modeling the UI as part of the software system helps to reduce risk.

Although both GUI design as well as software engineering create models before implementation, they do so independently and they rarely combine their respective models into a complete view of the system. If they did, synergies could be achieved, for instance the resulting model could be analyzed to eliminate inconsistencies and usability issues in an early stage of development. When joining the two approaches, the UML is an appropriate foundation due to its precise semantics, versatile extension mechanism and dominant market share.

Extending a method from the field of software development to the creative work of designers bears the risk that designers are reluctant to constrain their informal method of working with layout ideas to a more rigid and formal one. To avoid this, the new method should resemble existing practice as much as is sensible and provide an immediate benefit to all of its users.

In essence, graphical user interfaces consist of an interactional or behavioral part and a presentational or layout part. While interaction and behavior can be modeled using UML's behavior diagrams, layout cannot. Although the structural diagrams can be used to model the basic structure of a GUI, they are not suited for modeling layout issues. The reason for this lies in the UML metamodel: The layout of a diagram does not bear semantic meaning.

By its very nature UML is a visual (i. e. graphical) modeling language for various aspects of object oriented software systems. In order to facilitate interchange of model data among modeling tools UML is accompanied by the specification of the *XML Metadata Interchange* (XMI) format [12]. However, this mechanism laid out in UML 1.x solely supports the definition of elements in a model. While this is important for tools that check consistency of a model or generate code, this information is not sufficient for graphically oriented tools, including UML tools themselves. These shortcomings of UML 1.x have been corrected by the official standardization process by accompanying UML 2.0 with an additional specification part [14] which extends the syntactical metamodel in order to facilitate the interchange of graphical information about models.

UML diagrams, similar to UML models, may be described by means of a *metamodel*. The term metamodel here is used in the same way the UML does it throughout its specification, as a model of a model defining some aspects of the structural semantics. The metamodel itself is formulated re-using the language it describes, which is in our case UML. UML 2.0's diagram interchange approach adds a separate metamodel for diagram information to those already present.

Based on the metamodel introduced by UML 2.0 it is possible to store and transfer UML compliant models including their structural information combined with certain aspects of presentation. These aspects include information about spatial arrangement, sizes and also coloring of the graphical elements constituting a model.

As UML 2.0 is a relatively new standard, the options it provides for modeling GUIs still have to be investigated. While earlier approaches had difficulties in integrating layout information into their metamodels firmly, this is not a problem anymore with UML 2.0 for the reasons described above. Our contribution is to see how UML 2.0 can be used for GUI layout by exploiting its profile extension mechanism.

For the look of the elements defined in the profile, we have analyzed sketches made by graphics designers and extracted the most basic screen elements, which were then abstracted and integrated into the profile metamodel as stereotype icons [2]. Our approach thus integrates into existing solutions and practice nicely by conforming to the UML specification and by mimicking designers' sketches.

The remainder of this paper is structured as follows: After this introduction we will discuss related work which as been published recently. Section three will introduce the structure of the profile proposed and discuss the relationship to UML 2.0's diagram interchange. Finally, an example of the application of the proposed profile for modeling the layout of a Web interface is presented and an outlook on future work is given.

2   Related Work

In recent years, research has emphasized modeling the interactional and navigational part of user interfaces.[3–5] Apart from these, there are two approaches that include the notion of modeling GUI layout.

UML-based Web Engineering (UWE) [1, 6] uses the extension mechanisms provided by the UML to create a UML profile for hypermedia design. The approach uses specific stereotypes to model the navigational and presentational aspects of web applications. The presentational model contains frames, dynamic areas and primitives like text, images and audio/video. These are arranged to roughly reflect the desired layout of the final screen. Layout information is not authoritative and is not established in the extension's metamodel. The diagram is meant to model *only the structural organization of the presentation, . . . and not the layout characteristics.*

OMMMA-L[16] is a UML-based language for modeling multimedia applications. It extends UML with elements and diagrams to model time-dynamic behavior and screen layout. In OMMMA-L, the logical structure of an application and its "interactive control" is modeled using plain UML. Time-dynamic arrangement of media objects and GUI layout is modeled using new elements and diagrams. GUI layout is modeled using the presentation diagram, which allows *an intuitive description of the layout, i. e. the spatial arrangement of visual objects at the user interface.* The presentation diagram shows the layout of the user interface using bounding boxes. A bounding box is a virtual area on the screen that has size and position and is either interactional or visualizational. Interactional object may allow user interaction or trigger events, visualizational objects passively present text, images etc. OMMMA-L provides a solution to model the complete user interface of an application, including GUI layout, but does not include layout information in its metamodel.

Both approaches create their own notation, disregarding established design-ers practice. UWE does not regard layout information as essential and thus only makes weak demands on how to interpret the layout of diagrams. OMMMA-L takes layout information more important, but its metamodel also does not in-corporate it.

Some research exists in the field of sketch recognition for document layout and user interfaces, most remarkably DENIM[7] and the work of Pinto-Albuquerque et al.[15]. These approaches focus on using sketching as a new input method for creating user interface wireframes. In contrast to them, we will provide a grammar for wireframes that is based on the UML metamodel, so diagrams created with our profile will look more uniform than freeform sketches. Our profile is independent from any input methods; in fact it could be used with a sketch-recognition algorithm as in [7] or [15].

3   A UML 2.0 Profile for Modeling GUI Layout

The profile for modeling GUI layout information using standard UML diagrams extends UML's present modeling capabilities in a manner which is conformant to the official UML specification. In detail, UML's well-known class diagrams are extended to cover more meaning by adding a set of stereotypes defined by the GUI layout profile.

The semantic information expressed by adding stereotypes to UML's prede-fined constructs is combined with spatial information added to the UML meta-model by the most recent release of UML.

Additionally, the set of stereotypes defined by the GUI layout profile which is offered for usage within UML models is accompanied by graphical symbols which may be used instead of the textual representation.

Based on this, class diagrams which conform to the profile outlined below are well suited for describing both visual as well as semantic aspects of a GUI layout.

3.1   Profile Structure

Prior to creating the profile metamodel, we have examined sketches made by de-signers in the early stages of user interface design. This provided several valuable results:

- A common practice among graphics designers exists of how to draw screen elements.
- Some elements of a layout can be omitted in a drawing if they are less important for the purpose of the screen.
- Not only whole screens are sketched; often, the basic layout is finished and only micro-layout issues have to be resolved. In this case, the screen areas are drawn isolated from their surrounding elements.

Our understanding of screen layout originates from a static view of screen contents: The contents of a screen form a two-dimensional area with pixels as the units of the coordinates. If a GUI provides layered objects (e. g. overlapping windows), a screen thus provides a flattened view of them, just as the user perceives them statically. Hence, each screen area can display zero or one screen element at a time. It is not possible for a screen area to display two screen elements at once, for instance an image and a link. However, one screen element can have multiple functions on a screen; using the above example, it can serve as an image and as a link at the same time, allowing composite functionalities like nested HTML tags.

By questioning the designers and by analyzing their sketches, we have identified the most important functions an area on a screen can perform and how these are commonly drawn. We have structured them into our metamodel in a way to group similar elements and permit future extensions of the profile. The icons of the stereotypes we introduce have been abstracted from the sketches to mimic their look.

The structure of the profile we propose is shown by figures 1 and 3. Technically speaking the profile consists of a set of stereotypes applicable to UML's standard model element Class. The stereotypes defined by the profile for GUI layout are organized in a hierarchical manner in order to emphasize their semantics. Furthermore, stereotypes which require the presence of another stereotype or type of stereotype (i. e. generalized stereotype) are interrelated by UML associations, all of which are subsets of existing UML metamodel associations following a restriction of UML profiles.

In order to separate concerns, the profile metamodel has been split into the two subpackages GUILayout and References, which are combined using package merge. While the GUILayout package (Fig. 1) contains all stereotypes needed for modeling static GUI layout, the References package (Fig. 3) contains additions to the stereotypes of the GUILayout package that enable modeling of navigational structure.

3.2   Layout Package

The central class of the profile is *ScreenArea*, which represents a coherent area within the GUI. It is modeled as a stereotype (technically: a class stereotyped by UML's standard stereotype named stereotype) of the standard metamodel class Class which stores information about its size and relative position using two DataTypes from diagram interchange metamodel, Dimension and Point, respectively. The general notation for ScreenArea and its subclasses is a simple box. A ScreenArea can either be used as a container for other ScreenAreas or provide a part of the functionality of the user interface. Accordingly, ScreenArea has two concrete subclasses:

ContainerScreenArea is a concrete subclass of ScreenArea that can contain other ScreenAreas, forming a nested hierarchy of ScreenAreas. Its attribute isVisible specifies whether the ContainerScreenArea is meant to create a visual partitioning of screen space or if it is a purely logical construct. In the former case,

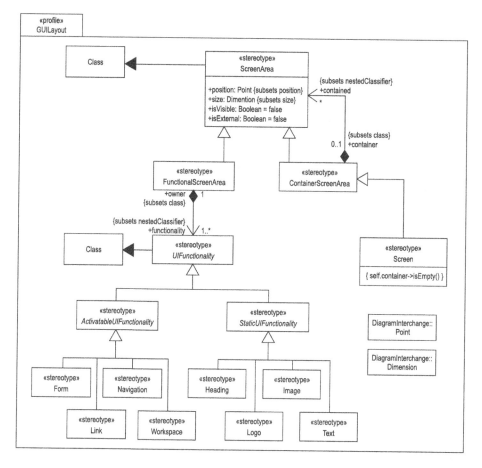

Fig. 1. Structure of the GUILayout Package

it has a solid border and its instances have a visual representation, in the latter case its border is dashed and its instances have no visual representation.

A *Screen* is a special kind of ContainerScreenArea: It may not be contained in any ContainerScreenArea, thus it is the root of the ScreenArea hierarchy. A Screen contains all elements of the GUI that are displayed at one point of time, and is drawn as a box with the top horizontal line drawn in bold.

A *FunctionalScreenArea* is a ScreenArea that provides certain functionalities; therefore, it is associated with one or more UIFunctionalities. *UIFunctionality* is an abstract stereotype of Class that represents one functionality of the user interface. Concrete subclasses are classified into ActivatableUIFunctionalities and StaticUIFunctionalities. *ActivatableUIFunctionalities* have behavior and can be part of or trigger an interaction; *StaticUIFunctionalities* statically display an UI element. Form, Link, Navigation and Workspace are the concrete subclasses of ActivatableUIFunctionality, Heading, Image, Logo and Text are concrete subclasses of StaticUIFunctionality. The notation of each of these concrete stereo-

Table 1. UIFunctionalities as sketches and icons

Stereotype	Icon	Sketched	Description
form			request information from the user
heading			short headline in a larger or otherwise distinct font
image			static image, movie or animation
link			navigable link to other screens
logo			pictorial corporate design element
navigation			provides links to all main parts of the system
text			continuous text with any alignment
workspace			interactively manipulating data

Fig. 2. Two FunctionalScreenAreas associated with multiple UIFunctionalities each

types is derived from the sketches graphics designers prepare while developing a screen design (Table 1).

A FunctionalScreenArea that is associated with a UIFunctionality stereotype is drawn by drawing the stereotype icon within the FunctionalScreenArea's box at the same size as the box. In other words, the stereotype icon must occupy the whole box of its owner. If a FunctionalScreenArea is associated with multiple UIFunctionalities, the corresponding stereotype icons are drawn on top of each other so all stereotypes are always displayed. Figure 2 shows how this is done. FunctionalScreenAreas can be collapsed to the stereotypes they own. In this case, their notation consists of the stereotype icons without the ScreenArea's bounding box.

The semantics of the subclasses of StaticUIFunctionality are straightforward and need not be explained, and the semantics of the ActivatableUIFunctionalities are discussed in the next section.

A ScreenArea that is abstract in the model cannot be instantiated (i.e. displayed on the real user interface). Instead, it must be specialized by another ScreenArea. By inheriting position, size and container from its superclass, such a specialized ScreenArea can be displayed on the user interface instead of its superclass during runtime. This means that by subclassing ScreenAreas dynamic areas on the screen whose layout varies over time can be modeled. If a ScreenArea that is part of a Screen is subclassed by a second ScreenArea, the subclassing ScreenArea can be drawn separately, i. e. all elements that hierarchically lie above the more general ScreenArea can be omitted (see Fig. 5).

3.3   References Package

The References subpackage introduces navigational links between ScreenAreas. All ActivatableUIFunctionalities can have associated ScreenAreas to which they link or which are displayed when the owning ScreenArea is activated, for instance by clicking it with the mouse. This is modeled using a *Reference*, a stereotyped Association that has been constrained to be binary and navigable in one way from source memberEnd to the reference memberEnd. The two subclasses of Reference specify two types of references: *LinkReference* specifies a direct link that originates from an ActivatableUIFunctionality and points to a ScreenArea. *ScreenFlow* specifies the order in which Screens are displayed during a user interaction sequence, and always leads from one Screen to another.

A *Form* is a set of input fields that requests some information from the user and links to the ScreenAreas that display the result of the form processing. A *Workspace* is an area that allows interactive editing of data or media. The editing pane of a word processor and the four viewports of a CGI application are examples of Workspaces. Due to the complexity of Workspaces, they can display other ScreenAreas at any time as determined by the model. A *Link* is a navigable link that points to a ScreenArea. When an instance of Link is clicked, the ScreenArea it links to is displayed. A *Navigation* is a set of links to all major parts of the software system modeled.

We have extended the informal modeling language observed in the work of screen designers with the two elements Workspace and Navigation in order to improve expressiveness of the GUI profile. Their icons are based on simple metaphors and are easily comprehensible. A Navigation is substantially different semantically from a group of Links: In a Navigation the link targets are chosen to cover all major parts of the system, while in a group of links no such restriction exists. Thus, a Navigation is one of the most important functionalities in a Screen and needs to be recognized quickly if usability is of any importance. Hence we have created a separate notation for Navigation to distinguish it from link groups. The visual representation of an instance of Workspace often is a blank area and would otherwise have to be modeled using an empty ContainerScreenArea, omitting all of its semantics.

We are aware of the fact that a major part of user interface design is about form design. However, we believe that exact form layout is beyond the scope of a modeling language. In addition, many software development tools provide visual tools for rapid development of forms, so creating them using a modeling tool does not yield much benefit.

3.4   Relationship to UML 2.0 Diagram Interchange

UML 2.0's diagram interchange specification allows adding information about spatial arrangement, size and color to every model element which is defined

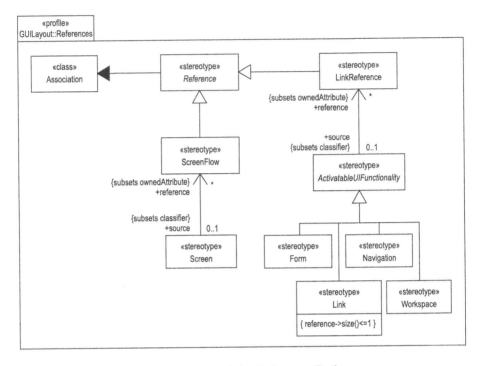

Fig. 3. Structure of the References Package

as a subclass of the metamodel class Element. This is especially true for the standard class Class predefined by the metamodel to serve as abstraction of all classes explicitly modeled within a class diagram.

Since all stereotypes defined by the GUI profile described above are applied solely to instances of the metamodel class Class in turn all GUI elements are equipped by diagram information automatically.

For defining graphical layouts using the presented GUI profile, we rely on this inherent feature of UML 2.0 and re-use the existing layout information for describing dimensions and arrangement of stereotyped classes. In essence, the spatial data which is part of every UML 2.0 compliant class diagram instance can be interpreted as information describing the layout of the visual components of the GUI to develop.

Eventually, simple adjustments (more precisely: linear scaled transformations) of dimensions occuring have to be done, but all information necessary for generating first sketch GUI descriptions are present within UML 2.0's metamodel instance already.

4   Example

When a new design is to be created, the designer first sets the general page layout using ContainerScreenAreas. Usually, this layout will be shared by sev-

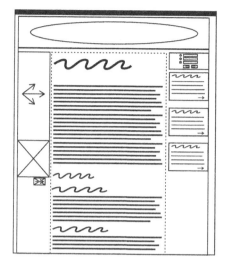 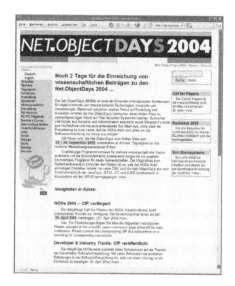

Fig. 4. The model of a screen and its real life instance

eral Screens. While some parts of a layout vary from screen to screen depending on the screen's purpose, some elements like navigation appear on all screens. Therefore in the next step, the designer identifies these FunctionalScreenAreas that appear on all variations of a Screen and models them with their functionalities. The Screen thus created can be used as a template or design guideline for following Screens and to present the first design draft to the customer. The ContainerScreenAreas that have been left empty so far can be designed separately by creating specialized ScreenAreas. In Fig. 5, the abstract ScreenArea News is specialized by three ScreenAreas with different layouts. Each one of them can be displayed instead of News without the designer having to model three complete screens.

Often the lead designer will create the initial page layout and is joined by additional designers when the details of specific Screens are modeled. For each subsequent Screen, only the ScreenAreas that differ from the first one are modeled by subclassing the original ScreenAreas with specialized ones. Figure 4 shows the model of a screen and its real life instance.

Creating a model of a screen using our profile as opposed to sketching on paper or creating a high-fidelity mockup helps the designer to focus on high-level aspects of the system without getting lost in detail. Instead of producing intermediate artifacts that are discarded later, they immediately create artifacts that can be used for communicating layout issues and as a basis for later work.

5   Conclusion

We have developed a UML 2.0 profile to support the modeling of GUI layout. This profile facilitates integration of GUI development into UML-based software

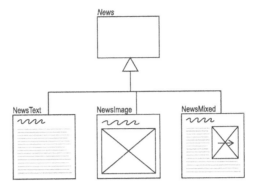

Fig. 5. ScreenArea generalization

projects, reducing the risk of fatal design flaws. To capture layout information in diagrams, we have used the Diagram Interchange specification, which is part of UML 2.0. The profile defines a hierarchical nesting of screen areas to represent the layout of a particular screen. Using graphical stereotypes it is possible to create a functional overview of a screen that is similar to designers' sketches.

As our profile incorporates UML's Diagram Interchange, the diagrams including all layout information can be stored as XML data using XMI. These data can be transformed with XSLT into an XML dialect for GUIs like the User Interface Markup Language (UIML)[11] or the XML User Interface Language (XUL)[8] to generate prototypical applications from the modeled Screens.

Sketch recognition is a promising method of adapting application look and feel to graphics designers' practice. Our profile does the same for UML models, and it is a logical conclusion to apply both our profile and sketch recognition abilities into a prototype application.

As software development is often driven by development processes, it is important to find out how the profile can be applied in existing processes, e.g. the Rational Unified Process.

Our next steps will be to refer to ScreenAreas from other diagrams like Activity or Use Case Diagrams. For example, an ObjectNode can represent a ScreenArea instance and the information it presents to the user; using Activity-Partitions, a detailed and expressive model of user interface interaction including user actions, system reactions and the ScreenAreas involved can be created.
Every UseCase can be associated with the Classifier whose behavior it specifies. This can be utilized to associate a ScreenArea with a UseCase. We hope to find more combinations with other diagrams like these two that can be created without altering the metamodel and apply them in future internal projects.

References

1. Baumeister, H., Koch, N., Mandel, L.: Towards a UML extension for hypermedia design. In UML99 The Unified Modeling Language - Beyond the Standard, LNCS 1723, Fort Collins,USA, October 1999. Springer Verlag. (1999)

2. Blankenhorn, K.: A UML Profile for GUI Layout, Master's Thesis, University of Applied Sciences Furtwangen, Department of Digital Media (2004)
3. da Silva, P. P., Paton, N. W.: UMLi: The Unified Modeling Language for Interactive Applications. In Proc. <<UML>> 2000 - The Unified Modeling Language: Advancing the Standard. LNCS Vol. 1939. Springer (2000), pp. 117–132
4. Dolog, P., Bieliková, M.: Hypermedia Modeling Using UML. In: Hanacek, Petr: Proc. of ISM'2002, April 2002 (2002)
5. Gorshkova, E., Novikov, B.: Exploiting UML extensibility in the design of Web information systems, In Proc. DB&IS'2002, Tallinn, Estonia, June 2002 (2002), pp. 49–64
6. Koch, N.: Software Engineering for Adaptive Hypermedia Systems: Reference Model, Modeling Techniques and Development Process. PhD. Thesis, Ludwig-Maximilians-Universität München, UNIDRUCK Verlag (2001)
7. Lin, J. et al.: DENIM: Finding a Tighter Fit Between Tools and Practice for Web Site Design, In Proc. of CHI 2000, The Hague, The Netherlands, April 2000 (2000), pp. 510–517
8. Mozilla.org: XML User Interface Language (XUL) 1.0, http://www.mozilla.org/projects/xul/xul.html (2001)
9. Myers, B. A.: Why are Human-Computer Interfaces Difficult to Design and Implement? Carnegie Mellon University Technical Report CMU-CS-93-183 (1993)
10. Newman, M. W., Landay, J. A.: Sitemaps, Storyboards, and Specifications: A Sketch of Web Site Design Practice. In: Boyarski, D., Kellogg, W. A.: Proc. of the Conference on Designing Interactive Systems, DIS 2000, New York City, August 2000 (2000), pp. 263–274
11. OASIS: User Interface Markup Language (UIML) Specification, http://www.oasis-open.org/committees/documents.php?wg_abbrev=uiml (2004)
12. Object Management Group (ed.): XML Metadata Interchange (XMI) Specification v1.2, Framingham, USA, http://cgi.omg.org/docs/formal/02-01-01.pdf (2002)
13. Object Management Group (ed.): UML 2.0 Superstructure Final Adopted Specification (ptc/03-08-02) http://www.omg.org/cgi-bin/apps/do_doc?ptc/03-08-02 (2003)
14. Object Management Group (ed.): UML 2.0 Diagram Interchange Final Adopted Specification (ptc/03-09-01) http://www.omg.org/cgi-bin/apps/do_doc ?ptc/03-09-01 (2003)
15. Pinto-Albuquerque, M. et al.: Visual Languages for Sketching Documents. Proc. of VL 2000, Seattle, September 2000 (2000), pp.225–232
16. Sauer, S., Engels, G.: Extending UML for Modeling of Multimedia Applications. In Hirakawa, M., Mussio, P. (eds.): Proc. 1999 IEEE Symposium on Visual Languages, September 13-16, 1999, Tokyo, Japan, IEEE Computer Society (1999), pp. 80–87
17. Shneiderman, B.: Designing the User Interface, Third Edition. Addison Wesley, Reading, Massachusets (1997)
18. van der Veer, G., van Vliet, H.: A Plea for a Poor Man's HCI Component in Software Engineering and Computer Science Curricula. Computer Science Education, Vol 13, no 3 (Special Issue on Human-Computer Interaction) (2001), pp 207–226

Reconciling Feature Modeling: A Feature Modeling Metamodel

Valentino Vranić

Institute of Informatics and Software Engineering
Faculty of Informatics and Information Technology
Slovak University of Technology, Ilkovičova 3, 84216 Bratislava 4, Slovakia
vranic@fiit.stuba.sk
http://www.fiit.stuba.sk/~vranic

Abstract. Feature modeling, a conceptual domain modeling technique used mainly in domain engineering, proved as useful for representing configurability of concepts by dealing explicitly with commonality and variability. This paper introduces feature modeling for multi-paradigm design as an integrative approach and evaluates other approaches to feature modeling. These approaches differ mainly in the notation of feature diagrams, but there are also differences regarding the basic notions. The commonalities and variabilities of the domain of feature modeling are concisely expressed using feature modeling itself in the form of a feature modeling metamodel which may serve both for further reasoning on feature modeling and as a basis for developing feature modeling tools.

1 Introduction

Feature modeling is a conceptual domain modeling technique in which concepts are expressed by their features taking into account feature interdependencies and variability in order to capture the concept configurability [1].

A *domain* is understood here as an area of interest [2]. Two kinds of domains can be distinguished based on their role in software development: application and solution domains [2]. An *application domain*, sometimes denoted as a problem domain [2], is a domain to which software development process is being applied. A *solution domain* is a domain in which a solution is to be expressed (usually a programming language).

The origins of feature modeling are in FODA method [3], but several other approaches to feature modeling have been developed. Feature modeling has been used to represent models of application domains in many domain engineering approaches to software development beside FODA such as FORM [4], ODM [5], or generative programming [1].

Feature modeling is used also in *multi-paradigm design with feature modeling* (MPD_FM), a method introduced in [6] that follows the same process framework as Coplien's multi-paradigm design [2], where it was adapted to express both application and solution domain concepts in order to simplify finding a correspondence and establishing the mapping between the application and solution

M. Weske and P. Liggesmeyer (Eds.): NODe 2004, LNCS 3263, pp. 122–137, 2004.

domain concepts in transformational analysis. Feature modeling used in $\mathrm{MPD_{FM}}$ is based on Czarnecki-Eisenecker feature modeling [1]. However, it introduces the following new concepts: concept instantiation with respect to feature binding time, representing concept instances visually using feature diagrams, concept references, parameterization of feature models, expressing constraints and default dependency rules as logical expressions, and a dot convention for referring to concepts and features.

The rest of the paper is structured as follows. First, Sect. 2 introduces feature modeling for multi-paradigm design as an integrative approach to feature modeling. Next, Sect. 3 evaluates other approaches to feature modeling. Finally, based on this analysis, Sect. 4 presents a feature modeling metamodel as a feature model. Sect. 5 concludes the paper and proposes the issues for further research.

2   Feature Modeling for Multi-paradigm Design

Feature modeling is a conceptual domain modeling technique in which concepts are being expressed by their features taking into account feature interdependencies and variability in order to capture the concept configurability [1]. Feature modeling presented in this section is based on the Czarnecki-Eisenecker feature modeling [1], which has been adapted and extended to fit the needs of $\mathrm{MPD_{FM}}$.

A *concept* is an understanding of a class or category of elements in a domain. Individual elements that correspond to this understanding are called *concept instances*.

A *feature* is an important property of a concept [1]. A feature may be *common*, in which case it is present in all concept instances, or *variable*, in which case it is present only in some concept instances. The features connected directly to a concept or feature are being denoted as its *direct features*; all other features are its *indirect features* [1].

Any feature may be isolated and modeled further as a concept, therefore being a feature is actually a relationship between two concepts. However, the concepts identified only in the context of other concepts, i.e. as their features, will be referred to as features exclusively in order to emphasize the main concepts in a domain.

A feature model consists of a set of feature diagrams, information associated with concepts and features, and constraints and default dependency rules associated with feature diagrams. A *feature diagram* is a directed tree whose root represents a concept and the rest of the nodes represent its features.

2.1   Feature Diagrams

Each concept is presented in a separate feature diagram. A feature diagram is drawn as a directed tree with edge decorations. The root represents a concept, and the rest of the nodes represent features. Edges connect a concept with its features, and a feature with its subfeatures.

Concept instances are represented by configurations of concept features, which are achieved by a selection of the features according to their variability. A feature can be included in a concept instance only if its parent has been included. A concept instance *must* have all the mandatory features and *can* have the optional features.

There are two types of edges used to distinguish between *mandatory* features, ended by a filled circle, and *optional* features, ended by an empty circle. A concept instance *must* have all the mandatory features and *can* have the optional features.

The edge decorations are drawn as arcs connecting disjunct subsets of the edges originating in the same node. There are two types of arcs, an empty and filled one, used to denote *alternative features* and *or-features*, respectively. Exactly one feature can be selected from the set of alternative features, and any subset or all of the features can be selected from the set of or-features. If optional, each selected alternative or or-feature may still be left out.

A concept or feature may be *open*, which means it is expected to have new direct variable subfeatures. This is indicated directly in feature diagrams by introducing the open concept or feature name in square brackets and optionally by ellipsis at its subfeatures.

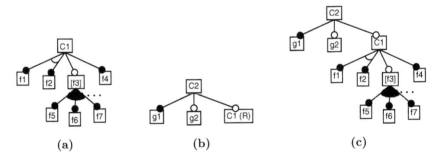

(a)   (b)   (c)

Fig. 1. Feature diagram examples.

An example of a feature diagram with different types of features is presented in Fig. 1a. Features f_1, f_2, f_3, and f_4 are direct features of the concept C_1, while other features are its indirect features. Features f_1 and f_2 are mandatory alternative features. Feature f_3 is an optional feature. Features f_5, f_6, and f_7 are mandatory or-features. Feature f_3 is open; ellipsis indicates that new features are expected in the existing group of or-features.

A concept can be referenced as a feature in another or even in its own feature diagram, which is equivalent with the repetition of the whole feature diagram of the concept. Figure 1b presents the feature diagram of the concept C_2 that refers to the concept C_1. Figure 1c presents the same diagram, but with the reference C_1Ⓡ expanded. To distinguish concept references from the rest of the features in a feature diagram, the Ⓡ mark[1] is being put after the name of a concept reference.

---

[1] For technical reasons, it will be presented as (R) in diagrams.

Additional information may be associated with concepts and features, which depends on the application, so it should be as configurable as possible[2]. A concept reference may be associated with its own information as any other feature, but the information associated with the concept it references applies to it, too.

2.2 Constraints and Default Dependency Rules

Feature diagrams define the main constraints on feature combinations in concept instances. Since feature diagrams are represented as trees, in all but simplest cases it is impossible to express all the constraints solely by a feature diagram. Additional constraints are expressed in a list of constraints associated with the feature diagram. Also, a list of default dependency rules is associated with each feature diagram in order to specify which features should or should not appear together by default.

Constraints and default dependency rules are specified by predicate logic expressions formed out of specific and parameterized names of concepts and features (see Sect. 2.3), and commonly used logical connectives (e.g., not ¬, and ∧, or ∨, xor $\underline{\vee}$, implication ⇒, and equivalence ⇔), commonly used quantifiers (e.g., universal quantifier ∀ and existential quantifier ∃), and parentheses. A feature name f in constraint or default dependency rule expressions stands for $is\_in\_instance(f)$, a predicate which is true if f is embraced in the concept instance, and false otherwise.

The intention of using predicate logic to express constraints and default dependency rules is to avoid ambiguities natural language is prone to. At this stage, the automated evaluation of the constraints and default dependency rules has not been considered, although that would certainly be useful.

Feature names in expressions should be qualified to avoid name clashes, but since each expression is associated with a specific feature diagram, the domain and concept name are unnecessary. To avoid repeating long qualifications, as in $A.B.C.x \vee A.B.C.y$, the common qualification may be introduced in front of the expression, e.g. $A.B.C.(x \vee y)$.

Constraints. A list of constraints associated with a feature diagram is a conjunction of the expressions it consists of. Thus, for a concept instance to be valid, all the constraints associated with the feature diagram must evaluate to true. Obviously, in case of a contradiction among the constraints, it is impossible to instantiate the concept.

Constraints express mutual exclusions and requirements among features, i.e. they determine which features cannot appear together and which must appear together, respectively. A single constraint may express both mutual exclusions and requirements.

Constraints have numerous equivalent forms, but they should be kept in the form which is as comprehensible as possible. Bearing this in mind, mutual

---

[2] Such a configurability has been implemented in AmiEddi, a feature modeling editor (available at [19]), through so-called metamodel editor [21, 22].

exclusions may be expressed by connecting features with xor, while requirements may be expressed as implications or equivalences, depending on whether the requirement is bidirectional or not.

As has been said, the main constraints are expressed directly in feature diagrams and thus need not be repeated in the information associated with them. However, sometimes it may be needed to change a feature diagram constraint to associated one, or vice versa. In a feature diagram, a mutual exclusion is expressed by alternative features. A requirement is expressed by a variable subfeature whose parent is also a variable feature: the subfeature *requires* its parent to be included. Also, a requirement may be expressed by or-features: at least one feature is *required* from a set of or-features.

Default Dependency Rules. A list of default dependency rules associated with a feature diagram is a disjunction of an implicit (not displayed) *true* and the expressions it consists of. The implicit *true* disjunct in a list of default dependency rules assures that it always evaluates to *true*.

Default dependency rules determine which features should appear together by default. Default dependency rules are applied at the end of the process of concept instantiation if there are variable features left such that no explicit selection has been made among them. Which of these features will be included in the concept instance is decided according to the default dependency rules.

2.3   Parameterization in Feature Models

A *parameterized name* of a concept or feature has the form: $p_1p_2 \ldots p_n$, where for each $i \in [1, n]$ p_i is either a parameter or specific string and where exists $j \in [1, n]$ such that p_j is a parameter. For each parameter, a set of possible strings that may be substituted for it has to be defined in its description. Parameters are introduced in $<>$ brackets to distinguish them from specific strings.

Name parameterization enables to reason more generally about concepts and features. An example of a parameterized name is *Singular Form<i>*, where *<i>* is a natural number. The specific names corresponding to this parameterized name are: *Singular Form1*, *Singular Form2*, etc.

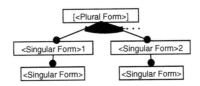

Fig. 2. Dealing with plural forms using a parameterized concept.

Name parameterization is the only way to express constraints and default dependency rules about subfeatures of an open feature because their number is unknown. Consider the feature diagram in Fig. 2 (ignoring the parameterizations of *<Singular Form>* and *<Plural Form>* for the moment). The feature

<Plural Form> is open; further direct variable subfeatures of the form *<Singular Form><i>*, where *<i>* is a natural number, are expected at it. The parameterized name *<Singular Form><i>* is exactly how all these features may be referred to.

A *parameterized concept* or *feature* is a concept or feature whose name is parameterized. Parameterized features may appear only in feature diagrams of parameterized concepts; otherwise, the feature model would be inconsistent since it would define a set of different feature diagrams for a single concept. For the same reason, parameterized concepts may not be referenced in feature diagrams of specific (i.e., non-parameterized) concepts.

Figure 2 shows an example of a parameterized concept. The name *<Plural Form>* is a plural form of *<Singular Form><i>.<Singular Form>*. Using a parameterized concept, we avoided drawing a separate feature diagram for each concept.

2.4   Representing Cardinality in Feature Models

Parameterized concepts are capable of representing UML style cardinalities represented by a comma separated list of the *minimum..maximum* cardinality pairs [7]. This may be achieved by a feature diagram in Fig. 3a with the following constraint which will assure the appropriate number of features according to the specified cardinality:

$$\bigvee_{<i>=1}^{<n>} ((\text{max}<i>\neq * \Rightarrow \bigvee_{<j>=<min<i>>}^{<max<i>>-<min<i>>+1} \bigwedge_{k=1}^{i} <C><k>) \wedge$$
$$\wedge (\text{max}<i>= * \Rightarrow \bigwedge_{k=1}^{<min<i>>} <C><k>))$$

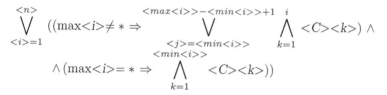

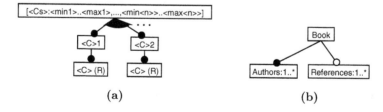

(a)   (b)

Fig. 3. Parameterized concept for representing cardinality (a) and an example of its application (b).

The parameter *<Cs>* is the plural form of the parameter *<C>*. Note that parameters *<min<i>>* and *<max<i>>* are in fact doubly parameterized. This is to enable the parameterization of the number of *minimum..maximum* cardinality pairs.

The values allowed for both minimum and maximum cardinalities are natural numbers. Also, an additional value denoted by an asterisk is allowed for the maximum cardinality value meaning "many," as in [7]. Zero cardinality is achieved by referencing the concept $<Cs>:<min1>..<max1>,...,<min<n>>..<max<n>>$ as an optional feature.

This parameterized concept may be applied to any domain by including it in the feature model of the domain. Next, the set of the singular and plural forms of concept names corresponding to each other (representing possible values for $<C>$ and $<Cs>$, respectively) has to be defined. Obviously, a feature model must include the concepts singular form concept names refer to. Finally, specific concept name and a set of *minimum..maximum* cardinality pairs should be substituted. An example is shown in Fig. 3b; a book has at least one author, and it may have zero (modeled by the optionality of *References:1..**) or more references.

2.5   Concept Instantiation

An instance I of the concept C at time t is a configuration of C's features which includes the C's concept node and in which each feature whose parent is included in I obeys the following conditions:

1. All the mandatory features are included in I.
2. Each variable feature whose binding time is earlier than or equal to t is included or excluded in I according to the constraints of the feature diagram and those associated with it. If included, it becomes mandatory for I.
3. The rest of the features, i.e. the variable features whose binding time is later than t, may be included in I as variable features or excluded according to the constraints of the feature diagram and those associated with it. The constraints (both feature diagram and associated ones) on the included features may be changed as long as the set of concept instances available at later instantiation times is preserved or reduced.
4. The constraints associated with C's feature diagram become associated with the I's feature diagram.

A concept instance is represented by a feature diagram derived from the feature diagram of the concept by showing only the features included in the concept instance. A concept instance is regarded further as a concept and as such may be considered for further instantiation at later instantiation times. During instantiation, a concept reference may appear in a concept instance as any other feature if it is not replaced by the diagram of the concept it references prior to instantiation.

3   Other Approaches to Feature Modeling

Feature modeling originates from Software Engineering Institute (SEI), where it was used in FODA method [3] developed there, which became a part of their

MBSE method. Recently, MBSE has been replaced by PLP approach [8, 9], which also employ feature modeling. An adapted version of FODA feature modeling is also a part of FORM method [4].

Since the publishing of FODA in 1990, several approaches have adopted FODA feature modeling, often in an adapted version [10, 1, 11]. Some work has been devoted primarily to extending feature modeling as such (with respect to UML) [12, 13], or even to formalize it [14].

Czarnecki-Eisenecker feature modeling [1] generalized FODA feature modeling notation and accepted a more general notion of a feature from ODM approach in which features are associated with particular domain practitioners and domain contexts [5], i.e. a feature is any concept instance property important to some of the stakeholders [1]. Such an understanding of a feature has been adopted also by FORM [4], a direct ancestor of FODA.

Czarnecki-Eisenecker feature modeling is also more abstract than FODA or FORM feature modeling. In Czarnecki-Eisenecker feature modeling, relationships between a feature and its subfeatures don't have any predefined semantics; the relationship is fully determined by the semantics of subfeatures. FORM feature modeling defines three types of relationships of a feature to its subfeature: composed-of, generalization/specialization, and implemented-by. Moreover, each feature is classified as a capability, operating environment, domain-technology, or implementation technique feature[3]. According to their type, features are placed into one of the four layers feature diagrams are divided into. On the other hand, Matthias Riebisch argues against the classification of features according to FORM and proposes to classify features into functional, interface, and parameter features [15]. Therefore, it seems that it is better not to enforce such predefined feature categories in feature modeling.

Concept instantiation with respect to feature binding time (see Sect. 2.5) is a generalization of concept instantiation as proposed in [1]. Compared to the set representation proposed in [1], even if the features are qualified as proposed in Sect. 2, feature diagrams are a more appropriate way to represent concept instances. Moreover, they enable to represent concept instantiation in time.

The following sections discuss other solutions to referencing concepts, representing constraints and default dependency rules, and representing cardinalities.

3.1   Concept References

The problem of coping with complex feature diagrams has been recognized already in [1], where complex diagram are divided into a number of smaller diagrams, which then may be referred to in the main diagram by introducing their roots.

Concept references, introduced by MPD$_{FM}$ feature modeling, are a logical extension of this idea. MPD$_{FM}$ feature modeling specifies how the information associated with the concept applies to its references and how it may be adapted to the needs of a particular reference.

---

[3] This classification has been proposed already in [3], but since FODA was concerned with user visible features, it dealt only with (application) capabilities.

Concept references enable a concept to reference itself (directly or indirectly). This enables feature diagrams to be viewed as trees while being in conformance with the fact that feature diagrams in general are directed graphs.

To refer to a concept or features unambiguously, a common dot convention is used in MPD$_{\mathrm{FM}}$ feature modeling. A similar convention is used in FeatuRSEB [10], though without taking into account domain names, which may lead to ambiguities when talking about concepts and features from several domains.

3.2   Representing Constraints and Default Dependency Rules

In MPD$_{\mathrm{FM}}$, constraints and default dependency rules are expressed concisely as logical expressions. Logical expressions are capable of expressing both mutual exclusions and requirements among features. In fact, a single logical expression may encompass both types of the constraints. In FODA feature modeling, as well as in Czarnecki-Eisenecker feature modeling, constraints are expressed by explicitly stating which feature is mutually exclusive or requires which other feature.

In [16], constraints are written in an adapted version of Object Constraint Language (OCL) used in Unified Modeling Language [7]. It is merely a matter of preference whether to use OCL syntax or traditional mathematical symbols for logical connectives (e.g., implies vs. $\Rightarrow$). However, in [16], constraints are also accompanied by the information to be passed to the developer who instantiates the concepts that, for example, another feature has to be selected. This significantly reduces the readability of constraints. Better, such messages could be generated or a whole constraint could be passed instead.

Incorporating messages to developers significantly reduces the readability of such constraints. Moreover, such messages to the developer may be generated or, even better, a whole constraint may be passed instead.

The proposed form of expressing constraints and default dependency rules may be applied also to the constraints expressed directly by feature diagrams. This way, a whole feature diagram may be represented as a set of logical expressions. For the purpose of a graphical representation, a set of views of the feature diagram could be then defined. For each view, the relationships that should be shown would have to be specified with respect that the feature diagram should be a tree. The new constraints for the feature diagram could be then calculated to avoid duplicity (some of the constraints would be expressed in the feature diagram). In order to distinguish the primary relationships between the features expressed in a feature diagram from the constraints associated with it, one of the views could be denoted as primary.

The need to represent feature diagrams in a graphically independent form has been identified also in [17]. The formalized feature modeling proposed in [14] actually relinquishes the feature diagrams completely, and with them the primary relationships between the features, too.

3.3   Representing Cardinalities

In the original Czarnecki-Eisenecker feature modeling, introducing feature cardinalities was strongly avoided arguing that since the only semantics of an edge is whether to assert a feature or not, cardinality would only mean to assert it several times, which is useless [1, p. 117]. Instead, to model the cardinality as a feature was recommended. In spite of this, a later work proposes to use the UML-style cardinalities with features [18]. Also, a generalized form of alternative and or-features is introduced in which the number of features which may be included is specified also as a cardinality (which does not contradict to the original Czarnecki-Eisenecker feature modeling)[4].

As has been demonstrated in Sect. 2.4, plural forms of the concepts and cardinality in general can be specified by parameterized concepts without compromising the principles of feature modeling. If preferred, UML cardinalities can be used instead, provided they are defined as a notational extension with respect to the parameterized concept.

4   A Feature Modeling Metamodel

The domain of feature modeling is understood here as a domain of the tools that support feature modeling as a central activity in software development. The feature modeling based methods, such as generative programming, FODA, FORM, FeatuRSEB, and feature modeling for multi-paradigm design, all have in common the central role of a feature model from which traceability links to other models are provided. The variability lies in the notations of feature modeling employed by different methods. The systems built in the domain would represent feature modeling CASE tools suitable for individual methods (possibly groups of methods).

Based on the information presented in the previous sections, a metamodel of the feature modeling will be proposed in this section. The metamodel will be expressed using feature modeling itself in order to capture the variability of feature modeling notations and to describe the core concepts of feature modeling in a concise way. The purpose of this metamodel is to provide a basis both for further reasoning on feature modeling and for developing feature modeling tools. Therefore, the metamodel embraces features that express functionality, too.

The concepts identified in the domain of feature modeling are: feature model, feature diagram, node, feature, partition, associated information, AI item, AI value, constraint, default dependency rule, and link. The model also includes the parameterized concept *Plural Form* introduced in Sect. 2.3, where *<Singular Form> <i>.<Singular Form>* is a reference to one of the following concepts: *Feature Diagram, Node, Feature, Link, Constraint, Default Dependency Rule,* or *AI Value*. Dynamic binding of *Plural Form* features is assumed. In the rest

---

[4] These extensions are implemented in Captain Feature (available at [20]), in which the whole feature modeling notation should be configurable through a metamodel represented by a feature model [23, 18], but its editing is not possible.

of the concepts, dynamic binding is indicated where applies; otherwise, static binding is assumed.

4.1 Feature Model and Feature Diagram

A feature model (Fig. 4) represents the model of a domain obtained by the application of feature modeling. It consists of a set of feature diagrams (*Feature Diagram Set*). and it may have a set of links to other modeling artifacts (*Link Set*). Feature diagrams in a feature model may be normalized [1] (*Normalize*), but this applies only to those feature modeling notations that embrace or-features.

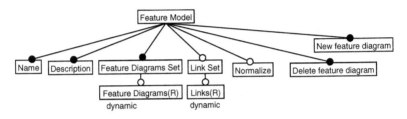

Fig. 4. *Feature Model* concept.

A feature diagram (Fig. 5) presents a featural description of a concept graphically. An additional constraint that applies to *Feature Diagram* is that a root may not be a concept reference:

¬*Root.Node.Reference*

A feature diagram contains a set of nodes (*Node Set*) and a set of features (*Feature Set*). It may be represented by a directed tree (*Tree*). In this case, a feature diagram describes the features of a domain concept represented by its root node (*Root.Node*®). An operation of adding a feature to a feature diagram represented as a tree (*Tree.Add feature*) should preserve the tree structure. A feature diagram may also be considered to be a connected directed graph.

A set of constraints (*Constraint Set*) and default dependency rules (*Default Dependency Rule Set*) may be associated with a feature diagram, which is needed by some approaches to feature modeling. Also, a feature diagram may have a set of links to other modeling artifacts (*Link Set*). A feature diagram may be normalized (*Normalize*).

4.2 Node and Feature

Feature diagram nodes (Fig. 6) represent concepts in general sense (as explained in Sect. 2), which have they own names (*Name*), and concept reference nodes (*Reference*). It may have a set of links to other modeling artifacts (*Link Set*). Some approaches to feature modeling allow feature diagram nodes to be marked as open, which means that new direct features of a node are expected (*Openness*).

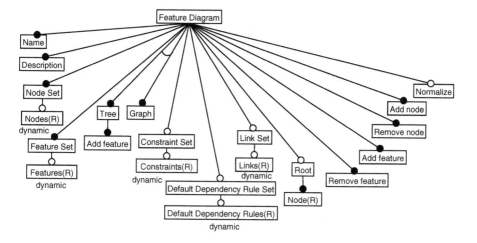

Fig. 5. *Feature Diagram* concept.

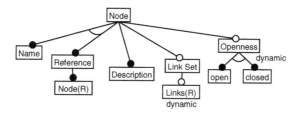

Fig. 6. *Node* concept.

A feature is a relationship between two nodes (Fig. 7). It describes the variability of a subfeature (*Subfeature*) with respect to its superfeature (*Superfeature*): the subfeature may be mandatory (*mandatory*), i.e. it must be included in a concept instance, or it may be optional (*optional*), i.e. it may be included in a concept instance.

In some approaches to feature modeling, relationships between nodes are named (*Name*) or may have a type specified (*Type*). Also, a feature may have a set of links to other modeling artifacts (*Link Set*).

4.3   Partition

Features originating in one node may be divided into a set of disjunct partitions (Fig. 8) marked by arcs in feature diagrams. The features in a partition are presumed to be alternative, i.e. to have xor semantics (as in FODA). Some approaches (e.g., Czarnecki-Eisenecker notation and MPD$_{FM}$) employ also or-features, so the features in a partition may be either alternative or or-features (*Type*). Other approaches (e.g. [18]) employ cardinality, which enables to specify the number of features (maximum and minimum) in a partition that may be selected (*Cardinality*). Some approaches to feature modeling allow partitions to

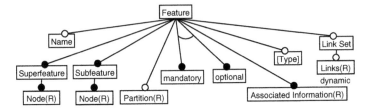

Fig. 7. *Feature* concept.

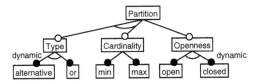

Fig. 8. *Partition* concept.

be marked as open (similarly to openness of a node in a feature diagram), which means that new direct features in a partition are expected (*Openness*).

4.4 Associated Information and Related Concepts

Different approaches to feature modeling, and different applications of it, too, require different information to be associated with features. The concept of associated information (Fig. 9) captures this demand by a fully configurable set of items associated information consists of (*AI Items*®).

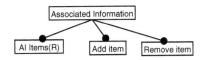

Fig. 9. *Associated Information* concept.

An associated information item (Fig. 10a) applicability may depend on the optionality of a feature with which it is associated (*Applicability*). There are two kinds of an associated information item: textually expressed ones (*Textual*) and those represented by a value selected from the extensible set of available values (*Selectable*). The concept of an associated information value (Fig. 10b) represents such a value.

4.5 Constraint and Default Dependency Rule

Constraints (Fig. 11a) express mutual exclusions and requirements among features beside those specified by the feature diagram. They may be specified either

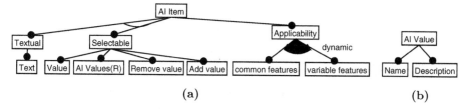

Fig. 10. *AI Item* (a) and *AI Value* (b) concepts.

Fig. 11. *Constraint* (a) and *Default Dependency Rule* (b) concepts.

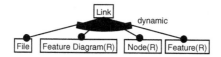

Fig. 12. *Link* concept.

as logical expressions (*Logical expression*), textually (*Textual*), or in a FODA-like form (see Sect. 3.2).

Default dependency rules (Fig. 11b) determine which features should appear together by default in concept instances. They may be specified either as logical expressions (*Logical expression*) or textually (*Textual*).

4.6 Link

A link (Fig. 12) enables to connect a feature model or its parts to its own nodes and features, or to other models. These models include feature models, in which case a link may be more specific and point to a feature diagram in that model, or a node or feature in that diagram. An additional constraint that applies to *Link* concept is that a link may not lead to a node and feature simultaneously:

Node $\veebar$ *Feature*

5   Conclusions and Further Research

This paper brings several improvements into feature modeling. Concept instantiation is defined with respect to instantiation time with concept instances represented by feature diagrams. Parameterization in feature models enables to reason more generally about concepts and features and to express constraints and default dependency rules about subfeatures of an open feature. Constraints and default dependency rules are represented by logical expressions. Concept references enable to deal with complex feature models. A dot convention enables referring to concepts and features unambiguously. A parameterized concept which enables to represent cardinality in feature modeling is introduced.

Other approaches to feature modeling have been evaluated and compared with feature modeling for multi-paradigm design. Based on this analysis, a feature modeling metamodel has been proposed. The metamodel shows how the commonalities and variabilities of the domain of feature modeling may be modeled by feature modeling itself. This metamodel may serve both for further reasoning on feature modeling and as a basis for developing feature modeling tools.

Further research topics include enhancing parameterization in feature modeling with respect to binding time/mode and expressing feature models fully in the form of constraints (as logical expressions) with defined primary constraints that are to be presented visually (in feature diagrams).

Acknowledgements

The work was partially supported by Slovak Science Grant Agency VEGA, project No. 1/0162/03.

References

1. Czarnecki, K., Eisenecker, U.W.: Generative Programing: Principles, Techniques, and Tools. Addison-Wesley (2000)
2. Coplien, J. O.: Multi-Paradigm Design for C++. Addison-Wesley (1999)
3. Kang, K.C., et al.: Feature-oriented domain analysis (FODA): A feasibility study. Technical Report CMU/SEI-90-TR-21, Software Engineering Institute, Carnegie Mellon University, Pittsburgh, USA (1990).
4. Kang, K.C., Kim, S., Lee, J., Kim, K., Shin, E., Huh, M.: FORM: A feature-oriented reuse method with domain-specific reference architectures. Annals of Software Engineering 5 (1998) 143–168
5. Simos, M.A.: Organization domain modeling (ODM): Formalizing the core domain modeling life cycle. In: Proc. of the 1995 Symposium on Software reusability, Seattle, Washington, United States, ACM Press (1995) 196–205
6. Vranić, V.: Feature modeling based transformational analysis in multi-paradigm design. Submitted to *Computers and Informatics (CAI)*, December 2003.
7. Object Management Group: OMG unified modeling language specification, version 1.5 (2003).
8. Chastek, G., et al.: Product line analysis: A practical introduction. Technical Report CMU/SEI-2001-TR-001, Software Engineering Institute, Carnegie Mellon University, Pittsburgh, USA (2001).
9. Software Engineering Institute, Carnegie Mellon University: A framework for software product line practice – version 3.0.
   http://www.sei.cmu.edu/plp/framework.html. Last accessed in June 2004.
10. Griss, M.L., et al.: Integrating feature modeling with the RSEB. In Devanbu, P., Poulin, J., eds.: Proc. of 5th International Conference on Software Reuse, Vicoria, B.C., Canada, IEEE Computer Society Press (1998) 76–85

11. Geyer, L.: Feature modelling using design spaces. In: Proc. of the 1st German Product Line Workshop (1. Deutscher Software-Produktlinien Workshop, DSPL-1), Kaiserslautern, Germany, IESE (2000)

12. Riebisch, M., et al.: Extending feature diagrams with UML multiplicities. In: Proc. of the 6th Conference on Integrated Design and Process Technology (IDPT 2002), Pasadena, California, USA, Society for Design and Process Science (2002).

13. Clauβ, M.: Modeling variability with UML. In: Proc. of Net.ObjectDays 2001, Young Researchers Workshop on Generative and Component-Based Software Engineering, Erfurt, Germany, tranSIT (2001) 226–230

14. Jia, Y., Gu, Y.: The representation of component semantics: A feature-oriented approach. In Crnković, I., Larsson, S., Stafford, J., eds.: Proc. of the Workshop on Component-based Software Engineering: Composing Systems From Components (a part of 9th IEEE Conference and Workshops on Engineering of Computer-Based Systems), Lund, Sweden (2002).

15. Riebisch, M.: Towards a more precise definition of feature models. In M. Riebisch, J. O. Coplien, D.S., ed.: Modelling Variability for Object-Oriented Product Lines, Norderstedt, BookOnDemand Publ. Co. (2003) 64–76

16. Streitferdt, D., et al.: Details of formalized relations in feature models using OCL. In: Proc. of the 10th IEEE Symposium and Workshops on Engineering of Computer-Based Systems (ECBS'03), Pasadena, California, USA, IEEE Computer Society (2003) 297–304

17. Lee, K., et al.: Concepts and guidelines of feature modeling for product line software engineering. In Gacek, C., ed.: Proc. of 7th International Conference (ICSR-7). LNCS 2319, Austin, Texas, USA, Springer (2002)

18. Czarnecki, K., et al.: Generative programming for embedded software: An industrial experience report. In Batory, D., et al., eds.: Generative Programming and Component Engineering: ACM SIGPLAN/SIGSOFT Conference, GPCE 2002. LNCS 2487, Pittsburgh, PA, USA (2002) 156–172

19. Czarnecki, K., Eisenecker, U.W.: Generative programming – methods, tools, and applications. http://www.generative-programming.org. Last accessed in March 2004.

20. Captain Feature: Project page. https://sourceforge.net/projects/captainfeature. Last accessed in March 2004.

21. Blinn, F.: Entwurf und implementierung eines generators für merkmalmetamodelle. Master's thesis, Fachhochschule Zweibrücken, Fachbereich Informatik (2001) In German. Available at http://www.informatik.fh-kl.de/~eisenecker (last accessed in March 2004).

22. Czarnecki, K., et al.: Generative programing: Methods, techniques, and applications. Slides and notes of the tutorial given at Net.ObjectDays 2003 (2003)

23. Bednasch, T.: Konzept und implementierung eines konfigurierbaren metamodells für die merkmalmodellierung. Master's thesis, Fachhochschule Kaiserslautern, Standort Zweibrücken, Fachbereich Informatik (2002) In German. Available at http://www.informatik.fh-kl.de/~eisenecker (last accessed in March 2004).

Feature-Oriented Development
of Software Product Lines:
Mapping Feature Models to the Architecture

Periklis Sochos, Ilka Philippow, and Matthias Riebisch

Technical University Ilmenau, Process Informatics, Postfach 10 00 565
98684 Ilmenau, Germany
{Periklis.Sochos,Ilka.Philippow,Matthias.Riebisch}@tu-ilmenau.de
http://www.theoinf.tu-ilmenau.de/~pld

Abstract. Software product lines (PLs) present a solid approach in
large scale reuse. Due to the PLs' inherit complexity, many PL methods
use the notion of "features" to support requirements analysis and domain
modelling (e.g. FODA, FORM, FeatuRSEB). Nevertheless, the link between features and architecture remains weak in all methodologies, with
a large impact on the traceability of high-level concerns in respect to
lower-lever architectural structures. This paper provides an analysis on
the state of the art of feature-oriented PL methodologies from the point
of view of the linkage between feature models and architecture. Based on
the identified shortcomings it introduces an approach to allow a strong
mapping between features and architecture. The approach makes use of
extensions in the feature modelling techniques and adopts plug-in architectures as a means of mapping feature structures and at the same time
satisfying the demanded PL variability and flexibility.

Keywords: Software product lines, product line methods, feature modelling, separation of concerns, feature-architecture mapping, generative
programming, plug-in architectures.

1 Introduction

Software product lines (PLs) replace the various separately-developed systems
of a domain. Thus PLs embed at least the additive complexity present in each
of these systems, posing a challenge in their development and demanding extensive variability. Additionally, PLs must follow all principles of modern software,
being flexible, extendible and maintainable. In order to keep a balance between
these requirements and virtues, PLs must adhere to a high level of abstraction:
alone the variability and size of PLs impose the use of explicit domain modelling
techniques and the development of a solid architecture. Many PL development
methodologies have established "features" and "feature modelling" for this purpose e.g. FODA, FORM, FeatuRSEB.

In the current PL methods, the high level of abstraction obtained by feature
domain analysis is constrained to the simplification and representation of the
PL requirements or as a vague guide for design.

M. Weske and P. Liggesmeyer (Eds.): NODe 2004, LNCS 3263, pp. 138–152, 2004.

This paper aims to clarify the state of the art feature-oriented PL methods' insufficiencies in respect to the linkage between feature models and architecture and to present an approach to "bridge" the gap between these two artifacts. The proposed methodology involves the adoption of a modular plug-in architectural structure in synergy with feature modelling techniques. The method bears the name "Feature-Architecture Mapping" (FArM-reads farm).

Section 2 provides a rational for the selection of features as the main abstraction construct and the importance of a *strong* mapping between feature models and architecture. Section 3 illustrates the development of the main feature-oriented PL methods up to this point. Sections 4 until 7 analyze the previously identified methodologies from the point of view of the linkage between feature model and architecture. In section 8 an overview of the development process of FArM is presented. Finally, sections 9 and 10 provide the conclusions and further work.

2   Feature Models and Architecture in Software Product Lines

Software product lines centralize upon the idea of designing and implementing a family of systems to produce qualitative applications in a domain, promote large scale reuse and reduce development costs.

2.1   The Role of Features

Achieving these goals in the space of a domain makes the need of preserving a high level of abstraction even more evident. Based on this rational, the concept of a *feature* is introduced.

A formalized definition of a feature in the software field is given in [7]: "*a logical unit of behavior that is specified by a set of functional and quality requirements*". Adding to this, comes the definition of features from [18]: "*A feature represents an aspect valuable to the customer...*".

Furthermore, features may be structured in *feature models*. These are hierarchical tree illustrations of features. There exist many variants of feature modelling conventions (see [7], [11], [21], [22], [24]). A sample feature model of an IDE (Integrated Development Environment) PL showing the previously mentioned conventions, with the *multiplicity* extension (see [18] and [19]), is given in figure 1.

Summarizing, features may serve as a means of:

- modelling large domains
- managing the variability of PL products
- encapsulating system requirements
- guiding the PL development
- driving marketing decisions
- future planning
- communication between system stakeholders

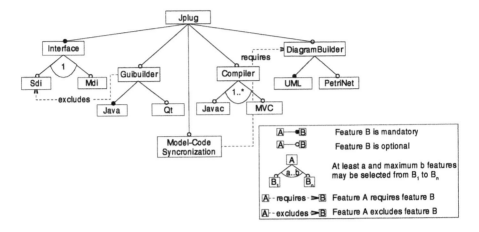

Fig. 1. A sample feature model

2.2 The Role of Feature Model and Architecture Mapping

During the design phase of a PL, one needs to identify all important aspects of the system and based on the imposed quality requirements, to device the main architectural abstractions and the connections between them.

In order to achieve a long-life, maintainable system, one must adhere to the rule of *separation of concerns* i.e. achieve such an architectural structure, where ideally each architectural component encapsulates exactly one *concern*. In PLs, that would ideally be one *feature*[1].

Nowadays, software technologies (e.g. Object-Orientation) make it extremely difficult to achieve a pure one to one relation between feature models and architectures [28]. Therefore, it is vital for the PL system to achieve, if not a pure one to one relation, at least a strong mapping between features and architectural components.

3 Feature-Oriented Product Line Methods

With the term *Feature-Oriented* product lines we stress the fact that this paper is concerned with the PL methods making intensive use of the notion of features and feature modelling. Looking at the evolution of PL methods in relation to each other, one could extract the picture shown in figure 2.

Rather than providing a complete reference to all possible variations of the feature-oriented methodologies, this paper concentrates on those methods using features as a main artifact in their processes, having a wide industrial acceptance and providing sufficient documentation.

---

[1] Experience from real life [14] shows that high maintainability may be achieved, when at least a one-to-many relation between features and architectural components is present.

Fig. 2. Development of Feature-Oriented Product Line Methods

The identified methods are FODA (Feature-Oriented Domain Analysis), FeatuRSEB (Featured RSEB), HyperFeatuRSEB (Hyper Featured RSEB), GenVoca and FORM (Feature-Oriented Reuse Method). Note that the RSEB (Reuse-Driven Software-Engineering Business) [15] method is provided only for completeness. It is based mainly on use-cases and therefore it is not explicitly analyzed in this paper.

4   FODA and FORM

FODA is a domain analysis method. It focuses on providing a complete description of the domain features, paying less attention on the phases of design and implementation [1]. The feature modelling notation used in FODA does not include the representation of basic processes in a system's architecture, e.g. interactions between architectural components implementing features. Furthermore, FODA lacks a concrete description of the transition from a feature model to an architecture.

FORM comes as a concretization of the FODA processes. It provides guidelines for the creation of the feature model, design and implementation phases. In [27] FORM's authors provide a description of these phases. As presented in this source, FORM performs an analysis of a domain's features and attempts to provide a mapping between features and architectural components: *"By designing each selectable feature as a separate component, applications can be derived easily from product-line software. If there is difficulty in establishing this relation, the feature must be refined into specific features so that features can be easily mapped into architectural components."*

FORM provides no concrete description of the above mentioned process. Furthermore, feature interactions are superficially addressed by FORM. No explicit support is provided by the method for the construction of an architecture to conform to the structure of a feature model. FORM's main focus, as given in [23], is not providing a clear mapping between the feature model and the architecture, rather concretizing the FODA processes of design and analysis from a marketing perspective.

FODA and FORM remain vague on the matter of mapping feature models to architectural elements. FODA concentrates on the modelling of the domain concepts and FORM does not place enough focus on describing such a process.

5   FeatuRSEB

FeatuRSEB merges the RSEB and the FODA methods. Its main goal is to provide a central model for the synchronization of the RSEB processes and at the same time model the commonality and variability within the RSEB. This is achieved through the introduction of the feature model.

FeatuRSEB is divided, as most PL methods, into two main processes, namely, Product Line Engineering and Product Engineering, where the former develops the PL assets and the latter makes use of them to build PL products.

The Product Line Engineering phase is initiated by storing all requirements of the product line in a common repository in the form of use-cases. The PL requirements are also ordered in features on a feature model. Features and use-cases are linked with traceability links. The PL architecture is derived from the use-cases following the "Layers" architectural pattern [8], where each layer consists of components containing object-oriented classes. Traceability links are then assigned between the derived classes and their use-cases.

Thus FeatuRSEB performs the mapping between feature models and architectural elements exclusively through traceability links pointing to use-cases, which in turn point to classes within the architectural elements.

This way of mapping a feature model to the architecture, although it does present a step towards the right direction, has a number of disadvantages. Namely, the number of traceability links in a PL very soon becomes extremely large. The creation, management and maintenance of the traceability links, even for a normal sized PL, is an overwhelming task and its resolution is not addressed by FeatuRSEB.

6   HyperFeatuRSEB

HyperFeatuRSEB combines the Hyperspace and FeatuRSEB methods. It utilizes Hyperspace techniques to map features to architectural component. Because of this fact, this section will explore HyperFeatuRSEB in more detail. Before considering specific aspects of HyperFeatuRSEB, section 6.1 will provide the needed terminology for the Hyperspace Approach.

6.1   The Hyperspace Approach

The Hyperspace Approach [28] was developed by IBM to achieve a *multiple-separation of concerns*. A concern can be anything that is of importance to the system stakeholders, from requirements to features or implementation details.

The Hyperspace approach allows the definition of a multi-dimensional *hyperspace*, where all concerns are included. A *hyperslice* may encapsulate one of these concerns, and the combination of many hyperslices through *integration relationships* yields a product containing all desired concerns, defined as a *hypermodule*.

These concepts can be easier understood by means of an example throughout the description of the HyperFeatuRSEB method.

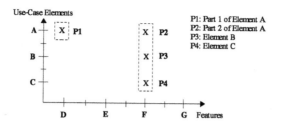

Fig. 3. A two-dimensional hyperspace. A hyperslice is marked with a dashed line and encapsulates exactly one feature

6.2   The HyperFeatuRSEB Method

HyperFeatuRSEB [5] identifies the problem of separation of concerns in FeatuRSEB and integrates FeatuRSEB with the Hyperspace approach after providing a UML extension of this method, the HyperUML [6].

HyperFeatuRSEB's structure is similar to that of FeatuRSEB. This time FeatuRSEB's use-cases are broken down to actors, use-cases and activity diagrams. Each of these use-case elements are assigned to their belonging features and are ordered in a two-dimensional hyperspace, as shown in figure 3.

The product line engineering derives the PL's common architecture from the complete use-case model. Separate processes, coordinated by the PL engineers, derive the object model for each hyperslice (i.e. feature) from the partial use-cases within each hyperslice.

Thus, we have one hyperslice (i.e. feature) containing the object model elements belonging to it, which assures a one to one relation between feature model and architectural elements. The inadequacies of this method are illustrated through an example.

Figure 4 shows a partial feature model of a PL made with HyperFeatuRSEB and the respective hyperslices encapsulating the parts of the architectural elements for each feature.

As shown in figure 4, if a customer chooses to have an IDE (Integrated Development Environment) with an Sdi (single document interface), the "empty" method `GetSelectedText()` in the `Core` hyperslice, marked by the Hyperspace construct **Unimplemented**, will be replaced by the "implemented" `GetSelectedText()` method in the `Sdi` hyperslice. When the customer selects the Mdi (Multi document interface) feature, the respective substitution will take place.

As a result, the end product will contain either the implementation of the Sdi or the Mdi feature.

6.3   HyperFeatuRSEB and the Hyperspace Approach Open Issues

The shortcomings of the methods become evident when a "non-additive" change occurs. With the term non-additive, we mean, for example, a change that causes

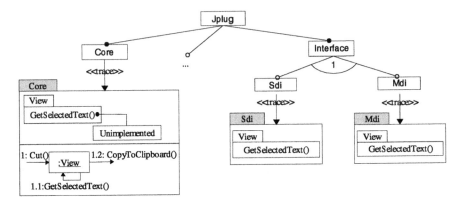

Fig. 4. A partial feature model for an IDE product line, along with the features' hyperslices from an architectural perspective

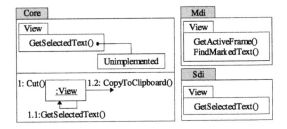

Fig. 5. A non-additive change within a hyperslice causes cascading changes in other hyperslices (i.e. features)

a method to be removed and replaced by others. Such a change can be seen in figure 5.

The implementation of the `GetSelectedText()` method of the Mdi feature in figure 4 needs to be removed and replaced by the `GetActiveFrame()` and `FindMarkedText()` methods, as shown in figure 5. A hyperslice is "encapsulated", so a change of its internal structure is perfectly legal.

If a customer now chooses the Mdi feature, the `View` class in the `Core` and Mdi hyperslices can not be *merged* anymore. The `GetSelectedText()` method in the `Core` has to be changed in accordance to the Mdi's feature methods to `GetActiveFrame()` and `FindMarkedText()`. But now merging the `Core` and `Sdi` features is not possible anymore. This means that the Sdi feature must also be changed and surprisingly in an absurd way.

This example has led us to the following conclusions:

Maintainability. In the work on HyperFeatuRSEB [5] a software product line has been implemented to illustrate the strengths and weaknesses of the method and serve as a means of comparison to the FeatuRSEB method.

An analysis on the source code of this system has shown that the PL has 1243 such unimplemented methods from overall 4197, shared between various combinable features, in other words: *"1 out of 3 method changes causes at least 2, at most 19, on average 4 features to change"*.

The way of the Hyperspace approach to create a separation of concerns has led to an extreme sensitization of the underlying system's architecture to non-additive changes. This points out the poor maintainability of the produced product lines.

Feature Interaction. Hyperslices must have *declarative completeness* [28]: a hyperslice *must* contain all structure (e.g classes, methods, etc) definitions or partial implementations of all other hyperslices to which they refer to. This fact enforces the inclusion of identical, unimplemented methods, belonging to other hyperslices. Therefore, hyperslices are not encapsulated from their environment, on the contrary, they illustrate high coupling, since small changes in a hyperslice cause changes in other hyperslices. These interactions are neither explicitly modelled in HyperFeatuRSEB, nor are they taken into consideration in the system's development.

Tool Support. The tool support needed for the creation and management of hyperspaces, as well as for the definition, development, maintenance and management of hyperslices is not provided at the moment. The HyperJ tool accessible from the IBM web site [30] and described in [29] is still in an immature phase and not in the position to support a PL development process. There is clear need for professional case tool support for the method's implementation.

7   Aspect-Oriented Programming and GenVoca

Other generative programming techniques could also be used to provide a separation of concerns. This section examines the Aspect-Oriented Programming and the GenVoca approaches.

7.1   Aspect-Oriented Programming

One could also achieve a separation of concerns using the Aspect-Oriented Programming technique [25] and effectively perform an integration with one of the aforementioned PL methodologies, as in HyperFeatuRSEB.

Aspect-Oriented Programming makes use of *aspects*. These are code descriptions of a concern, which are weaved into the system and respectively affect its behavior. There exists a special grammatical syntax [26], as well as a possible UML extension [20] for the modelling of an aspect-oriented implementation.

One of the issues with this approach is that the aspect-modules are difficult to understand and maintain. The developers need to maintain the system's code and also the extra developed aspects, "inflating" the system's complexity.

7.2 GenVoca

The GenVoca [2] method is based on similar principles as the Aspect-Oriented Programming and the Hyperspace approach. Systems are built from layers containing programs [3]. Each program implements a feature. Combinations of layers allow the addition of the programs' functionality to compose a working system. The whole process is supported by the Jakarta tool suite [16].

The GenVoca modelling of PL systems is performed by means of a formal algebraic notation [3]. It is based mainly upon the same principles of class composition as the Hyperspace approach and therefore bares the same problems. Finally, the Jakarta tool suite proves to be in an immature state to support the actual development of a product line [5].

8 Feature-Architecture Mapping – FArM

The methodology presented in this section of the paper introduces solutions based on the identified deficiencies of the state of the art PL methodologies. It strives to achieve an efficient mapping between feature models and the architecture and at the same time preserve the qualities of a PL, like enhanced maintainability, ease of evolution and simplified product generation.

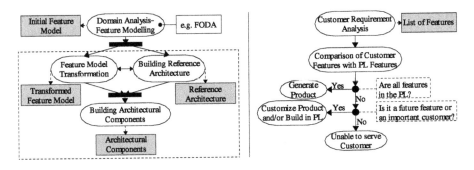

Fig. 6. The FArM Product Line and Product Engineering workflows

8.1 Process Overview

FArM is divided into a Product Line Engineering and Product Engineering phases effectively managing the PL's development complexity. FArM's workflows for the Product Line and Product Engineering phases are illustrated in figure 6.

FArM may be applied right after the domain modelling stage of a PL's development cycle. The current state of the method supports the FODA domain analysis method [21].

After the development of an initial feature model, FArM proceeds with two concurrent bidirectional processes, namely the Feature Modelling Transformation and Building Reference Architecture processes. The result of these processes is a transformed feature model compliant with the newly built PL's reference architecture. The latter is a plug-in architecture.

At this point, each identified feature is implemented in exactly one architectural (plug-in) component in the Building Architectural Components process, following the guidelines defined in the transformed feature model and reference architecture artifacts.

In FArM's Product Engineering phase needs to be pointed out that if the customer's requirements are satisfied by the product line features, the product will be *generated* by simply plugging the feature-components to the plug-in platform.

8.2   Product Line Engineering

This section takes a closer look at the Product Line Engineering phase of FArM and its processes.

Feature Model Transformation. The Feature Model Transformation process receives the initial feature model and performs a transformation based on predefined *transformation rules*. The goal of this process is to allow a logical ordering of the features and model the product line's feature interactions, as well as providing a complete list of possible non-costumer related features. The Feature Model Transformation is based upon the PL's requirements and high-level architectural decisions. This process runs concurrently with the Building Reference Architecture process, maintaining a bidirectional communication link among the two processes.

The transformation of the initial feature model is performed through the use of predefined transformation rules. These can lead to **adding** features, **integrating** features within other features, **dividing** features and **reordering** the hierarchy of features on the feature model.

FArM transformation rules are based on:

- **Grouping Features**: Grouping features must illustrate a logical relation to their sub-features (e.g. Interface–Mdi-Sdi in figure 1).
- **Quality Features**: Quality features must be integrated inside functional features (e.g. "performance" in an IDE could be integrated as a time limitation on the model-code synchronization feature and/or other features).
- **Architectural Requirements/Implementation Details**: The PL itself may impose the existence of a variety of architectural structures through requirements or implementation details. These should in turn yield features in the feature model to retain the one-to-one relationship between feature model and architecture (e.g. a "security" feature in the IDE PL to prevent unregistered use of the software, is mainly a concern of the developers. Thus it must be implemented is the PL architecture and reflected as a feature in the feature model, although it is not a customer visible feature.).
- **Interacts Relationships**: When referring to interacts relationships, we concentrate on the communication between features for the completion of a task. Transformations based upon such communication support the developers in

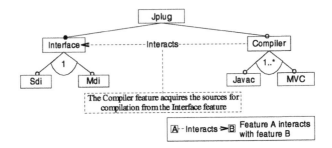

Fig. 7. An interaction relationship in a FArM transformed feature model.

the explicit modelling of the extra-hierarchical relationships between features and also transferring this knowledge to the system's architecture. Interacts relationships support also the design for maintainability as well as PL end-product instantiation.

The modelling of feature interactions is implemented in FArM through an extension to the feature model, namely the *interacts relationship*. An example of an interacts relationship is shown in figure 7. Information related to a FArM interacts relation can be of a textual or formal form (e.g. OCL) and must avoid going into implementation details. These are documented in the feature's respective architectural component's documentation.

All transformation rules defined within the Feature Model Transformation process strive to achieve a balance between the initial feature model and the changes needed to allow a strong mapping to the architecture, preserving the nature of the initial features.

Building Reference Architecture. FArM's reference architecture is a plug-in architecture. The root feature of the feature model representing the product line is the architecture's plug-in platform. Each feature is implemented in exactly one plug-in component and adheres to the platform's plug-in format.

During this phase the developers have the task of defining the plug-in format and communication protocols for inter-component communication. Based on the requirements placed upon each feature and the needed interactions, each component is assigned and commits to the implementation of an interface to provide services to other components.

Messages sent to a parent component/feature are transmitted to the proper sub-component/feature, allowing the decoupling of the components and providing the needed flexibility for instantiating PL products.

The advantages of such a plug-in architecture, from the perspective of establishing a strong mapping between feature models and architectures are:

- Allowing automatic product generation: Features plugged into the plug-in platform instantly compose PL products.
- Allowing the encapsulation of features in plug-in components.

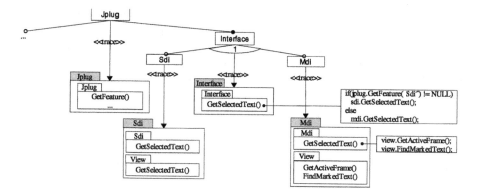

Fig. 8. A FArM solution to the maintainability issues of HyperFeatuRSEB

– Decoupling of the features is achieved through the hierarchical plug-in structure.
– Component interfaces allow the modelling of feature interactions.

8.3   Feature-Architecture Mapping Solutions

Based on the description of FArM, this section will illustrate the solutions to the identified problems in the state of the art feature-oriented methodologies from the perspective of the mapping between feature models and architecture.

Feature Model-Architecture Transition. FArM's main goal is to clarify the transition from a feature model to an architecture. This is achieved through a detailed description of the Feature Model Transformation and Building Reference Architecture processes, as well as the introduction of transformation rules and the support for the creation of the PL's architecture.

The state of the art methodologies analyzed in the previous sections provide insufficient description of the needed steps for this transition.

PL Maintainability. HyperFeatuRSEB's maintainability issues are resolved within FArM through the use of a modular plug-in architecture.

Figure 8 illustrates the solution to the maintainability problem introduced in section 6.3. Now, each plug-in component representing a feature, defines an interface to allow the interaction between features. A change in the inner parts of the Mdi feature has no effect on the feature's interface.

Feature Interaction. The issue of feature interactions is identified and accepted by FArM as a part of the PL system. It is therefore integrated within the development process in the Feature Model Transformation and Building Reference Architecture processes. Explicit modelling of the feature interactions is performed through the feature model extension *interacts* relationship and its reflection in the plug-in components' interfaces. Furthermore, this process can be supported from related work on resolving feature interactions [9], [31].

None of the state of the art methodologies directly addresses the issue of feature interactions. In FODA, FORM and FeatuRSEB this issue is not a separate part of the development process, while the Hyperspace approach in HyperFeatuRSEB claims to achieve a "clear" separation of concerns, neglecting feature interactions and causing the maintainability problems already discussed.

Tool Support. FArM requires the use of a case tool for the development of the plug-in architecture and a feature modelling tool for construction and maintenance of the PL feature model. For both tools exist sufficient (semi-)commercial software solutions [17], [10], [12].

The issue of sufficient tool support was identified as one of the problems in the HyperFeatuRSEB and the GenVoca methods.

9   Conclusions

This paper has explored the main feature-oriented PL methodologies from the point of view of the linkage between feature models and architecture. Based on the identified shortcomings, an approach is introduced to allow a stronger mapping between a PL's feature model and architecture.

More precisely, although FODA and FORM provide a number of guidelines, their focus is not placed directly upon the resolution of a weak mapping between feature models and architecture. FeatuRSEB performs a mapping through the heavy use of traceability links, providing little support for the creation, management or maintenance of such constructs.

The integration of generative programming techniques in product line methodologies, like Aspect-Oriented Programming and GenVoca, proves to be insufficient for the development of a product line. Maintainability problems and complexity in the aspect-modules, as well as lack of modelling principles and sufficient tool support in the GenVoca environment, denote these issues.

HyperFeatuRSEB uses the Hyperspace approach to isolate features within hyperslices. The result of this process carries a number of disadvantages, e.g. low maintainability and immature tool support.

The Feature-Architecture Mapping method (FArM) introduced in this paper identifies the nature of the problems prevailing in the aforementioned methodologies and supports the mapping of features to the architecture with existing technologies.

Explicit feature modelling processes with well defined transformation rules support the smooth transition from a feature model to the architecture. The interaction between features is documented on different levels: on the model level through the feature model extensions of the *interacts* relationships, and on an architectural level in the interfaces of the respective plug-in components.

Furthermore, support for the development of a flexible and maintainable product line architecture is provided through the proposed plug-in structure.

Figure 8 shows the flexible nature of the FArM architecture: the `Interface` feature serves as a switch mechanism between the `Sdi` and `Mdi` features, thus enabling an automatic product instantiation. The method supports the generation of PL products, while the maintainability and the system's complexity remain manageable. Finally, the method allows the use of commercial tools.

10   Further Work

The next steps in the development of the Feature-Architecture Mapping (FArM) method include:

- The support of more domain analysis methods for the creation of the initial feature model.
- The formal definition of transformation rules for the transition from the feature model to the architecture.
- Integration of feature interaction resolution techniques in the FArM processes.
- The development of a process specifically for the support of the definition of component interfaces in respect to feature interactions.

A number of features from the IDE product line presented in the examples have already been implemented with FArM. An industrial case study is taking place at the point of this writing in the domain of mobile phones. More specifically, the plug-in platform of the Blackberry handheld is used for the development of client components with the FArM method. Publications will follow on this theme. Further work will also include the implementation of the method in various other domains, e.g. real-time system's, medical domain, etc. Finally, future work includes the precise definition of the method's limitations.

References

1. Atkinson, C: Component-based product line engineering with UML. Addison-Wesley (2002)
2. Batory, D. and Geraci, J. B.: Composition Validation and Subjectivity in GenVoca Generators. IEEE Transactions on Software Engineering (23)(2), 67–82 (1997).
3. Batory, D.; Lopez-Herrejon, E. R.; Martin J.: Generating Product-Lines of Product-Families, Automated Software Engineering Conference, Edinburgh, Scotland, 81–92 (2002)
4. Blackberry Handheld, http://www.blackberry.com/
5. Boellert, K.: Object-Oriented Development of Software Product Lines for the Serial Production of Software Systems (Objektorientierte Entwicklung von Software-Produktlinien zur Serienfertigung von Software-Systemen). PhD Thesis, TU-Ilmenau, Ilmenau Germany (2002)
6. Philippow, I.; Riebisch, M.; Boellert, K.: The Hyper/UML Approach for Feature Based Software Design. In: The 4th AOSD Modeling With UML Workshop. San Francisco, CA (2003)
7. Bosch, J.: Design & Use of Software Architectures - Adopting and Evolving a Product Line Approach. Addison-Wesley (2000)
8. Buschmann, F.: Pattern-Oriented Software Architecture: A System of Patterns. John Wiley & Sons (1996)

9. Calder, M.; Kolberg, M.; Magill, M.H.; Reiff-Marganiec, S.: Feature Interaction – A Critical Review and Considered Forecast. Elsevier: Computer Networks, Volume 41/1 (2003) 115–141
10. Captain Feature, http://sourceforge.net/projects/captainfeature
11. Czarnecki, K.; Eisenecker, U.W.: Generative Programming. Addison-Wesley (2000)
12. DOME (DOmain Modelling Environment), http://www.htc.honeywell.com/dome/
13. Griss, D.; Allen, R. and d'Allesandro, M.: Integrating Feature Modelling with the RSEB. In: Proceedings of the 5th International Conference of Software Reuse (ICSR-5) (1998)
14. Pashov, I.: Feature Based Method for Supporting Architecture Refactoring and Maintenance of Long-Life Software Systems. Phd Thesis. Technical University of Ilmenau, Ilmenau, Germany, 2004 (submitted)
15. Jacobson, I.; Christerson, M.; Jonsson P.; and Oevergaard, G.: Object-Oriented Software Engineering: A Use Case Driven Approach. Addison-Wesley (1992).
16. Jakarta Tool Suite. www.cs.utexas.edu/users/schwartz/
17. Rational Rapid Developer, http://www-306.ibm.com/software/awdtools/rapiddeveloper/
18. Riebisch, M.: Towards a More Precise Definition of Feature Models. In: Workshop at ECOOP. Books On Demand GmbH, Darmstadt, Germany (2003) 64–76
19. Streitferdt, D.; Riebisch, M.; Philippow, I.: Formal Details of Relations in Feature Models. In: Proceedings 10th IEEE Symposium and Workshops on Engineering of Computer-Based Systems (ECBS'03). IEEE Computer Society Press, Huntsville Alabama, USA (2003) 297–304
20. Suzuki, J. and Yamamoto, Y.: Extending UML with Aspects: Aspect Support in the Design Phase. In Proceedings of the Aspect-Oriented Programming Workshop at ECOOP '99 (1999).
21. Kang, K.; Cohen, s.; Hess, J.; Novak, W.; Peterson, A.: Feature-Oirented Domain Analysis (FODA) Feasibility Study. Technical Report CMU/SEI-90-TR-021, Software Engineering Institute, Carnegie Mellon University, Pittsburgh (1990)
22. Kang, KC; Kim, S.; Lee, J.; Kim, K.; Shin, E.; Huh, M: FORM: A Feature-Oriented Reuse Method with Domain-Specific Reference Architectures. Annals of Software Engineering, 5 (1998) 143–168
23. Kang, KC; Lee, J. and Donohoe, P.: Feature-Oriented Product Line Engineering. IEEE Software, Vol. 9, No. 4, Jul./Aug. (2002) 58–65
24. Kang, KC; Lee, K.; Lee, J.: FOPLE - Feature Oriented Product Line Software Engineering: Principles and Guidelines. Pohang University of Science and Technology (2002)
25. Kiczales, G.: Aspect-Oriented Programming. Springer-Verlag, In Proceedings of the 1997 European Conference on Object-Oriented Programming (ECOOP '97), (1997) 220–242
26. Kiczales, G.: Getting Started with AspectJ. Communications of the ACM (44)(10), (2001) 59–65
27. Kang, KC.; Lee, K.; Lee, J. and Kim, S.: Feature-Oriented Product Line Software Engineering: Principles and Guidelines. In: Domain Oriented Systems Development: Practices and Perspectives. Taylor & Francis (2003) 19–36
28. Ossher, H.; Tarr, P.: Multi-Dimensional Separation of Concerns and the Hyperspace Approach. In: Software Architectures and Component Technology. Kluwer Academic Publishers (2001)
29. Tarr P. and Ossher, H.: Hyper/J User and Installation Manual (2001)
30. Multi-Dimensional Separation of Concerns: Software Engineering using Hyperspaces. www.research.ibm.com/hyperspace/
31. Zave, P.: FAQ Sheet on Feature Interaction. AT&T (1999)

Managing Product Line Variability by Patterns

Jürgen Meister[1], Ralf Reussner[2], and Martin Rohde[1]

[1] Oldenburg Research and Development Institute
for Computer Science Tools and Systems (OFFIS)
Escherweg 2, 26121 Oldenburg, Germany
{meister,rohde}@offis.de
[2] Department of Computing Science
University of Oldenburg
Escherweg 2, 26121 Oldenburg, Germany
reussner@informatik.uni-oldenburg.de

Abstract. Software product lines have a demonstrated potential for cost-effective development of software families. Product lines have to support and coordinate variabilities between the different members of the product family. However, it is also known that the management of these variabilities and the concurrent evolution of product line architecture and single products are still challenging tasks [1]. This organizational overhead often prevents small and medium enterprizes with limited software development staff from adopting product lines. This paper introduces three classes of product line variability and discusses their impacts to product line architectures. In particular, we discuss the management of these variabilities, by introducing a pattern-based product line architecture and an associated pattern language for statistical analysis software.

1 Introduction

Product lines have the potential of great productivity gains compared to single product development (e.g., [1]). These gains stem from systematically dealing with commonalities and variabilities of related software products. Shared commonalities of these products are factored out in product line architecture and, on code level, in frameworks. Differences between the related products form variation points of the product line architecture. Although in principle, variation points should be modeled in domain model first, and later be implemented in architecture, usually new variation points occur during the development and application of product line architecture. The main reasons for this are (a) new or changed requirements often specific to single customers and (b) broadening the domain of the product line to cover new usage scenarios in general (which also results in new requirements). In both cases, this means that a product line is not automatically by itself a long-term asset (as it is often called in literature) but has to evolve steadily.

The evolution of the product line architecture can be either that a new variation point is introduced without affecting much of the rest of the architecture (*local variability*), or that the whole product line architecture has to be adapted

M. Weske and P. Liggesmeyer (Eds.): NODe 2004, LNCS 3263, pp. 153–168, 2004.
© Springer-Verlag Berlin Heidelberg 2004

as a whole to accomplish the new requirements (*global variability*). Obviously, the global variability is the more challenging task associated with higher costs due to a considerable effort in restructuring the product line architecture while the local variability most often can be accomplished by the addition or deletion of simple architectural elements or the configuration of plug-in elements. In larger organizations, specialized teams of experienced developers are solely dedicated to product line evolution while other teams are responsible for the actual software product implementation and evolution. However, small and medium enterprizes (SMEs) usually have not the staff and financial capabilities of organizing several teams. Much more, a single group of developers has to deal with development and evolution of product line and products simultaneously. What is actually needed for SMEs is a light-weight organization of product line development. Unfortunately, the common approach of eXtreme Programming (XP) [2] does not support product line development, as the steady refactoring of designs and architectures (if made explicit at all) of single products. Of course, many product lines stem from single products (or sets of single product) which often have been developed without any architectural modeling at all and have been generalized to a product line later. However, when starting with product lines, one cannot abandon explicit architectural modeling and a kind of top-down product development adhering to explicitly modeled architectures. Therefore, XP seems to be a bad starting point for product line development in our view.

In this paper, we present a pattern-based approach to product line development. This approach consists of (a) the usage of patterns and architectural styles [3] in the product line architecture, and (perhaps more importantly) (b) a pattern-language [4,5] guiding the instantiation of single products out of the product line. Although pattern as a design technology seem to have nothing to do with the organization of product line evolution, we claim that pattern-based product line development supports light-weight product line development and is therefore particularly suitable for SMEs. This is because:

- Patterns provide well thought of design solutions with well understood properties. In particular, it is documented how to vary a pattern in case of changing design forces [3,5]. As a consequence, the use of patterns and styles in product line architectures directly shows how to deal with global variability of a product line.
- Single patterns are concerned with different aspects of the software which are often expressed in the different architectural views [6]. This enables the separation of variabilities. Particularly interesting is how global variation requirements are accomplished by single patterns.
- The pattern language documents the dependencies between the patterns used in the product line architecture and gives advice on the order of pattern application.

Here, we discuss how global variation of a product line is supported by the application of patterns and the selection of alternative patterns or pattern variants. In particular, we discuss the PAC and the microkernel pattern [3] as well as several patterns for concurrent and networked systems [5].

To illustrate our approach we are describing a product line architecture for statistical analysis software and an associated pattern language. However, this architecture serves not only as an example for the role of patterns in general but also represents a value by itself. This is because current statistical analysis software does not reflect its different application domains in a satisfying manner, such as business intelligence, public health, and other domains. Hence, a generic product line architecture is still lacking and the MUSTANG architecture [7] used in this paper as an example is one of the first of its kind.

The contribution of this paper is threefold:

1. Pattern-based product line development is introduced. The role of patterns and pattern languages during product line evolution and product instantiation is analyzed in detail.
2. In particular, different kinds of product line variability are discussed their relationship to architectural views are described.
3. The design decisions for a product line architecture for statistical analysis software are discussed with a special emphasis on presented variability types.

This paper is organized as follows. For setting the stage for using patterns and pattern languages to accomplish global variability, in section 2 we first discuss variability of product lines and their relationship to the architectural views in general. In section 3 we discuss how patterns support global variability by demonstrating the application of patterns for a product line architecture for statistical analysis software. In section 4 we present the resulting pattern language guiding the instantiation of the product line to actual products. In section 5 we present several applications of the product line (i.e., several of its actual products). In section 6 we conclude and discuss the role of an outstanding process model for empirical evaluation and a quantification of the benefit of pattern usage. Related work is given within the whole paper where appropriate.

2   Product Line Variabilities

Software requirements are divided in functional and qualitative ones. The qualitative requirements are subdivided in development and operational requirements [8]. Thus, product line developers must consider the following different variability types.

1. *Functional variability* is visible for the customers by varying feature sets in products. Product line instances vary in (a) the amount of implemented features, (b) the kind of feature composition and collaboration, and (c) the varying feature implementations (often also affecting qualitative properties).
2. *Development variability* is relevant from a software engineering perspective and refers to modifiability, extensibility and maintainability.
3. *Operational variability* predefines variabilities of particular products in operation concerning performance, scalability, safety, etc.

Functional variability regarding the amount of features (a) and the used version of the features (c) is locally restricted to few interrelated elements of a product line architecture. The global variability (i.e., functional (b), development and global variability) concerns product line architecture as a whole. Therefore it must be possible to instantiate customized product architectures from the product line architecture.

Software architectures provide design plans of systems, and an abstraction helping to manage the complexity of systems. As a design plan, the architecture defines a structural plan that describes the elements of the system, their composition and collaboration to fulfill the requirements. As an abstraction, the architecture encapsulates implementation details of the software within an element of an architecture. Software architectures separate different aspects of systems in different views. Hofmeister [6] differentiates four views of architectures. Figure 1 shows this architecture views and their dependencies to the various kinds of software requirements.

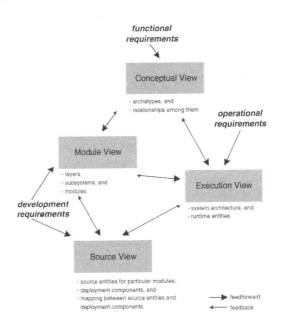

Fig. 1. Impacts of Software Requirements on Architectures

The conceptual view describes the semantic concept of a software product according to functional requirements. The module view is derived from the conceptual view. Here, the elements of the conceptual view are separated into layers, subsystems and modules, to fulfill the desired development requirements (e.g., modifiability, portability). At the same time, a suitable system/hardware architecture is defined by the execution view to meet the operational requirements. Runtime entities of the system architecture and module view entities are semantically linked to each other. In the code view (a) code components for elements of module view are specified, (b) runtime entities are mapped to platform specific deployment components and (c) build configurations of deployment components from code components are defined.

Variability types are related to these architecture views as follows.

- The *conceptual view* describes the system in terms of its domain elements and the relationships among them. Bosch [8] names such architecture elements as archetypes. Archetypes are determined only by functional requirements. They form the most stable part of the software and are changed in limited ways only. In product lines the conceptual view has to provide the desired functional variability [9] accordingly to functional requirements of product line instances.
- The *module view* defines layers, subsystems, modules and the relationships among them. The module view is a refinement of the conceptual view, that maps archetypes to subsystems and modules. The module view has to provide the *development variability*, especially technological flexibility and maintainability.
- The *execution view* maps modules to runtime entities, and shows how these are mapped to the system architecture. The product line architecture often has to support different system architectures to enable the required operational variability.
- In the *code view* the runtime entities are mapped to deployment components (e.g., Executable, DLL), modules are mapped to source entities, and it is defined how deployment components are produced from source components. This view facilitates the technological variability (as a subclass of development variability), because the choice of appropriate application server technology may be changed subsequently.

Thus, the instantiation of product architectures requires following transformations. At first, the conceptual view of the product line architecture must be transformed in order to fulfill the functional requirements. Secondly, the module and the code views of the product line architecture have to be modified according to development requirements of the product. At last, operational requirements have to be incorporated. Operational requirements of a software product demand a specific system architecture. Especially, distributed system architectures determine the module mapping to execution components in the code view. Therefore, the code and if necessary the module views must be aligned with selected system architecture. Furthermore, system architectures impact portability issues regarding to middleware frameworks. Therefore, operational requirements may influence the development requirements, too. In our projects, we realized that pattern-based architectures enable the desired variability for product lines and that associated pattern languages support required transformations.

3   Pattern-Based Product Line Architecture for Statistical Analysis Software

The term statistical analysis software refers to software used to perform data analysis. Data analysis is the extraction of knowledge out of data by using statistical methods [10]. DW (data warehouse) software or OLAP (on-line analytical processing) tools can be seen as a kind of "general purpose" statistical analysis software. Besides these important general domain, many current statistical analysis software products specialize their functionality and user guidance accordingly to (a) their application domain, (b) their user group and (c) their actual statistical methods. This enumeration of variability motivates well the use of product lines for statistical analysis software.

In this section we introduce a pattern-based product line architecture for statistical analysis software. The PAC and the microkernel architectural pattern enable the required functional variability of the product line architecture. The PAC pattern enables architecture variations for implementation of specialized interaction workflows during product instantiation. The microkernel pattern facilitates the embedding of specialized statistical functions. Beside the functional variability, a high degree of development variability is achieved by a recursive application of the microkernel pattern. Applying patterns for distributed and concurrent data processing facilitates the support of different system architectures by the product line for fulfilling desired operational variability.

3.1   Functional Variability

Systems for statistical analysis on multidimensional data like DW systems or scientific and statistical databases are used in BI (business intelligence) [11], public health [12,13] and other application domains. The BI application domain subsumes general purpose statistical analysis software tools (e.g., OLAP tools, BI portals) and specialized software products for miscellaneous domain areas like controlling, performance management, customer relationship management, etc.. In public health and other application domains there is also a trend toward customized statistical analysis software for particular application domains.

Statistical analysis software support different analysis processes, depending on (a) application domain and particular domain area, (b) user groups and their habits, and (c) statistical methods. Analysis processes itself consist of several single steps, named interactions. These interactions are attached to interaction classes: data selection, statistics, visualization, and navigation. Interaction workflows in analysis processes can vary notably. Moreover, different domains generally use different statistical methods. Statistical methods apply one or more statistical functions accordingly to an interaction workflow, in order to solve an analytical task. Hence, the product line has to facilitate the concurrent usage of different interaction workflows in a single software product and has to support extensibility mechanisms to embed specialized statistical function libraries.

Support of Different Interaction Workflows. The interaction workflows can differ in user guidance and, if required, in different user interfaces for the same interaction classes. Interaction classes can be realized by PAC agents. Higher-level PAC agents combine lower-level agents into a specialized analytical product according to the requirements of the particular interaction workflow.

The PAC pattern is an agent-based architectural pattern [3, 14] that structures interactive software as a hierarchy of cooperating agents. Every agent is responsible for a specific aspect of application functionality. An agent consists of three components: presentation, abstraction and control. Presentation and abstraction components separate user interactions from functional core and abstract interactions of the interaction model. Intra-agent communication between presentation and abstraction components, and inter-agent communication between agents is handled by the control component.

We are particularly interested in the partitioning semantically interrelated functionality among single PAC agents and in the building of new product features (or products) by hierarchical linking of PAC agents. The agents of a product constitute a tree-like hierarchy of PAC agents, with one top-level agent, several intermediate-level agents and even more bottom-level agents. Each agent depends on all higher-level agents. The top-level agent provides the kernel functionality of the software. Bottom-level agents represent self-contained semantic concepts on which users of the system can act. Intermediate-level agents group lower-level agents together to form a higher-level semantic concept on which user can operate, or coordinate lower-level agents to perform task execution.

The statistical analysis software itself is realized by the top-level agent who initializes the hierarchy of agents, implements the basic processes, and encapsulates the execution of statistical methods on multidimensional data. The bottom-level agents encapsulate the possible instantiations of interaction classes, e.g., for selecting data sets, configuring statistical methods and visualizing results. Intermediate-level agents can combine several visualizations (e.g., traffic light, pie chart and table) of a multidimensional data set for example to a panel and implement an application-specific interaction workflow.

The hierarchical structure of agents forces the distribution of different semantic concepts and interactions to separate agents. As a consequence, the development of dedicated data models and user interfaces for new products is relied only on a few agents. Each of these agents implements missing semantic concepts and interactions which may also be reused for the instantiation of further products. Using the PAC architecture pattern we achieve the following objectives:

- New interaction features are implemented by independent agents.
- Higher-level agents combine existing and new agents to semantic coherent software components and finally to new software products.
- Modifying single agents has no side-effects for other agents.

Due to the functional flexibility of an agent-based architecture, a diversity of different analytical software products can be instantiated, fulfilling different user group requirements and supporting domain specific user interfaces and user guidances.

Statistical Analysis on Multidimensional Data. Depending on the application area different libraries of statistical functions have to be implemented for the product line. The statistical functions must be exchangeable on demand. The microkernel pattern enables this functional flexibility realizing specialized statistical libraries as internal servers.

The microkernel pattern is originally developed to support the design of small, efficient and portable operating systems and to enable their extension by new services. It also serves as a socket for plugging in functional extensions and for coordinating their collaboration [3]. The microkernel itself contains the fundamental services for an application domain. Core functionality, that cannot be implemented in the microkernel without increasing its complexity, is separated into internal servers. External servers implement their own views with different policies of the underlying microkernel. The microkernel pattern is generally used to develop several applications that use similar programming interfaces all building on the same kernel functionality.

The functional core of our product line – **M**ultidimensional **S**tatistical Data **A**nalysis E**ngine** (MUSTANG) [7] – is responsible for statistical calculations on multidimensional data and is structured by microkernel pattern. MUSTANG contains two internal servers. The first internal server – *multidimensional engine* – provides multidimensional data sets. The second internal server – *statististical library* – provides product-specific statistical functions. The MUSTANG microkernel itself supports basic services for the application of statistical functions on multidimensional data sets. The external server MUSTANGFacade hides the complexity of MUSTANG from the application developers by an appropriate encapsulation of the microkernel's services.

3.2   Development Variability

Depending on the kind of permanent storage of multidimensional data, the data management of statistical analysis software can be categorized into relational, multidimensional and hybrid. Relational data storage makes the management of huge data sets possible. Systems for multidimensional data storage have a higher performance in multidimensional querying and calculation but they can handle only comparatively small amounts of data. Therefore, relational and multidimensional approaches are often combined to hybrid systems. Hybrid systems save the whole data set in a relational DBMS (database management system) and manage those parts of the data set in multidimensional systems which constitute the performance of the application.

The data management of statistical analysis software is still insufficiently standardized and it will remain this way in the foreseeable future because the particular approaches have their pro and cons depending upon deployment scenarios and because the competitive vendors cannot agree on common standards, like e.g. SQL. Hence, a product line architecture has to support a high level of technological modifiability in order to support the appropriate data management technology for each software product and to ensure long-term maintainability. Consequently, a product line for analytical software should be able to provide the different approaches for managing multidimensional data. One can achieve this technological flexibility by a recursive application of the microkernel pattern (cf. Fig. 2). The multidimensional engine has altogether three variation points, each realized as an internal server. The *data warehouse connector internal server* implements features to connect and query relational DWs. The

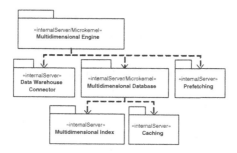

Fig. 2. Recursive Applying of Microkernel Pattern

multidimensional database internal server supports multidimensional storage of data sets. The *prefetching internal server* provides plug-in interfaces for caching of multidimensional data sets as optional feature for hybrid data management. With the appropriate combination of the internal servers the multidimensional engine supports relational, multidimensional or hybrid data storage.

The multidimensional database has two variation points. First, it must be possible to integrate suitable index structures for the administration of multidimensional data. The choice of adequate index structures depends on a number of factors, such as the number of dimensions, the concrete dimension structure, and other criteria. For this reason, it is beneficial to use several internal servers with different index structures concurrently. Furthermore, different approaches for caching of multidimensional data sets may be used. The optional prefetching component tries to predict and execute future queries and to cache the results. Since there are many different strategies and algorithms for this purpose, this functionality should be implemented as an exchangeable internal server.

The mediator [15] and the component configurator [5] design patterns are used as assistant patterns. The multidimensional engine implements the hybrid data storage by applying the mediator pattern to control the cooperation of DW converter, the multidimensional database and the prefetching internal server. The component configurator pattern is used for exchanging DW connectors, multidimensional index structures or the prefetching components at runtime.

Furthermore, the support of (industry) standards for data exchange is a common requirement. OLE DB for OLAP and MDX (multidimensional data exchange) define the "Microsoft" standard for querying multidimensional data. The OMG's metadata standard, CWM (common warehouse metamodel), supports XML based exchange of meta data between individual tools in complex DW systems. Both standards can be supported by implementing external servers.

3.3   Operational Variability

Besides the discussed functional and development variability, the performance and the scalability in terms of the data volume and the number of concurrent users are important operational requirements. The operational variability can only be achieved, if the product line architecture is aligned with an adequate system architecture by applying of appropriate architectural and design patterns. Statistical analysis software is generally used in the following scenarios.

- *PDA:* The user replicates a small multidimensional data set on his PDA, to examine the data set outside the office.
- *Desktop:* Desktop solutions are an alternative in environments with only few users and medium sized data sets. Such applications are used for example in epidemiology [13] or in small and medium sized enterprises.
- *Application server:* Statistical analysis software adopt generally the following distributed system architectures [11].
  - *Basic:* This version is typical for environments with few users and large data sets which cannot be mastered by a desktop PC anymore. Executive information systems often demand this system architecture.
  - *Concurrent users:* Management information systems must handle multiple parallel user queries which often operate only on small data sets.
  - *Parallel data processing:* In decision support systems the number of end-users is generally small. However, very large data sets must be handled, so that load balancing by concurrent data analysis is required.

A distributed deployment of the functional core must fulfill the following requirements: (a) the distribution of the kernel functionality must be transparent, both for the client and the server components, i.e., no changes of interface signatures are allowed, (b) the server must be able to process concurrent client requests, and (c) load balancing of concurrent user requests by parallel data processing on redundantly available computing resources should be possible. For this purposes we introduce the *concurrent proxies architectural pattern* in the following. This concurrent proxies pattern is an advancement of the remote proxy design pattern, which supports several proxies concurrently. The concurrent proxies decouples method invocation from method execution to enhance concurrency and simplify synchronized access to a shared service component. This component resides in its own process and also can run on a remote machine without any modification of component signatures. Figure 3 shows the structure of the concurrent proxies architectural pattern. A *Proxy* provides the interface of the original component to the clients and ensures (possibly remote) access to original component. The *Servant* contains the original service component. At runtime, the proxy transforms the client's method invocations into *MethodRequests*[1]. However, these requests are forwarded to the *RequestDemultiplexer*. The RequestDemultiplexer demultiplexes simultaneously arriving method requests to the appropriate servant for execution. After that, the MethodRequest dispatches the associated method on the Servant. Clients can obtain the result of a method's execution via a *Future*.

For demultiplexing method requests one can use the reactor, proactor or leader/followers architectural patterns [5]. These patterns use the operating system mechanisms for synchronous or asynchronous communication, in order to

---

[1] Concepts for decoupling method execution from method invocation (Method-Request/Future) are borrowed from the active object design pattern [5].

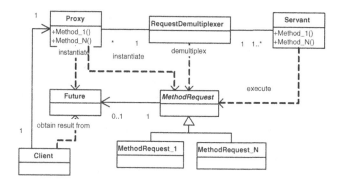

Fig. 3. Concurrent Proxies Architectural Pattern

realize efficient event based communication between several clients and a server. These patterns implement the request handling according to the following basic scheme: arriving events (i.e., MethodRequests) are received by the operating system handle, assigned to an event handler (i.e., Servant) by a demultiplexer and passed on to the associated hook method of the event handler by a dispatcher (i.e., MethodRequest) for execution.

The reactor architectural pattern implements synchronous detecting, demultiplexing and dispatching of service requests to the servants. The demultiplexer waits for indication events, demultiplexes them to associated servants, and than dispatches the appropriate method on the servant. Sometimes the method must save the arrived notification event and wait for missing data which is completed with the following notification events. The servant is blocked in the meantime and data processing cannot start until all data is received. Because of this blocking, the reactor pattern does not scale in order to support a large number of concurrent clients or long-duration client requests. Thus, the reactor pattern is applicable only in scenarios with mostly short communication. However, since in our application domain large data sets must often be exchanged and long-duration calculation requests are processed, this pattern is usually not suitable for statistical analysis software.

The proactor architectural pattern allows to detect, demultiplex and dispatch service requests asynchronously. Communication with clients is handled by an asynchronous operation processor which is usually provided by the operation systems. After the complete transmission of an asynchronous operation, a completion event is activated. When the completion event has arrived, the proactor demultiplexes the asynchronous operation and dispatches the appropriate method to the servant. Because of the relocation of the communication to an asynchronous operation processor, the event handler (i.e., servant) is not blocked by communication tasks. Hence, this pattern tendentiously supports a large number of parallel clients. However, a very large number of parallel accesses and numerous long-duration client requests can also lead to bottlenecks.

The leader/followers architectural pattern provides a concurrency model. In this concurrency model multiple threads take turns in sharing a set of event sources to detect, demultiplex, dispatch, and process service requests, that occur on the event sources. The leader thread waits for an event to occur on a set of event sources. Other threads – the followers – can queue up waiting to become the leader. After the leader thread detects an event from the event source set, it first promotes a follower thread to become the new leader. It then processes the event, i.e., demultiplexes and dispatches the event to the corresponding servant that performs method execution. After execution, the processing thread reverts to the follower role and waits to become the leader thread again. Multiple processing threads can execute methods concurrently, while the current leader waits for new events. Processing threads may demultiplex and dispatch client events with the reactor or proactor pattern.

With help of the concurrent proxies architectural pattern and the proactor respectively leader/followers pattern the product line can support different system architectures. As a result, individual microkernel components can be relocated transparently onto a dedicated application server. In distributed environments, the entire kernel functionality (i.e., MUSTANG microkernel) is typically located on an application server. This improves the performance of the software and allows the shared use of multidimensional data. With sufficient client computing power the load of the application server may be decreased by relocating statistical computations onto the clients. For this purpose, the MUSTANG microkernel and the internal server with statistical functions are located in the client processes whereas the internal server with its multidimensional engine is deployed on the application server. Beyond that, many further constellations are also conceivable.

4   A Pattern Language of Product Line Design for Statistical Analysis Software

When developing software applications with patterns, the sequence of pattern application is crucial for their successful integration [4, 5]. Therefore, in this section we introduce a pattern language for product line design of analytical software (cf. figure 4). The pattern language defines the relationships between the presented patterns and determines which patterns have to be applied first (and which later) to instantiate software products, in order to fulfill product-specific requirements. The presented pattern language also offers a good starting point for the development of product lines for other application domains.

PAC agents structure interactions and other features are visible to the user in a tree-based manner. By the selection of bottom-level agents with appropriate basic interactions respectively features and the integration of these agents into intermediate-level agents more complex software features are implemented. The top-level agent controls the instantiation of the agent tree and the collaboration of PAC agents with the kernel functionality.

The microkernel architectural pattern shapes the kernel functionality. With help of specialized internal servers, kernel functionality can be modified accordingly to the requirements of the specific product. Furthermore, software products

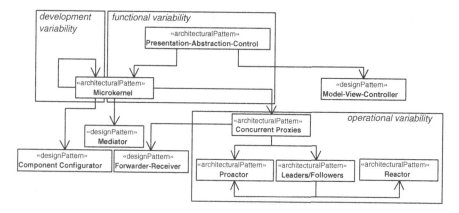

Fig. 4. Pattern Language of Product Line Design for Statistical Analysis Software

without user interfaces (e.g., alerting services) can use this pattern directly. As discussed above, the microkernel pattern enables together with the PAC pattern the functional variability of our product line, while the other patterns are used to ensure development and operational variability.

The MVC design pattern is used to realize concrete PAC agents, as it simplifies the implementation of their control components by uncoupling the intra- and inter-agent communication. In addition, it facilitates the use of more modern MVC based GUI libraries. The recursive application of the microkernel pattern for the realization of internal servers reduces dependencies from external systems, simplifies the deployment of alternative concepts for multidimensional data storage, and improves technological flexibility of functional core as a whole. In conjunction with the microkernel pattern the use of the mediator and the component configurator design patterns should be also considered. The mediator pattern implements coordination of co-operating internal servers, like DW connector and multidimensional database for the hybrid hybrid variant multi-dimensional engine. The component configurator pattern supports the dynamic reconfiguration of functional core at run-time.

The strict separation of communication and concurrency aspects from the functional core represents a fundamental requirement to the design of distributed multi-user software. The concurrent proxies architectural pattern allows the transparent decoupling of remote method execution from local method invocation. In multi-user environments the concurrent proxies pattern can utilize either the proactor pattern or the leader/followers pattern for the synchronization of concurrent requests, depending on the number of concurrent users and the range of data sets. Since the leader/followers pattern only structures the distribution of the demultiplexing and dispatching of requests on several threads, the demultiplexing and dispatching in single threads is attributed again to the reactor or proactor pattern. The concrete implementation of remote communication between the individual components of these patterns should be hidden by the forwarder-receiver design pattern.

5   Application of the Product Line Architecture

The presented product line architecture and the associated pattern-language is used in different projects. In this section we present two of them. CARESS is a statistical analysis application for cancer epidemiology [13]. Epidemiologists use CARESS, in order to perform explorative data analysis (EDA) on medium sized data sets. User interactions are implemented accordingly to the PAC pattern by agents as follows. Basic interactions, like the selection of data sets for investigations or the visualization of the result data sets, are realized by bottom-level agents (*data set selection, map, diagram, table*). The sequence of interactions during an investigation is controlled by an intermediate-level agent *investigation*. After the selection of a data set the user selects an appropriate visualization and parameterizes the chosen statistical function. Due to the use of CARESS for data exploration the user may alternate visualizations, statistical functions and data selections arbitrarily. The individual investigations can be combined into logical units by a superordinate intermediate-level agent *report*, in order to be able to store individual user analysis sessions as a whole. The top-level agent initializes the functional core and coordinates the execution of lower-level agents. The functional core implements an internal server with statistical functions for cancer epidemiology. The multidimensional data engine uses a relational DW for storing multidimensional data.

In another project we are implementing a cockpit application for continuous monitoring of key performance indicators for SMEs. Here we integrate the existing bottom-level agents for visualization (map, diagram, table) with an intermediate-level agent *cockpit*. This product line instantiation implements a simple OLAP based interaction workflow. The cockpit gives an overview of indicators and allows users to change the granularity of presented data. Users can neither change the data selection nor define new parameters for statistical functions. The functional core includes a component with statistical functions for financing. The multidimensional data engine manages medium sized data sets by a multidimensional database. All components of this application are integrated into a single process on the desktop. Thereby installation and administration efforts are minimized. In the medium-term this application will also be used in small multi-user environments. Hence, a distribution of the statistical processing and multidimensional data management with the help of the proactor pattern will be implemented.

6   Conclusions

In this paper we classify variabilities in product lines, associate variabilities to different architecture views and discuss the use of patterns for implementing a pattern-based product line architecture in the domain of statistical analysis. Functional variability of our product line architecture is provided by combination of PAC and microkernel architectural patterns. The recursive application of microkernel pattern enables development variability, especially technological flexibility. Operational variability generally demands an adequate distribution of modules between different computation nodes. For this purpose, we introduce the concurrent proxies architectural pattern. In combination with the appropriate demultiplexer pattern, this pattern supports a wide range of system architectures. Presented patterns are integrated into a pattern language. This pattern language predefines instantiation paths for concrete product architectures.

There are a number of different approaches to design product line architectures. Generally the product line architecture and the software architectures of its instances are identical up to the missing components. The functional variability of the products is achieved by using of alternating component implementations and by selective omitting of components. This approach does not provide operational and development variability explicitly. Furthermore the functional variability is often supported insufficiently by these approaches (cf. varying interaction workflows). Therefore we use the pattern-based architecture for our product line. The domain archetypes and relations between them define the "core" conceptual architecture of the product line. In our example we vary this architecture functionally by the application of the PAC architectural pattern in order to implement product-specific interaction workflows. According to global variability further transformations of the product line architecture may be required in order to derive an appropriate code view for every product of the product line. As shown in our example, pattern languages predefine transformation paths for the instantiation of product architectures from the product line architecture. The proposed approach for handling variability in product lines is suitable especially for small development teams and immature application domains. In comparison to other product line approaches (like, e.g. [16]) the pattern-based approach needs relatively small development efforts in advance and retain a high degree on modifiability and maintainability. Therefore we are able to extend the product line architecture iteratively and to integrate the changes in the application domain into the product line architecture contemporary.

However, many issues remain unsolved. For example, an incremental-iterative development process for product lines is still an open issue. The need of such a tailored process model exists not only for practical reasons, but also arise from a researcher's perspective. A clear process model would also enable the lacking broader experimental validation of the reported benefits of using patterns to support global variability. Such a process would enable the repeated development of pattern-based product lines. Much more, it makes the development of pattern-based product lines comparable to the development of product lines based on generalization of existing products (such as described in [8, 16]). Tracking the costs during development and maintenance of patterns based product lines and comparing these costs with the costs of developing and maintaining comparable generalized product lines will form the base of an experimental validation of our results.

References

1. Clements, P., Northrop, L., Northrop, L.M.: Software Product Lines : Practices and Patterns. Addison-Wesley Pub Co (2001)
2. Beck, K.: Extreme programming explained. Addison-Wesley (2000)
3. Buschmann, F., Meunier, R., Rohnert, H., Sommerlad, P., Stal, M.: Pattern-Oriented Software Architecture – A System of Patterns. Volume 1. John Wiley & Sons, New York (1996)
4. Buschmann, F.: Applying patterns. Technical report, POSA, http://www.posa.uci.edu (2000)
5. Schmidt, D., Stal, M., Rohnert, H., Buschmann, F.: Pattern-Oriented Software Architecture – Patterns for Concurrent and Networked Objects. Volume 2. John Wiley & Sons, New York (2000)
6. Hofmeister, C., Nord, R., Soni, D.: Applied Software Architecture. Addison-Wesley (1999)
7. Koch, S., Meister, J., Rohde, M.: Mustang – a framework for statistical analyses of multidimensional data in public health. In: Proceedings of the 17th International Conference Informatics for Environmental Protection, Cottbus (2003) 635 – 642
8. Bosch, J.: Design & Use of Software Architectures – Adopting and Evolving a Product-Line Approach. Addison-Wesley (2000)
9. Van Gurp, J., Bosch, J., Svahnberg, M.: On the notion of variability in software product lines. In Kazman, R., Kruchten, P., Verhoef, C., van Vliet, H., eds.: Proceedings of the Working IEEE/IFIP Conference on Software Architecture (WICSA'01), IEEE Computer Society (2001) 45–54
10. Hand, D.J.: Intelligent data analysis: Issues and opportunities. In: Advances in Intelligent Data Analysis – Reasoning about Data. 2nd International Symposium (IDA). Springer (1997) 1–14
11. Tiedrich, A.II.: Business intelligence tools: Perspective. Technical report, Gartner, Inc. (2000)
12. Kamp, V., Wietek, F.: Intelligent support for multidimensional data analysis in environmental epidemiology. In Desai, B., Eagelstone, B., eds.: International Database Engineering and Applications Symposium (IDEAS'97), IEEE Computer Society Press (1997) 180 – 190
13. Meister, J., Rohde, M., Appelrath, H.J., Kamp, V.: Data-warehousing in public health. it - Information Technology **4** (2003) 179–185
14. Coutaz, J., Nigay, L., Salber, D.: Agent-based architecture modelling for interactive systems. In Palanque, P., Benyon, D., eds.: Critical Issues in User Interface Engineering. Springer-Verlag (1995)
15. Gamma, E., Helm, R., Johnson, R.E., Vlissides, J.: Design Patterns – Elements of Reusable Object-Oriented Software. Addison-Wesley Professional (1997)
16. Weiss, D.M., Lai, C.T.R.: Software Product-Line Engineering – A Family-Based Sorftware Development Process. Addison Wesley (1999)

UnSCom: A Standardized Framework for the Specification of Software Components

Sven Overhage

Dept. of Software Engineering and Business Information Systems
Augsburg University, Universitätsstraße 16, 86135 Augsburg, Germany
`sven.overhage@wiwi.uni-augsburg.de`

Abstract. This paper proposes a standardized framework for the specification of components, which focuses on providing the information necessary to facilitate component development, discovery, and composition. To be applicable in all these fields, the Unified Specification of Components (UnSCom) framework ties together a mix of different specification aspects and unifies the specification of components using a single, coherent approach. The framework is based on the notion of *design by contract* which it extends to component-based software engineering by introducing service and composition contracts. It supports the specification of composition contracts, which describe the required and provided interfaces of components on various contract levels. These contract levels are thematically grouped into colored pages: white pages contain general and commercial information, yellow pages comprise component classifications, blue pages describe the required and provided functionality, green pages comprise the architectural design of the required and provided interfaces, and grey pages describe the required and provided quality.

1 Introduction

Building new applications by merely browsing component repositories, discovering a set of compatible components, and composing them using connectors promises to contribute a lot of advantages to the field of today's application development [1, 2], among those a shorter time to market, increased adaptability and scalability and, as a result, reduced development costs [3].

When analyzing this rather simple-sounding central paradigm of component-based software engineering in detail, however, it becomes obvious that it introduces a variety of methodological challenges: how to determine the *compatibility* of components, how to deal with *incompatibilities* between components, how to deduce *application properties* based on component properties before composition, and, finally, how to support the *composition* of components? The persistence of these complexities indicates that we might just be witnessing the dawn of a *composition crisis*. In order to eliminate them, especially the development of a substantiated composition methodology, which will provide a mix of methods and tools to manage component discovery and composition, becomes a critical success factor of component-based software engineering.

M. Weske and P. Liggesmeyer (Eds.): NODe 2004, LNCS 3263, pp. 169–184, 2004.
© Springer-Verlag Berlin Heidelberg 2004

Such a composition methodology has to support a variety of different tasks and, in particular, provide methods and tools to support component certification, component search, compatibility checks, adaptor generation, and the prediction of application properties (see figure 1). Most of these methods and tools are dependent on appropriate information about components, which they respectively utilize to support a specific task. The required information about components has to be provided in the form of specifications in order to avoid the costly evaluation, testing, or even reverse-engineering of components, which usually does not provide accurate information, requires the acquisition or development of components in advance, and, moreover, is almost impossible for black-box components [4, 5].

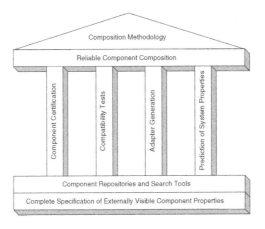

Fig. 1. Elements of a component composition methodology [6–8].

For these reasons, the provisioning of component specifications, which ideally contain all the required information about the provided services and context dependencies of a component, becomes an important prerequisite for the development of a composition methodology. This paper proposes a *standardized* specification framework, which unifies existing approaches and thereby predetermines both the content of component specifications as well as the notations to be used. It has been designed to serve as the basis for the development of a coherent composition methodology. Using the introduced framework as a common source of information, it becomes feasible to distribute the development of methods and tools among multiple specialized parties and, because they all make use of a single set of specifications, nevertheless facilitate the emergence of a homogeneous methodology.

The proposed specification framework is called *Unified Specification of Components (UnSCom)*. It based on the notion of *design by contract* [9], which it extends to satisfy the needs of component-based software engineering by introducing service and composition contracts. The UnSCom framework fulfills a variety of principal requirements, which are being elaborated in the following section, and introduces a set of contract levels that have partly been identified by a standardization project at the German Society of Informatics (GI) [10]. They are being discussed in detail in section 3. After a summary of related work in section 4, the paper is being concluded with a brief outlook on remaining tasks to complete the proposed Specification framework and related activities to form a composition methodology in the longer-term.

2   Principal Requirements

In order to serve as a basis for the development of a composition methodology, a specification framework ideally should fulfill the following requirements:

1. It ought to *completely describe* the (externally visible) properties of a component that are being utilized by methods and tools of the composition methodology. In other words, one should be able to perform all the various tasks that belong to a composition methodology (see figure 1) on the basis of the provided component specifications.
2. The framework has to *strive for a balance* between the expressive power and usability of component specifications. In general, specification formalisms that support the description of more complex facts also are more difficult to evaluate and utilize for static, composition-time tasks. This applies, e.g., to static compatibility checks between components, which depend on the existence of efficient algorithms to compare specified facts.
3. It has to *be normative* and precisely determine what is to be specified (the specification content) and which notations have to be used to denote specifications (the specification formats). Establishing such a normative framework ensures the homogeneity of component specifications, so that they may be utilized by tools.
4. The framework should *provide a modular structure* so that additional specification perspectives can be integrated as backward-compatible extensions simply by adding new modules. Moreover, some of the composition tasks may not require all of the provided specifications and, thus, methods and tools should be allowed to make use of specific parts only.
5. It should *make use of well-established, industry compatible notations* whenever this is feasible. Even though this may introduce some sub-optimal concepts, both the support by industrial tools and the probability that the framework will get accepted as a practical software engineering standard are enhanced.
6. The framework ought to *provide both human- and machine-understandable* specifications. In order to enable tool-supported component discovery and composition, formal (machine-understandable) specifications are to be preferred compared to informal (natural) languages. On the other hand, specifications should nevertheless be simple enough for a human programmer to understand and use, since supporting tools may not (yet) be available.

3   The Unified Specification of Components Framework

Based on the before-mentioned principal requirements, the Unified Specification of Components (UnSCom) Framework is now being elaborated. It is founded upon the central notion of composition and service contracts, which are derived from the well-known principle of *design by contract* [9]. Design by contract currently plays an important role in functional programming and object-oriented programming (OOP), where it is used to specify *service contracts*.

A service contract describes the pre-conditions, which must be established by the client prior to calling a service, as well as the post-conditions that the service guarantees to fulfill provided that it was called with the pre-condition satisfied [9]. A service contract can be used without modifications to specify the properties of a component service as well.

Specifying service contracts that contain *run-time constraints* is crucial but, however, not sufficient to support component-based software engineering. Because components (as opposed to classes) are units of independent deployment [1], one also has to make explicit what in particular a component offers to and what it expects from its deployment context (i.e. other components) to find out whether it can be used for composition with others [1]. Offerings and context dependencies of a component are to be specified as component interfaces [1, 2]. Thereby, it has to be considered that a component usually makes its offers in return for satisfying its context dependencies only (see figure 2). Hence, one also has to specify the *composition contract* of a component, which contains *deployment-time constraints* and consists of a set of required interfaces as well as a set of provided interfaces [2, 11, 12].

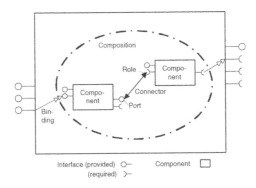

Fig. 2. Conceptual component and composition model (based on [13]).

Such a composition contract prescribes which interfaces must be made available by the deployment context before a component may be used and, in addition, specifies the interfaces that the component offers to the environment provided that is was composed with the required interfaces satisfied. To describe the services contained in the provided and required interfaces in more detail, composition contracts may contain service contracts, which thus are parts of composition contracts. In general, a composition contract may be specified on various contract levels by describing the component interfaces from different point of views [14].

The UnSCom specification framework, which is being elaborated within this paper, focuses on supporting the specification of composition contracts and provides a detailed description of the required and provided interfaces of components. It aims at achieving complete descriptions of composition contracts by introducing various contract levels, which in part have been approved by a standardization project located at the German Society of Informatics [10].

The introduced contract levels have been devised from a classification schema (see figure 3) that, on the horizontal axis, discriminates the different development stages during the development process and, on the vertical axis, lists the specification (modeling) views that are commonly used to (completely) describe the characteristics of software artifacts [2, 15–19]. Note that the classification schema also covers service contracts and introduces them as (part of) a specific composition contract level.

	Functionality / Concepts (domain-related)	Architectural Design / Interfaces (logical)	Implementation / Quality (physical)
Static View (Structure)	Information Objects (Entity Model)	Type Declarations, Properties (Attributes)	Usability, Maintainability, Portability
Operational View (Effects)	Functions (Operations Model)	Events, Methods, Exceptions, Assertions	Functionality
Dynamic View (Interactions)	Processes (Flow Model)	Interaction Protocols	Reliability, Efficiency

Fig. 3. A classification schema introduces various contract levels for the specification of composition contracts.

Each development stage uses a different perspective on components and, accordingly, contributes specifications with a specific content: the domain-related perspective describes the *functionality* that is either being required or provided at the interfaces of a component. It usually has been determined during domain modeling and is specified in the form of domain-related concepts (either in the form of a lexicon or a domain model) [11]. The logical perspective describes the *architectural design* of the required and provided interfaces [2, 11] that is utilized by component models like, e.g. the CORBA Component Model [20]. The architectural design is specified in the form of signature lists, assertions, and protocols. Finally, the physical perspective describes the *quality* which is either being required or provided at the interfaces of a component. It is predetermined by the component implementation and specified as ISO 9126 conformant quality characteristics [21, 22].

Orthogonal to that, each specification view puts the focus on a specific part of a development perspective: the static view focuses on specifying the *structure* (arrangements) of a software artifact, the operational view concentrates on describing the *effects* of its operations, and the dynamic view documents the temporal variability of a software artifact over time by specifying its *interactions*.

The resulting nine composition contract levels, which have been identified using the classification schema, form the core of the UnSCom specification framework. It is complemented with general and commercial information about components as well as classifications that facilitate component discovery (see figure 4).

The UnSCom framework structures component specifications using a thematic grouping into colored pages that was taken over from the UDDI specification framework [23] and has been extended to cover all of the introduced composition contract levels: *white pages* provide general and commercial information about components, *yellow pages* contain component classifications, *blue pages* hold information about the required and provided functionality of components, *green pages* contain the architectural design of the required and provided interfaces, and, finally, *grey pages* contribute information referring to the required and provided implementation quality.

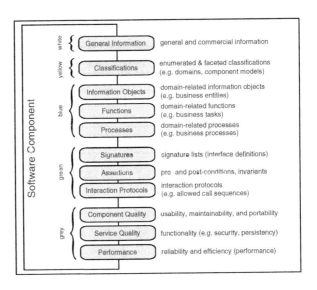

Fig. 4. The overall structure of the Unified Specification of Components Framework comprises eleven different perspectives.

The UnSCom framework introduces various specialized, (preferably) well-established, formal, and platform-independently applicable notations to denote specifications on the eleven levels. Moreover, it introduces different notation-mixes to adequately present component specifications to different target groups: a set of textual specification formats (UnSCom/T) is used to present component specifications to programmers, a set of graphical notations based on UML 2.0 [24] (UnSCom/G) is used to present component specifications to designers, and, finally, an XML format (UnSCom/X) is used to exchange component specifications between different tools. In addition, a special mix of standardized notations may be used to describe XML Web services (WS-Specification [25]). All introduced notation-mixes are integrated using a common meta-model, which is part of the framework core and can be used to translate component specifications between the mentioned formats.

In the following, the UnSCom framework is being elaborated in more detail and an example specification is provided to illustrate the various perspectives. The example specification describes a component that offers services from the general ledger domain similar to [26]. In order to achieve a more compact representation, it makes use of the textual notations contained in UnSCom/T.

3.1   White Pages: General and Commercial Information

The white pages provide general and commercial information, which, among others, is useful to assess the suitability of components. General information comprises the component name, its unique identifier, version, description, producer, and the administrative contacts one is able to get into touch with (e.g. to ask for additional information).

Name: Oversoft General Ledger
Version: 1.0.3755
Identifier: 206B2F65-E7BC-47a0-8DCF-4E34347322AA
Producer **Identifier**: AEFBE5B6-A13F-4ca4-B322-32ADB89EA14C **Name**: Oversoft Software **Means of Communication** (type: e-mail): info@oversoft.biz **Means of Communication** (type: phone): +49 6003 810260 **Address Line** (type: city): Rosbach **Address Line** (type: country): Germany
Distribution Channel **Identifier**: (type: internet download) **Price** (type: USD): 399.90 **Accepted Payment** (type: credit card) **Scope of Supply:** generalLedger.cab, setup.exe, setup.hlp
Terms of Use **Legal Agreement** (type: license agreement): Oversoft EULA ...

Fig. 5. The white pages contain general and commercial information.

Commercial information covers both the *conditions of purchase* and the *conditions of usage*. The conditions of purchase prescribe available distribution channels, which respectively consist of a distribution form, a price, accepted payment procedures, and a scope of supply (i.e. a list of artifacts included with the component shipping). The conditions of usage are determined by various legal agreements, e.g. a license agreement or a service agreement.

The information provided with the white pages is rather descriptive and usually denoted using natural language. To support precise and machine-understandable specifications, however, the specification framework prescribes the use of *taxonomies*, which have either directly to be used for specification or at least to classify the specifications that have been denoted in natural language. Figure 5 illustrates the use of taxonomies and provides an example specification.

3.2 Yellow Pages: Enumerated and Faceted Classifications

The yellow pages contain a set of enumerated and faceted component classifications [27]. These classifications provide information that is especially useful for component discovery and may be used to structure component repositories as well as to facilitate the development of methods to browse and search for components. For each classification, UnSCom provides a so-called *classification schema* in the form of a taxonomy, which can be used to specify component classifications.

Domain (type: UN/SPSC - General Ledger and Accounting)
Component Type (type: specialized component) Reuse Concept (type: logical) Component Model (type: Microsoft .NET 1.0)

Fig. 6. The yellow pages contain enumerated and faceted component classifications.

Principally, one is free to define arbitrary classification schemas. To enforce a minimum level of standardization, the UnSCom framework provides a standardized set of (enumerated) classification schemas to classify the application domain of components, e.g. UN/SPSC and NAICS (see figure 6). Moreover, it contains classification schemas to characterize the architectural component type (e.g. specialized component, framework, application etc.), the utilized component model, and the reuse concept (e.g. logical reuse, which means "provided as a redistributable", and physical reuse, which means "provided as a remote service").

3.3 Blue Pages: Information About
the Domain-Related Functionality

The blue pages describe the functionality that is either being required or provided at the interfaces of a component and usually has been determined during domain modeling. The explicit specification of the component functionality especially facilitates the process of component discovery during application-development [28]. It is specified in the form of a *lexicon* (which is also called a domain model [29]) and contains domain-related concept definitions as well as relationships between concepts (see figure 7) [2, 11].

The UnSCom framework supports the definition of three kinds of domain-related *concepts*: information objects (entities), functions (tasks), and processes. Information objects describe required or provided conceptual information and its structure (e.g. a balance or an account). Functions describe the required

Concept (type: information object): BALANCE
Short Definition: A BALANCE yields a comparison of ASSETS and LIABILITIES of a company at a special
                  date (CUTOFF DATE) based on a LEGAL REGULATION.
Relationship (type: specialization): US-GAAP BALANCE is a BALANCE.
Relationship (type: specialization): IAS BALANCE is a BALANCE.

Concept (type: function): ANNUAL ACCOUNTING
Short Definition: ...
Relationship (type: decomposition): ANNUAL ACCOUNTING consists of CLOSING OF ACCOUNTS.
Relationship (type: decomposition): ANNUAL ACCOUNTING consists of BALANCING.
Relationship (type: decomposition): ANNUAL ACCOUNTING consists of PROFIT & LOSS ACCOUNTING.

Concept (type: process): EXECUTE ANNUAL ACCOUNT
Short Definition: ...
Relationship (type: order): EXECUTE ANNUAL ACCOUNT starts with CLOSING OF ACCOUNTS.
Relationship (type: order): CLOSING OF ACCOUNTS is followed in sequence by PROFIT & LOSS ACCOUNTING.
Relationship (type: order): PROFIT & LOSS ACCOUNTING is followed in sequence by BALANCING.

Fig. 7. The blue pages describe the required and provided functionality.

or provided conceptual actions and their decomposition into sub-functions (e.g. annual accounting). Processes describe sequences of actions that have to be performed to achieve domain-related tasks (e.g. executing an annual account).

In addition, the UnSCom framework provides a set of predetermined *relationship types* to put concepts into relation: abstractions ("is-identical-to", "is-specialization-of" relationships etc.) determine a certain degree of identity between concepts and can be used to execute compatibility checks and specify specialization between concepts. Compositions (e.g. "is-part-of" and order relationships) are used to combine concepts and express compound structures.

From a more technical point of view, the resulting lexicon structure forms a lightweight domain-specific *ontology* (where the set of relationship types between concepts has been predefined by the UnSCom framework). By specifying ontologies, which describe the required and provided functionality, both the emergence of standards that address component functionality as well as the development of methods and tools that perform automated compatibility checks of component functionality will be facilitated, especially as the semantic web technology continues to evolve in the near-term future. In the long-term, this will help to eliminate or at least to uncover (and possibly adapt) domain-related incompatibilities between components (divergences in functionality) [4].

The proposed textual notation to specify domain-related information is *normative language*, an ontology definition language that is both machine- and human-understandable [19]. It uses a *standardized* form of natural language for specification and, e.g., predetermines patterns to build sentences (which put concepts into specific kinds of relationships, e.g. "A is a B." for concept specialization). While more popular and more complex notations (like, e.g. the Resource Description Framework) could be used to define ontologies as well, normative language especially facilitates the readability of ontology definitions by humans. For this reason, it is much less dependent on tools to visualize and process ontologies – since the semantic web technologies are still emerging, this currently is a crucial advantage.

Concept definitions not only form a domain lexicon but, in addition, can be used to characterize the component interfaces in more detail. By mapping concept definitions onto the architectural design of component interfaces, one is able to specify which particular architectural element yields a specific functionality: information objects can be mapped to type definitions, properties, parameters, and return values of services. Conceptual functions can be mapped to component services and events, and processes can be mapped to protocols (service invocation sequences). As a result, concept definitions can also be used to facilitate the identification and elimination of syntactic incompatibilities, and especially the process of signature matching [30], which concentrates on matching divergent signatures that provide the same functionality.

3.4   Green Pages: Information About the Architectural Design of Interfaces

The green pages describe the architectural design of the required and provided interfaces of a component [2, 11] which are composed of component services. This information is required to correctly invoke component service and utilized by component models, like e.g. the CORBA Component Model [20]. Both the static design and the basic part of the operational design of component interfaces is specified as *signature lists* which comprise various definitions: type and constant declarations, properties (attributes), services (methods), exceptions, and events (see figure 8). The proposed textual notation to specify signature lists is OMG IDL [20], which (in version 3.0) supports the definition of multiple required and provided interfaces for a component and provides mappings to many well-established programming languages.

In addition, the effects of required and provided services can be described in more detail by specifying *service contracts*, i.e. pre-, and post-conditions for each method [9]. While service contracts can be used to specify various kinds of information about component services, one has to keep in mind that, in general, this information only can be *heuristically* evaluated and utilized for static, composition-time tasks like compatibility checks between components [7]. This is due to the complexity of the task of theorem proving that has to be carried out in order to determine the compatibility of assertions and is not efficiently computable [9].

The principal notation to specify these so-called assertions is the Object Constraint Language (OCL [31]), a formal notation provided as part of the Unified Modeling Language (UML). An OCL expression firstly defines the context of a specification by linking it to an interface-method or a component (see figure 9). Thereafter, the respective assertions that apply to the context are listed. The pre-condition given in figure 9 states that `calculateBalance` can only be executed for an account that is known to the component. The post-condition guarantees that the quantity of an account (returned by `calculateBalance`) is the sum of the quantities that have been booked on this account up to the current date (decreases are considered as negative quantities and thus subtracted).

The specification of the architectural design of component interfaces is completed by specifying *interaction protocols*, which describe the legal orders of service invocations. Usually, services can not be arbitrarily invoked but have to

```
interface IGeneralLedger {
   typedef string accountNo;
   typedef double quantity;
   struct account {
      accountNo  n;
      quantity   safetyQuantity;
      quantity   reorderImgQuantity;
   };
   struct booking {
      accountNo  n;
      date       executionDate;
      string     orderNo;
      double     bookingQuantity;
   };

   exception notEnoughMoney {};

   void book(in booking b);
   void reserve(in booking b) raises notEnoughMoney;
   quantity calculateBalance(in accountNo n, in date z);
};


interface IDatabase {
   exception openConncectionFailed {};
   exception openTransactionFailed {};
   exception invalidSql {};

   void openConnection(in string database) raises openConnectionFailed;
   void openTransaction() raises openTransactionFailed;
   void closeTransaction();
   void rollback();
   void executeSql(in string sql) raises invalidSql;
};
```

Fig. 8. Signature lists describe the static and operational design of interfaces.

```
IGeneralLedger::calculateBalance(n:accountNo,z:date):quantity
   pre:  self.account->exists(k:account | k.accountNo = n)
   post: result = self.booking->iterate(b:booking; r:quantity = 0 |
            if b.accountNo = n and b.date <= z
            then
               r + b.bookingQuantity
            endif
         )
```

Fig. 9. The effect of component services is specified as assertions.

be called in a predetermined order that is difficult to identify solely on the basis of signature lists. Moreover, protocol specifications provide valuable information which can be utilized in composition methodologies (e.g. to generate protocol adapters [32] or predict application properties [12]).

The UnSCom framework currently supports the specification of protocols using *regular types*, which are based on finite state machines [33]. While finite state machines can efficiently be utilized for static, composition-time tasks like compatibility checks, their expressive power and preciseness, however, is limited: in general, it is unfeasible to specify orders of service invocations that depend on parameter values and, moreover, finite state machines only describe a superset of legal invocation orders that sometimes contains illegal ones, too (see [33] for details). This especially is not acceptable for the specification of protocols that are part of the provided interfaces.

For this reason, ongoing standardization work focuses on integrating a more expressive and precise protocol specification technique (e.g. based on temporal logic [10] or Petri-Nets [34]). In so doing, however, one has to ensure that protocol specifications can still be efficiently evaluated and used at composition-time.

```
Type Library
...
type Efficiency = contract {
   responseTime: decreasing numeric msec;
   throughput:   increasing numeric calls/sec;
}
```

```
ServiceLevel normalQuality
...
normalGLProfile for IGeneralLedger = profile {
   from book require Efficiency contract {
     responseTime < 50 msec;
     throughput > 100 calls/sec;
   }
}
normalDBProfile for IDatabase = profile {
   from executeSql require Efficiency contract {
     responseTime < 20 msec;
     throughput > 200 calls/sec;
   }
}
```

Fig. 10. The grey pages describe the required and provided quality.

3.5   Grey Pages: Information About the Implementation Quality

The grey pages describe the quality that is either being required or provided at the interfaces of a component. It is specified as a set of ISO 9126 conformant quality characteristics. The specification framework provides a library of quality characteristics based on the ISO 9126-1 standard [21], which defines quality characteristics, and the ISO 9126-2 standard [22], which defines external metrics to measure them. It supports the description of three kinds of quality: (static) *component quality* (consisting of the characteristics usability, maintainability, and portability), *service quality* (consisting of functionality), and (dynamic) *efficiency* (consisting of reliability and performance).

In contrast to functionality and architectural design, the required and provided quality characteristics usually cannot be specified as constants. In fact, the provided quality characteristics (at least) depend on the hardware a component will be deployed on as well as the quality provided by other components (i.e. the deployment context). Both hardware characteristics as well as the quality characteristics required from the deployment context usually are allowed to vary (within certain tolerances) without causing a component to stop offering functionality. The variability of hardware and required quality characteristics, however, also causes a variability of the provided quality characteristics. In order to support such variable quality characteristics, the framework introduces *service levels* as contract statements, which specify provided quality characteristics in dependence on specific (ranges of) hardware and required quality characteristics. In so doing, however, a composition contract may contain more than a single statement on the quality level.

The principal notation to denote quality characteristics is QML [35], which supports both the definition of quality characteristics as *contract types* as well as the specification of concrete quality measures as *contracts* (see figure 10). The UnSCom framework predetermines a library of ISO 9126 conformant contract types which can be used to specify quality characteristics. Moreover, the definition of additional contract types is possible. Because QML does not support the specification of hardware configurations, the UnSCom framework additionally introduces a set of specialized taxonomies to denote them in a standardized way (as part of service levels).

Like concepts, quality specifications can be mapped onto the architectural design of the component interfaces to describe which particular architectural element (in particular which component service) yields a specific quality characteristic. This mapping is directly supported by QML, which contains *quality profiles* to map quality specifications onto elements of the architectural interface design (see figure 10).

4   Related Work

Component specifications are widely acknowledged to be of key importance and, subsequently, have been addressed by various authors, who have proposed to use (semi-) formal methods to describe relevant component properties. Unlike in most of the more mature engineering disciplines, a generally accepted and supported specification standard to support component-based software engineering, however, still is missing.

This is due to the fact that most of the specification proposals have only been made to support a specific task of the component-based development process, e.g. component design and implementation [2, 11], component classification [27, 28], compatibility checks [33], component selection [36, 37], component adaptation [32, 30, 7], the design of application architectures [13], and the prediction of application properties [6, 12]. Concerning specific component properties, many of these "task-specific" specification proposals at least partially overlap, but they usually make use of different notations to describe them. Compared to these "task-specific" proposals, only a few authors have worked on establishing generic approaches that cover different component properties and try to completely describe components [1, 14].

The UnSCom framework has been designed to *unify* existing approaches to component specification and provide a standardized core set of component properties that is applicable to support many different tasks during the development process. It is based on the well-accepted principle of *design by contract* [9], which it extends to satisfy the requirements of component-based development. The UnSCom framework builds upon the contributions of the before-mentioned authors, unifies them within a single, coherent approach and develops them further.

Moreover, it theoretically motivates and justifies the specification of specific component properties by introducing a classification schema, which summarizes different specification perspectives and stages of the development process. In so doing, the UnSCom framework provides a stable and reliable basis for the development of methods and tools to support component development, discovery, and composition. Since most of the elements of a methodology to support component-based software engineering are still on the drawing board [8], however, it is likely that additional component properties will have to be specified to support newly identified development tasks. For this reason, the UnSCom framework also introduces a profile mechanism to support application-specific extensions.

5   Conclusions and Future Directions

The proposed specification framework is currently being evaluated in practice and some case studies have already been completed. Currently, tools to support the specification tasks are being implemented and, moreover, a component repository as well as a marketplace which both implement the UnSCom meta-model are being developed.

Ongoing work also concentrates on including a more expressive technique to specify required and provided interaction protocols as well as evaluating and introducing *parameterized composition contracts* [12], which have a potential to enhance the support for composition tasks like, e.g., the prediction of extra-functional application properties.

Building upon these specification tools and repositories, which will serve as a source to obtain UnSCom compliant component specifications, one of the central future directions will be to (jointly) design a *coherent methodology*, in which methods and tools utilize the provided specifications to support different development tasks. A strategic advantage of this approach will be the fact, that most of the provided methods and tools can be used by creating and providing a *single* specification only.

An important step to achieve this longer-term goal, however, will be to start standardization of component specifications at an international level. The UnSCom framework has been developed to contribute an initial proposal and open discussions in a broader interest group. Providing generally-accepted basic methodological standards like the proposed specification method is a key prerequisite to counter an approaching composition crisis and truly make component-based software engineering a mainstream approach.

References

1. Szyperski, C., Gruntz, D., Murer, S.: Component Software. Beyond Object-Oriented Programming. 2. edn. Addison-Wesley, Harlow (2002)
2. D'Souza, D.F., Wills, A.C.: Objects, Components, and Frameworks with UML. The Catalysis Approach. Addison-Wesley, Upper Saddle River, NJ (1999)
3. Brown, A.W.: Large-Scale, Component-Based Development. Prentice Hall, Upper Saddle River, NJ (2000)
4. Garlan, D., Allan, R., Ockerbloom, J.: Architectural Mismatch: Why Reuse Is So Hard. IEEE Software **12** (1995) 17–26
5. Weyuker, E.J.: The Trouble with Testing Components. In Heineman, G.T., Councill, W.T., eds.: Component-Based Software Engineering. Putting the Pieces Together, Upper Saddle River, NJ, Addison-Wesley (2001) 499–512
6. Wallnau, K.C.: A Technology for Predictable Assembly from Certifiable Components. Technical Report CMU/SEI-2003-TR-009, Software Engineering Institue (2003)

7. Zaremski, A.M., Wing, J.M.: Specification Matching of Software Components. ACM Transactions on Software Engineering and Methodology **6** (1997) 333–369
8. Crnkovic, I.: Component-Based Software Engineering – New Challenges in Software Development. Software Focus **2** (2002) 127–133
9. Meyer, B.: Object-Oriented Software Construction. 2. edn. Prentice Hall, Englewood Cliffs, NJ (1997)
10. Ackermann, J., Brinkop, F., Fettke, P., Frick, A., Glistau, E., Jaekel, H., Kotlar, O., Loos, P., Mrech, H., Ortner, E., Overhage, S., Raape, U., Sahm, S., Schmietendorf, A., Teschke, T., Turowski, K.: Standardized Specification of Business Components. Technical Report, German Society of Informatics (GI) (2002)
11. Cheesman, J., Daniels, J.: UML Components. A Simple Process for Specifying Component-Based Software. Addison-Wesley, Upper Saddle River, NJ (2001)
12. Reussner, R.H., Schmidt, H.W.: Using Parameterised Contracts to Predict Properties of Component-Based Software Architectures. In Crnkovic, I., Larsson, S., Stafford, J., eds.: Workshop on Component-Based Software Engineering, Lund (2002)
13. Shaw, M., Garlan, D.: Software Architecture: Perspectives on an Emerging Discipline. Prentice Hall, Englewood Cliffs, NJ (1996)
14. Beugnard, A., Jezequel, J.M., Plouzeau, N., Watkins, D.: Making Components Contract Aware. IEEE Computer **32** (1999) 38–45
15. Cook, S., Daniels, J.: Designing Object Systems. Object-Oriented Modelling with Syntropy. Prentice Hall, Englewood Cliffs, NJ (1994)
16. Davis, A.M.: Software Requirements. Objects, Functions, and States. Prentice Hall, Englewood Cliffs, NJ (1993)
17. Graham, I.: Migrating to Object Technology. Addison-Wesley, Wokingham (1994)
18. Olle, T.W., Hagelstein, J., MacDonald, I.G., Rolland, C.: Information Systems Methodologies. A Framework for Understanding. Addison-Wesley, Wokingham (1991)
19. Ortner, E., Schienmann, B.: Normative Language Approach: A Framework for Understanding. In Thalheim, B., ed.: Conceptual Modeling. ER '96, 15th International Conference on Conceptual Modeling, Berlin, Heidelberg, Springer (1996) 261–276
20. OMG: CORBA Components. OMG Specification, Version 3.0 02-06-65, Object Management Group (2002)
21. ISO/IEC: Software Engineering – Product Quality – Quality Model. ISO Standard 9126-1, International Organization for Standardization (2001)
22. ISO/IEC: Software Engineering – Product Quality – External Metrics. ISO Standard 9126-2, International Organization for Standardization (2003)
23. Cerami, E.: Web Services Essentials. O'Reilly, Sebastopol, CA (2002)
24. OMG: UML 2.0 Superstructure Specification. Adopted Specification ptc/03-08-02, Object Management Group (2003)
25. Overhage, S., Thomas, P.: WS-Specification: Specifying Web Services Using UDDI Improvements. In Chaudhri, A.B., Jeckle, M., Rahm, E., Unland, R., eds.: Web, Web Services, and Database Systems. NODe 2002 Web- and Database-Related Workshops. Volume 2593 of Lecture Notes in Computer Science., Berlin, Heidelberg, Springer (2003) 100–118
26. OMG: General Ledger Specification. OMG Specification, Version 1.0, Object Management Group (2001)
27. Prieto-Diaz, R.: Implementing Faceted Classification for Software Reuse. Communications of the ACM **34** (1991) 89–97

28. Vitharana, P., Zahedi, F., Jain, H.: Knowledge-Based Repository Scheme for Storing and Retrieving Business Components: A Theoretical Design and an Empirical Analysis. IEEE Transactions on Software Engineering **29** (2003) 649–664

29. Czarnecki, K., Eisenecker, U.W.: Generative Programming: Methods, Tools, and Applications. Addison-Wesley, Upper Saddle River, NJ (2000)

30. Zaremski, A.M., Wing, J.M.: Signature Matching: A Tool for Using Software Libraries. ACM Transactions on Software Engineering and Methodology **4** (1995) 146–170

31. OMG: Object Constraint Language. OMG Specification, Version 1.1 97-08-08, Object Management Group (1997)

32. Yellin, D., Strom, R.: Protocol Specifications and Component Adaptors. ACM Transactions on Programming Languages and Systems **19** (1997) 292–333

33. Nierstrasz, O.: Regular Types for Active Objects. In: Proceedings of the 8th ACM Conference on Object-Oriented Programming Systems, Languages and Applications (OOPSLA 93). Volume 28 No. 10 of ACM SIGPLAN Notices. (1993) 1–15

34. Petri, C.A.: Fundamentals of a Theory of Asynchronous Information Flow. In: Information Processing 62, IFIP (1962) 386–391

35. Frolund, S., Koistinen, J.: QML: A Language for Quality of Service Specification. Technical Report HPL-98-10, Hewlett-Packard Laboratories (1998)

36. Kontio, J.: A Case Study in Applying a Systematic Method for COTS Selection. In: Proceedings of the 18th International Conference on Software Engineering (ICSE), Los Alamitos, CA, IEEE Computer Society Press (1996) 201–209

37. Kiniry, J.R.: Leading to a Kind Description Language: Thoughts on Component Specification. Caltech Technical Report CS-TR-99-04, California Institute of Technology (1999)

A Cross-Platform Application Environment
for Nomadic Desktop Computing

Stefan Paal[1], Reiner Kammüller[2], and Bernd Freisleben[3]

[1] Fraunhofer Institute for Media Communication
Schloss Birlinghoven, D-53754 Sankt Augustin, Germany
stefan.paal@imk.fraunhofer.de
[2] Department of Electrical Engineering and Computer Science, University of Siegen
Hölderlinstr. 3, D-57068 Siegen, Germany
kammueller@pd.et-inf.uni-siegen.de
[3] Department of Mathematics and Computer Science, University of Marburg
Hans-Meerwein-Strasse, D-35032 Marburg, Germany
freisleb@informatik.uni-marburg.de

Abstract. The possibility to uniformly access the WWW using a standard web browser has fostered the development of *nomadic desktop computing*, allowing nomadic users to run their applications from nearly any location providing access to the Internet. In this paper, we propose an approach to nomadic desktop computing based on the idea of dynamically deploying and executing personalized applications on the desktop system currently used by a nomadic user. We present a *cross-platform application environment* that automatically adapts itself to the requirements and configuration of a nomadic desktop application and enables the seamless execution and migration of applications across heterogeneous desktop computer systems. The implementation of our approach is outlined and its use in ongoing research projects is demonstrated.

1 Introduction

The major goal of the Internet was to link spatially distributed computing resources in the real world into a virtual computing environment where their physical location becomes less important or even completely unknown to the user [1]. With the advent of the WWW, information published on HTML pages by web servers got transparently accessible from everywhere using an ordinary web browser. Subsequently, several proposals have been made to establish the web browser as the universal user interface for *nomadic desktop computing* [2]. Instead of deploying an application on each desktop system, it is centrally installed and executed on an application server [3]; a standard web browser on a desktop system is then used by the nomadic user to access the application on the application server, as shown in Fig. 1.

However, an HTML interface provided by a web browser can not really substitute the rich user interface of a native desktop application. Thus, several attempts have been made to provide a comparable user interface by implementing the *thin-client approach* and running a desktop Java applet [4]. This approach requires less administration effort due to the centralized installation of an application, but it heavily relies on the processing power of the application server and the availability of a permanent network connection to access the remote application.

M. Weske and P. Liggesmeyer (Eds.): NODe 2004, LNCS 3263, pp. 185–200, 2004.
© Springer-Verlag Berlin Heidelberg 2004

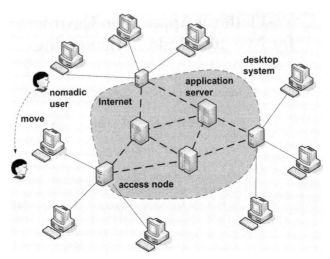

Fig. 1. A nomadic desktop computing scenario.

In this paper, we propose a different approach based on the idea of so called *nomadic desktop applications*. Instead of installing and executing applications on certain application servers, they are dynamically deployed and executed on the desktop system currently used by a nomadic user. In this scenario, a desktop computer system is alternately shared among different and unknown users. Thus, a fundamental problem is the dynamic and automatic adaptation of the current desktop computer to transparently provide a pervasive desktop environment to each user and application. Clearly, in practice it is not possible to prepare and maintain a single installation or configure all applications which might be used in advance. We address this basic problem by presenting a *cross-platform application environment*. It automatically adapts itself without user intervention to provide a suitable application environment for each deployed application across heterogeneous desktop computer systems. In addition, it enables the migration of application and user configurations among different hosts.

The paper is organized as follows. In section 2, we discuss the features and requirements of nomadic desktop computing and present related work. Section 3 presents our approach towards a cross-platform application environment and illustrates its realization in Java. The application of our approach is demonstrated in section 4. Section 5 concludes the paper and outlines areas of future work.

2 Nomadic Desktop Computing

In the following, we highlight the goals of nomadic desktop computing and identify the requirements to provide a suitable nomadic application environment. Then, we discuss related work and summarize our findings.

2.1 Goals

There are several models and visions of nomadic computing [2, 5, 6, 7], and many of them are mixed up with different variants of mobile computing, ubiquitous computing and pervasive computing. While some approaches are focusing on integrating computing systems into everyday scenarios and devices like car navigation systems or inventing new mobile devices like wearables, our focus is to particularly support nomadic users employing different desktop computing devices [2]. The basic idea is to enable people to use any desktop computer to run applications and to separate the one-to-one relationship between the *desktop computer* and the *nomadic user* as well between the *desktop computer* and the *desktop application*. Nomadic users can travel around and employ various desktop computers to work with their desktop applications, hence creating a *pervasive desktop environment*. Consequently, instead of having a desktop application installed on a single personal computer, the involved application has to travel with the nomadic user and become itself a *nomadic desktop application* which is dynamically deployed on unmanaged nodes, as shown in Fig. 2.

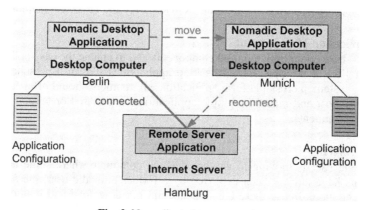

Fig. 2. Nomadic desktop computing.

A crucial problem in this scenario is to provide the illusion of a pervasive desktop environment that is independent of a specific host. This does not only include the automatic deployment and composition of application binaries, but also the migration of customized application configurations. In addition, the access to remote resources, such as the server application in Hamburg in Fig. 2, should be transparently reconfigured according to the current platform capabilities. The user should not be bothered with manual application configuration tasks but in contrast the desktop computer should adapt itself and provide a suitable application environment on the fly.

2.2 Requirements

The functional requirements of an application environment supporting nomadic desktop applications are as follows:

Runtime Environment

An application environment has to support nomadic desktop applications which may migrate to another desktop computer when the user moves. In effect, the desktop computer does not know in advance which application will be employed but it has to adapt itself and to provide a suitable runtime environment according to the platform capabilities and application requirements.

Self-management
While a desktop computer in a local network environment is well-known and can be easily managed, it is practically impossible to manage all possible desktop computers in a heterogeneous Internet environment. As a result, a potential Internet desktop computer has to self-manage the aspects of application deployment and composition as well as dynamic hosting and configuration of nomadic desktop applications.

Cross-Personalization
While traveling around, nomadic users and desktop applications pass different desktop systems. An important requirement for creating a pervasive desktop environment is the personal configuration and customization of the current desktop system [8]. With respect to current platform capabilities, each desktop system should offer a personalized application environment to the nomadic user and the desktop application.

Multi-application Management
In order to share commonly required components and to enable the easy collaboration and integration of multiple started desktop applications like in a personal desktop computing system, a cross-platform application environment should offer facilities to concurrently host and manage multiple applications in a shared or several separated runtime environments.

Resource Sharing
If a nomadic user is moving to another desktop computer where some application components have already been deployed by a former nomadic user, the application environment should reuse these components and not download and maintain exclusive copies for each application installation. Moreover, common configurations of the currently involved desktop computing systems should be shared among applications.

2.3   Related Work

In the following, we examine various approaches proposed in the literature to support the requirements of nomadic desktop computing.

Native Application Environments
A desktop computer is typically used exclusively by a single user. The installed operating system represents a *native application environment* bound to certain hardware. It is usually managed by a single administrator who ensures that all resources (e.g. libraries) are installed and properly configured in advance. This pre-installation is usually perfectly tailored to the needs of a single user and does typically not allow hot deployment of new applications. Instead, the administrator has to manually install and configure each application. Moreover, different computer systems are used, and the required application binaries as well as the capabilities of the installed operating system vary from version to version. Therefore, native application environments basically do not support seamless migration of an application to another host, e.g. a Linux binary can not be executed on a MS Windows system. Finally, native application environments are not expected to migrate application configurations across heterogeneous desktop systems, although there are approaches which synchronize user profiles

on a central server and retrieve them when the user logs in to another host, e.g. using Microsoft ADS, Novell NDS or LDAP [9]. As a result, nomadic desktop applications which rely on a native application environment and the related binary format can not be easily deployed across different desktop computers.

Virtual Application Environments

A different approach is so called *virtual application environment*. Instead of tightly coupling the application binaries with the operating system, they typically employ an intermediate application format. While some approaches like Flash or Shockwave [10] are typically tailored to be used as a plugin in a web browser, other approaches like Perl or Python [11] do not really support desktop computing with a graphical user interface. In contrast, Sun's Java comes with a full-fledged Java Runtime Environment (JRE) which provides a uniform application system across heterogeneous platforms. Actually, it is concurrently installed with a standard browser as a plugin and is thus available on nearly every desktop system. The introduction of Java applets allowed simple desktop applications to be deployed on desktop computer systems using a web browser. However, an applet could not be executed offline and independent of the browser. With the invention of Sun Java Web Start (JWS), the web browser was only needed for requesting an application but then it could be used offline as well as independent of the browser [12]. Furthermore, with Java Web Start, software deployment was simplified by introducing additional features such as automatic caching and updating of already downloaded components as well as sharing them across various desktop applications. Finally, application development was made as simple as developing a local application. There was no need to employ particular programming models as with Java applets. However, even though Java Web Start helped to seamlessly deploy Java applications across heterogeneous Internet nodes, it still lacks some important features required for a nomadic application system. First of all, there is no support for the migration of an application from one desktop system to another. In contrast, an application is independently installed on each desktop system and there is no synchronization with already existing configurations on another one. Moreover, it is not able to directly communicate with JAR repositories. Instead, a *Java Native Launch Protocol (JNLP)* configuration file must be downloaded and evaluated from a web server which can not be personalized by the user.

Remote Application Environments

Other approaches avoid deploying desktop applications at all and rely on a *remote application environment*. For instance, the project *Cooltown* is a Hewlett-Packard research project which follows the *smart space* solution of web-based nomadic computing [1, 13]. It utilizes existing standard Internet technologies like a web browser, HTTP, XML and URL. Thus, it avoids the inherent complications associated with ubiquitous computing, such as programming language, operating system and hardware dependencies. A similar approach called *crossware* was already proposed by Netscape in the mid-nineties but never reached broad acceptance [14, 15]. Another example is the *network computer* approach developed a few years ago mainly by Sun and Oracle [4]. The crucial idea was to replace a desktop computer by a computer system which basically consists of a screen, a keyboard and some memory. Instead of deploying and installing applications on each desktop computer, everything including the configurations and user profiles are managed on an application server which also provides processing power to execute the application. Similar to the XWindows system, the network computer is used to connect to the application server and to display the related user interface, following a *thin-client* approach. As a result, the user can access every application and all of her or his files from each connected network computer using a uniform desktop interface. In addition, the administration of the system is limited to a few application servers. Nevertheless, the original network computer approach did never receive widespread acceptance, possibly because network computers could not be used offline but only online. A variant is the use of a native operating system to provide a graphical user interface which is connected to an application running on a remote application server as in [16]. Instead of executing the application on the desktop, only the required display data is transferred from and to the application server. However, this also inherits the online problem and it is limited to a certain operating system supporting the user interface.

2.4 Summary

The presented approaches basically differ in their support for heterogeneous desktop systems. While native application environments are inherently bound to specific operating systems, virtual and remote application environments are actually independent of the underlying platform capabilities. Although MS .NET actually represents a virtual application environment, it is still only available as an attachment to MS Windows and can not be employed on different operating systems [17].

Furthermore, there is also a difference in the customization of the application environment according to personalized application configurations. Approaches based on Java Web Start do not support the modification of a given application configuration within a JNLP file. In contrast, native application environments may be independently customized but the resulting configuration is not always portable to another employed desktop system. Consequently, the personalized configuration options left on the formerly employed desktop system are lost. Concerning the sharing of resources such as downloaded components, there is also the problem that application systems typically provide a separated runtime environment to each deployed application. For instance, a Java application hosted by Java Web Start is usually isolated from other concurrently hosted applications and is not able to share common resources, e.g. already downloaded application components.

In summary, there are various approaches towards the distributed deployment of desktop applications. While they have proven their suitability in specific application scenarios, they typically introduce certain application models which are not suitable for all scenarios (such as Java applets and offline operation) or rely on fixed configurations (such as Java Web Start and its JNLP files). As a result, we think that there is still the need for a *cross-platform application environment* which is suitable to customize itself in a self-managed way according to the needs of the nomadic desktop application and the personalization of the nomadic user.

3 A Cross-Platform Application Environment

In this section, we present our approach towards a cross-platform application environment. We discuss its basic concepts and features concerning nomadic desktop applications. Finally, we illustrate its implementation and present an example of its use.

3.1 Conceptual Approach

A basic problem of nomadic desktop computing is the provision of a suitable application environment that is uniformly customized across different desktop systems following application-specific configuration requests and user-specific personalization options. We address this problem by separating platform, application and user related concerns and introduce various configuration options, as shown in Fig. 3.

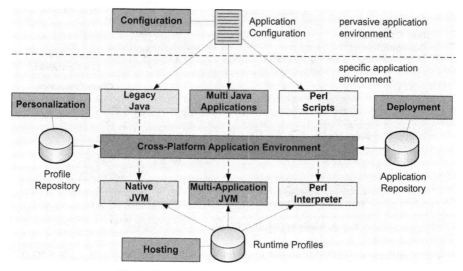

Fig. 3. Cross-Platform Application Environment.

The basic idea of our approach is to provide a pervasive application environment on top of a specific application environment which is customized by the *application configuration* passed by the nomadic user. In detail, particular *runtime profiles* are responsible for defining the hosting capabilities of the platform and are maintained by the platform administrator. The *application repository* is used by application developer to deploy application components and to describe the dependencies on other components. The *profile repository* contains the personalization for each nomadic user and nomadic application. In contrast to existing approaches, the cross-platform application environment does neither impose a single application model nor how the runtime environments are prepared or the required application components are deployed. It can be easily extended with additional runtime variants like Java or Perl whereby each extension is responsible for interpreting the passed application configuration and to prepare a suitable application environment.

3.2 Realization

Our current prototype of the proposed cross-platform application environment is implemented in Java and therefore greatly benefits from the uniform runtime environment provided by the Java Virtual Machine across heterogeneous operating systems and platforms. In addition, we have virtualized further aspects of nomadic desktop computing, such as the *deployment* and *composition* of Java applications. For instance, the composition of multiple Java applications within a single JVM is decoupled from the actual deployment scenario found on a certain platform, as shown in Fig. 4. Commonly used resources and classes can be shared and do not have to be loaded in separate JVM. Moreover, the collaboration of concurrently used applications is facilitated, e.g. exchanging data using object references.

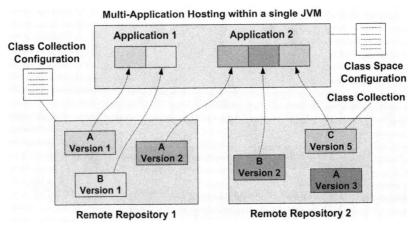

Fig. 4. Multi-application hosting within a single JVM.

Class collections [18] define the location as well as the content of a class repository. In turn, *class space* [19, 20] configurations are used to organize which classes may be loaded by the JVM, which are shared with and which are shielded from other concurrently loaded applications. Further, starting a single Java application by passing the class containing the static method *main* on the command line is not possible when multiple applications are hosted within the same JVM. Thus, we determine the *main* method using *Java Reflection* [21] and finally call it after having initialized the related application environment, as shown in fig. 5.

```
app = createClassSpace("application");
Class mainClass = app.loadClass(szMain);
String[] args = new String[mainArgs.size()];
mainArgs.toArray(args);
Object params[]={ args }; Class t[]={ String[].class };
Method meth = mainClass.getDeclaredMethod("main", t);
meth.invoke(null, params);
```

Fig. 5. Determining the main method using Java reflection.

In the first line, the class space is created and configured to host the application. After that, the application class containing *main* is loaded and the subsequent call with *invoke* is dynamically assembled and performed using Java reflection. Further details about *class collections* and *class spaces* are described in [18, 19, 20, 22].

Apart from the composition and hosting of multiple Java application, there is a related problem concerning the control of each application and its threads within a single JVM. The native JRE offers only little support for managing and signaling Java threads. For instance, there is no standard way to control a *foreign* thread or to process received signals in a pre-defined way, e.g. registering signal handlers. This means that for a multi-application environment there is no way to implement a common *task manager* to uniformly control various applications, threads and processes. In turn, an application can not be informed when a certain event is issued, e.g. when the application environment is shut down. As a solution, we developed a *managed thread model* which transparently wraps the original Java threads and provides synchronous and asynchronous access to each created thread within the JVM, as shown in Fig. 6.

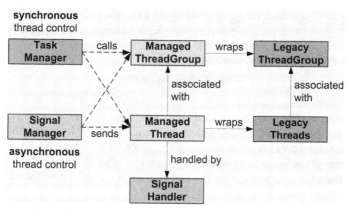

Fig. 6. Managed thread model and signal handling in Java.

The implementation is mainly based on the Java feature of *thread group inheritance* which automatically associates each newly created thread with the current thread group [23]. At the startup of the application environment, we create a particular managed thread group which is then able to address all later created threads. This way we can distinguish legacy and managed threads and can trigger callbacks that are used by the foreign thread to process asynchronous thread signals and synchronous thread control requests. In contrast to the native thread model where a thread is not longer allowed to call suspend, resume or stop, the managed thread model offers an alternative way to implement thread control. Of course, this assumes that the target thread is not refusing to be controlled but is regularly calling the signal handler method.

3.3   Use

A basic problem of a cross-platform application environment is its initial deployment on separately managed and remotely located computing systems. To this end, we distribute a Java-based management component with the Java Network Launch Protocol (JNLP). It is then used to load and start the requested applications as described in [20]. Thus, using the JNLP, the presented approach can be basically employed on any target system where a native Java Runtime Environment has been previously installed, e.g. as part of an Internet browser installation. If the nomadic user wants to move to another desktop computing system, he or she closes all applications and the application configuration is written back to the profile repository. He or she then moves and starts the cross-platform application environment on the next computer, the application profiles are retrieved from the profile repository and the user is able to start his or her applications again with personalized settings. In the following, we describe step-by-step how the actual cross-platform application environment is configured.

Step 1: Runtime Profiles (Platform Administrator)

Apart from launching Java applications within the same JVM as described in [20], we now use runtime profiles to specify additional runtime variants, as shown in fig. 7.

```
<application-runtime id="{8A750732}">
    <property name="runtime" value="native-java" />
    <property name="version" value="1.4.2" />
</application-runtime>
```

Fig. 7. Runtime profile.

The runtime profile is used to specify a common configuration setup which can be referenced by the application deployment, as depicted below. Its major objective is to configure runtime profiles depending on the resources of the underlying platform instead of the yet unknown applications. In the example above, we define a runtime profile for launching an application in a separate JVM using Java version 1.4.2.

Step 2: Collection Deployment (Component Developer)

We start with the deployment of a Java class collection. The developer has to create a class collection configuration with metadata about the collection, such as version property and where the Java classes can be actually downloaded. In addition, the required classes can be further selected by specifying regular expressions, as shown in Fig. 8. Only matching classes are loaded from the specified repositories.

```
<collection id="{553C6E73}">
    <property name="version" value="1.0" />
    <repository url="http://crossware.org/clock.jar" />
        <resource name="org/crossware/clock/.*"/>
    </repository>
</collection>
```

Fig. 8. Class deployment using class collections.

Step 3: Application Deployment (Application Deployer)

Next, the *application deployer* has to specify the required runtime environment in a separate application deployment configuration, as shown in Fig. 9. Along with that, she or he defines the required collections defined in the second step and which ones are shared or shielded using a class space configuration. The purpose of this separation is to enable the platform to look for alternative compatible collections in case the exact collection is not available on the current platform. In addition, the main class where the application execution starts has to be specified.

```
<application-environment id="{DC488997}">
    <runtime="native-java" />
    <main-class="org.crossware.clock.Main" />
    <classspace name="shared">
        <collection id="{553C6E73}" />
            <property name="version" value="1.0"/>
        </collection> </classspace>
    <classspace name="shielded">
        <collection id="{3283A542}">
            <property name="version" value="2.2"/>
        </collection> </classspace>
</application-environment>
```

Fig. 9. Application deployment.

Step 4: Application Configuration (Application Installer)

Another configuration is dynamically passed to a cross-platform application system when an application is to be deployed, e.g. a nomadic application migrating from one host to another. The application configuration shown in Fig. 10 contains a unique reference to the deployment description as well as a reference to the application profile. Both are evaluated by the cross-platform application environment and used to provide an appropriately configured runtime environment.

```
<application-configuration id="{5C015A86}">
    <deployment="{DC488997}"/> <profile="{DB92B18C}"/>
</application-configuration>
```

Fig. 10. Application configuration.

We want to point out that the application description does not contain any reference to the actual implementation, e.g. package name, JAR file location or name of the main class to start the application. Instead these settings are dynamically determined by the application environment evaluating the application deployment, collection deployment and runtime profile.

Step 5: Application Profile (Application User)

Finally, the application profile used for the personalization of an application installation is retrieved by the application system before the application is started. As shown in Fig. 11, the profile contains an individual display name and icon as well as certain parameters passed to the application.

```
<application-profile id="{DB92B18C}">
    <name="Clock" />
    <icon="class://org/crossware/clock/clock.png" />
    <args name="format" value="digital" />
</application-profile>
```

Fig. 11. Application profile.

This example represents only a simple view of the system. Of course, real collection configurations and application profiles are more complex than the mentioned ones. They are also usually not edited manually but with related tools.

3.4 Discussion

In this section, we highlight the basic features of the proposed cross-platform application environment with respect to nomadic desktop computing.

Separation of Concerns

We have identified various tasks for employing an application, such as deployment, composition, configuration, personalization and hosting of an application. Consequently, we have separated these concerns and provide options to customize each independently. In detail, the desktop computer system can be configured regardless of the nomadic desktop application. In turn, the application developer can also implement his or her application without actually knowing where it will be employed.

Extensible Runtime Support

Our cross-platform application environment is not limited to employ a certain runtime environment but is supposed to prepare and control arbitrary runtime environments as long as there is a suitable runtime profile available on the current platform. For this purpose, it can be extended with additional runtime configurator plugins. In effect, a particular application environment may be prepared and started in a separate process and window, e.g. executing a native C++ command line tool.

Self-managed Customization

The required customization and provision of a suitable runtime environment is performed without intervention of the nomadic user. This is a particular feature concerning a pervasive application environment that travels with a nomadic user and does not force him or her to manually configure and synchronize different application installations on each involved platform. Moreover, due to the diversity of platform configuration and capabilities, it would be actually not possible for the user to perform this task in heterogeneous environments such as the Internet.

Personalized Application Profiles

A basic objective of a pervasive application environment is cross-platform personalization. To this end, we have introduced a user-specific application profile which is used to maintain the application personalization independent of a particular desktop system and is synchronized with locally modified application profiles. Apart from personalizing a single application, it is also used to personalize selected settings specific to a certain host like the address of the proxy server.

Multi-application Management

The concurrent hosting of various applications is a typical feature of desktop computing, though it is often a complex task. Especially for Java applications we have introduced so called *class spaces* that allow organizing the classes of more than one Java application within the same JVM. Moreover, we have also invented a new thread control model that allows uniformly controlling and signaling *foreign* Java threads of concurrently loaded Java applications.

Resource Sharing

Commonly used resources like an XML parser can be shared among concurrently hosted applications in a multi-application environment. Apart from eventually downloading required components and the preparation of a suitable runtime environment, this does also not cause further performance overhead with respect to the execution of an application in a single platform environment.

4 Application of the Approach

In the following, we present a so called *Internet Application Workbench* which has been built as part of our cross-platform application environment to provide a graphical user interface. Currently, we use it in our project netzspannung.org [24] as an advanced workspace interface to access its document pools and start certain applications, as shown in Fig. 12.

The basic purpose of the workbench is to provide a uniform graphical interface to access nomadic desktop applications from arbitrary Internet hosts. For this purpose, the workbench is implemented in Java and initially deployed using Sun Java Web Start. It comes with a basic configuration for a Java application environment, e.g. the location of a Java application repository, as described in [18]. Thus, the user can immediately start to request and configure Java applications and run them within the workbench. In detail, the workbench can host multiple Java applications within the same JVM, which is realized by self-organizing Java class loaders using class spaces, as described in [19]. Concerning the way how users work with multiple applications within a native single desktop system, our Internet application workbench represents a *cross-platform desktop system* which is dynamically adapted to the current platform without bothering the user with manual configuration or installation tasks. In fact, the user is not aware of this adaptation and always gets the illusion of a pervasive application environment when moving across various desktop computers.

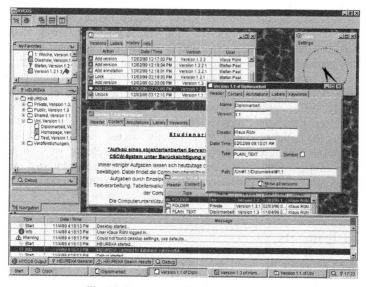

Fig. 12. Internet Application Workbench.

In addition, the user can further configure the application environment according to the platform capabilities as well as specific program settings like the path to a Perl interpreter. The workbench can then be used to some degree as a program launcher for running legacy applications in a separated process. It downloads the suitable application binary from a remote application repository, passes the appropriate program parameters to the operating system and controls the resulting process. However, the automatic migration of customized application configurations is typically not possible due to application specific approaches to store the configuration data.

5 Conclusions

In this paper, we have discussed the goals and requirements for nomadic desktop computing. Since existing approaches are either limited to fixed application scenarios, do not support the seamless migration of a desktop application and its configuration from one desktop system to another, or are not capable to synchronize user and multiple application profiles across various Internet hosts, we have presented our development of a cross-platform application environment that tackles these problems by separating the concerns of application deployment and composition, runtime customization and personalization by introducing various configuration files such as application descriptions, platform-specific runtime profiles and personalized profiles. Its implementation in Java, utilizing Java Web Start for the initial deployment on a new desktop computer system, was described. Finally, we have introduced a managed thread model that allows to uniformly controlling and signaling threads of multiple loaded Java applications. Our approach has been used to create an Internet application workbench that provides a uniform graphical interface across various Internet hosts. In effect, nomadic desktop users get the illusion of a pervasive application environment that travels with them and presents their personalized applications on different desktop computers in a uniform way.

There are several areas for future work. For example, the development of the cross-platform application environment is still going on. A major drawback of the current implementation is the lack of security features and protection against malicious applications. This problem could be solved by introducing cryptographic keys to protect downloaded and cached application components as well as application profiles. Another ongoing development is directed towards recommendation of application profiles. Currently, we investigate a recommender solution that evaluates existing profiles of other users which have already employed the same application and assists the user in creating the initial personalization. Finally, we use the current implementation only as part of our own research projects. After the first release, we want to test and evaluate it in further application scenarios, e.g. deploying the Internet Application Workbench as an advanced pervasive interface to netzspannung.org and its knowledge discovery tools [26].

Acknowledgements

The presented approach has been applied in the ongoing research projects CAT [25] and AWAKE [26] which are financially supported by the German Ministry of Education and Research (BMBF). The projects are conducted by the research group MARS of the Fraunhofer Institute for Media Communication, Sankt Augustin in cooperation with the University of Siegen and the University of Marburg, Germany. Special thanks go to Monika Fleischmann, Wolfgang Strauss, Jasminko Novak and Daniel Pfuhl.

References

1. Kindberg, T., Barton, J. A Web-Based Nomadic Computing System. Computer Networks. Vol. 35, Nr. 4. Elsevier 2001. pp. 443-456.
2. Amor, D. Internet Future Strategies: How Pervasive Computing Services Will Change the World. Prentice Hall 2001.
3. Zhu, J., Törö, M., Leung, V.C.M., Vuong, S. Supporting Universal Personal Computing on Internet with Java and CORBA. Concurrency: Practice and Experience, Vol. 10, Nr. 11-13. John Wiley & Sons 1998. pp. 1007-1013.
4. Gentner, D., Ludolph, F., Ryan, C. Designing HotJava Views. JavaSoft 1997. http://java.sun.com/products/hotjavaviews/hjv.white.html
5. Kleinrock, L. Nomadic Computing and Smart Spaces. IEEE Internet Computing. Vol. 4, Nr. 1. IEEE 2000. pp. 52-53.
6. Kleinrock, L. Breaking Loose. Communications of the ACM. Vol. 44, Nr. 9. ACM 2001. pp. 41-45.
7. Lyytinen, K., Yoo, Y. The Next Wave of Nomadic Computing. Information System Research. Vol. 13, Nr. 4. Informs 2002. pp. 377-388.
8. Wood, K. R., Richardson, T., Bennett, F., Harter, A., Hopper, A. Global Teleporting with Java: Toward Ubiquitous Personalized Computing. IEEE Computer. Vol. 30, Nr. 2. IEEE 1997. pp. 53-59.
9. Sheresh, D., Sheresh, B. Understanding Directory Services. Macmillan Computer Pub 1999.
10. Kerman, P. Macromedia Flash MX 2004 for Rich Internet Applications. New Riders Publishing 2003.
11. Wall, L., Christiansen, T., Orwant, J. Programming Perl. O'Reilly 2000.
12. Srinivas, R. N. Java Web Start to the Rescue. JavaWorld. IDG 2001. Nr. 7. http://www.javaworld.com/javaworld/jw-07-2001/jw-0706-webstart_p.html
13. Cooltown. HP Research Labs 2004. http://www.cooltown.com/cooltown/index.asp
14. Cusumano, M. A., Yoffie, D. B. What Netscape learned from Cross-Platform Software Development. Communications of the ACM. Vol. 42, Nr. 10. pp. 72-78. ACM 1999.
15. Andreessen, M. Building Crossware. Netscape Techvision 1997. http://wp.netscape.com/columns/techvision/crossware.html
16. Extent Solutions. http://www.exent.com/solutions/products.asp.
17. Meyer, B. .NET is coming. IEEE Computer. Vol. 34, Nr. 8. IEEE 2001. pp. 92-97.
18. Paal, S., Kammüller, R., Freisleben, B. Java Class Deployment with Class Collections. Proc. of the 2003 Int. Conf. on Objects, Components, Architectures, Services, and Applications for a NetworkedWorld. Erfurt, Germany., LNCS 2591, Springer-Verlag, 2003. pp. 135-151.
19. Paal, S., Kammüller, R., Freisleben, B. Java Class Separation for Multi-Application Hosting. In Proc. of the 3rd Conference on Internet Computing (IC 2002). Las Vegas, USA. CSREA Press, 2002. pp. 259-266.
20. Paal, S., Kammüller, R., Freisleben, B. Customizable Deployment, Composition and Hosting of Distributed Java Applications. Proc. of the 4th Int. Symposium on Distributed Objects and Applications (DOA 2002). Irvine, USA, LNCS 2519, Springer-Verlag, 2002. pp. 845-865.
21. Richmond, M., Noble, J. Reflections on Remote Reflection. Proc. of the 24th Australasian Computer Science Conference (ACSC 2001). IEEE 2001. pp. 163-170.

22. Paal, S., Kammüller, R., Freisleben, B. Separating the Concerns of Distributed Deployment and Dynamic Composition in Internet Application Systems. Proc. of the 5th Int. Symposium on Distributed Objects and Applications (DOA 2003). Catania, Italy., LNCS 2888, Springer-Verlag, pp. 1292-1311.
23. Venners, B. Inside The Java 2 Virtual Machine. McGraw-Hill. 1999.
24. netzspannung.org, Communication Platform for Digital Art and Media Culture. http://netzspannung.org
25. Fleischmann, M., Strauss, W., Novak, J., Paal, S., Müller, B., Blome, G., Peranovic, P., Seibert, C., Schneider, M. netzspannung.org - An Internet Media Lab for Knowledge Discovery in Mixed Realities. In Proc. of 1st Conference on Artistic, Cultural and Scientific Aspects of Experimental Media Spaces (CAST01). St. Augustin, Germany. pp. 121-129. Fraunhofer 2001.
26. AWAKE - Networked Awareness for Knowledge Discovery. Fraunhofer Institute for Media Communication. St. Augustin, Germany. 2003. http://awake.imk.fraunhofer.de

Agile Software Engineering: A New System for an Expanding Business Model at SCHUFA

Rainer Burkhardt[1] and Volker Gruhn[2]

[1] SCHUFA Holding AG, Wiesbaden, Germany
Rainer@Burkhardt.com
[2] University of Leipzig, Germany
Gruhn@ebus.informatik.uni-leipzig.de

Abstract. A software development unit called to renew or replace an existing corporate system may face some special problems in an established company with a lot of well-trained behavioral patterns and thought structures fitting to the legacy system only. The challenge is not just to be on a journey and reach the destination with the development team but keeping accompanied by the stakeholders during the travel. In this article we describe how Agile Software Engineering can be introduced to an in-house development structure of a company. We describe how agile process elements and model driven approaches can be combined in order to achieve a light weight, flexible and incremental software engineering process. We also show the resulting organizational structure of a development department and have a closer look to the management actions that must be taken to introduce agility to the internal team and the stakeholders all over the company.

1 Introduction

The German company SCHUFA has a 75 years history. Reorganized effective 2002 from a set of regional companies to an all-national and centralized AG with lots of shareholders – mainly banking corporations – it is still privately held. In an expanding market environment SCHUFA is a well known key player and market leader in the credit bureau business, has a tremendous pool of data on natural persons in Germany and is competing with international positioned companies like Experian, InFo-Score and others.

Nowadays, not a small set of companies face the situation, that a working IT system is processing some established business cases generating good profit. As technology and markets change, the need rises to rethink and rewrite the business model of companies in small steps. As crucial future capabilities of the IT system will be for the company's business success in the future as crucial the maintenance of the existing business presently is.

SCHUFA is one of these companies and addressed the importance of developing new markets while maintaining existing customers and shareholders by creating an in-house IT including a software development department.

M. Weske and P. Liggesmeyer (Eds.): NODe 2004, LNCS 3263, pp. 201–215, 2004.

The two major challenges for the SCHUFA IT have been and still are the ongoing developing and the going live of releases of the new system while maintaining the still productive and doing well legacy system – at least the not yet replaced parts. Thus, the legacy system business is focused on production demands and requirement while the new system business spans all project activities from early domain requirements to production demands as balancing optimizations and monitoring requirements from the production and operations teams.

Problems or challenges are accompanied by a lot of opportunities in our case. From the point of view of a software developer the most exciting one is to build and manage a new team for developing the new system. That newly hired team can feel relatively free of burdens that the legacy system and the long time employed staff have to carry. And these guys can use latest news and experiences from technology and science. This is not a statement like "throw away what you've learned – here is the new stuff"; because that is not what we think. Development in iterations and increments, building releases and modeling already have been a good choice earlier [2]. Now we had the chance to add lots of agility and omitted some predefined structure of processes and artifacts.

Agility is a really natural thing – at least for some of us. However, applying agile modeling and extreme programming in software development – as far as we have learned – is not a matter of laissez-faire. There is still an employment opportunity and need for managers in agile biospheres. Thus, an agile software engineering process contains activities on maintaining and selling as well as on controlling and educating the agile practices. The actions to be taken are headed toward the development team and the stakeholders. Concerning matters are the system, the architecture, and technological aspects.

The following chapter addresses the basic aspects of our approach. In the third chapter we refine the process on relationships and roles of stakeholders while we focus on the chosen organizational options as an environment in chapter four. The following two chapters explain how we applied our approach inside the development department of SCHUFA and how we lived the process in every day's business. Finally we summarize the lessons learned and left for future work.

2   The SEP Approach at SCHUFA

Software engineering processes (SEP) deal with artifacts and processes and try to give a handsome guideline to a development unit. A SEP is valuable if it is applied by the addressed unit, raises the quality of the produced software releases, helps to hit the goals of the projects and accelerates the velocity of the software production.

Introducing heavy weighted processes for about a decade, we learned that the first mentioned topic from above is crucial: the application of the process in a day by day business and by every member of the team.

We find it easy to trust a decision that already had proven to be the right one. Applying best practices is easy to argue because it uses knowledge from lessons learned earlier without paying the price again. Arranging the development in short cycles is one example: we can guarantee to have evidence available earlier and are able to evolutionary improve the development's processes. Thus, we take benefits from small steps and short cycles.

Combinations of iterative and incremental discipline-based development processes also use that nowadays (see [4]). So we decided to follow an evolutionary approach (see [5]).

Thus, light weight processes enable both: measurements to be taken soon and organizational effects to be effective early.

System

In migration from a legacy 3270 world to a via web accessible system an XML gateway addresses one of the most important objectives: get all SCHUFA customers shifted to the new system in a delimited time frame. Providing an extensible language and a 24x7 available service platform for contract partners to access today's and future's services from SCHUFA hands the technical means to the management and the sales force to connect new and existing customers to the SCHUFA system. All customers that are live at the XML Gateway my not take care if the demanded services are processed by the legacy system or some replacing component of the new system at SCHUFA.

Written in Java and already following the new architectural concepts that also are basics for the new system the XML gateway as the departments first productive service of the new system helped us train and improve the development and deployment processes and also helped us to find, fix and establish the new organizational structure. Via our XML gateway the complete set of services of the legacy system had been brought to the contract partner. However, our main internal interest in providing such an interface was to lay out a migration path for the existing (~5.000) and new (many) customers. We consciously left some work to do for others (outside the development) to execute the plan of getting all customers exclusively to that gate.

Our next steps to replace the Legacy System "just" had to replace the use cases of the acting production system by new solutions realized by components of the new system.

Architecture

Joining the company we discovered a remarkable technical oriented thinking from the IT division to the legal department and the sales division. Unfortunately the used technical terms mainly were bound to the long time existing legacy system implementation not to the domain. To learn the terminology of a company is one thing to make it accessible to new employees – and the SCHUFA hired a lot of new employees in that time – is sometimes completely different.

We anticipated that circumstances with an architectural metaphor. Since blade servers actually entered the mind of IT people we chose a similar design in three levels where the blades to be inserted are the software components (fig. 1).

The case is symbolizing the calling-type framework of the new system which is based on J2EE using *Container Managed Persistence* for *Entity Beans* and *Stateless*

Session Beans for the activities in a workflow written in UML's activity diagram notation and executed by the framework's workflow engine.

The lower level is capable to hold *Access Components*. These components encapsulate the access to subsequent systems, mainly the legacy system, the search engine,

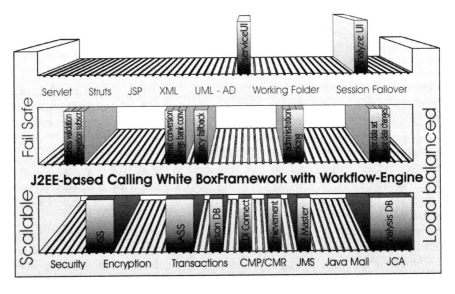

Fig. 1. Architecture of the New System.

the decision support system and via the database management system to the attached databases.

The mid level is the model-level of the architecture. So called *Activity Services* implement business components. We stereotyped these components to be *Organizational Components*, *Product Components* or *Workplace Components*. These components take remarkable advantage of detailed and well refined models. The static and dynamic structure is a crucial and sometimes immanent scope of rethinking, refactoring and rearchitecturing. As a result, sometimes the framework has to be extended. In all other cases the model of the application system is modified, altered or just enriched. We mainly used UML's *Class*, *Sequence* and *Component* diagrams (for dependencies). Sometimes in discussions we experienced *Deployment* diagrams to be helpful, especially to show which items we talk about are components residing inside the containers and which are located elsewhere referring the distinct machines.

The upper level is able to hold interface components. One is the above mentioned XML gateway. Most others are user interface components.

Architecture is a term that often appears as a homonym. The reader already noticed that the above given description is concentrating on software aspects that we call component architecture inside the department, following [2].

Development Team

Mixing expectations and experiences gave us a clear understanding of what the core tasks of the development team should be. We had to develop new products for the new system and to redevelop existing ones to stepwise replace the products from the legacy system. We had to maintain and improve the architecture and to do the concerning use-case spreading work. And we had to build new workplaces for internal employees.

Our work can be planned and the tasks to do can be ordered. However, there are some dependencies that rise the first time you go into the deep stuff – means: in modeling or programming sessions. Thus, *organizational* and *product components* sometimes turn out to use existing systems what pushes the appropriate *access component's* feature on top of the task stack. *Product* and *workplace components* sometimes turn out to force extensions to *interface components*, machine or user, causing the team to push the task to build a new version of that particular component to the top.

All these tasks not only cause effort in programming. Also involved is modeling, web design, database design, architecture, system technicians and production's concerns, quality aspects, requirements and of course all further communication to the stakeholders and management including reporting, best proved to be done by experienced project managers.

3 Addressing the Stakeholders

Stakeholders in XP terms are usually named just customers. While we focus on a corporate in-house development with SCHUFA here we are able to make some distinctions appropriate to that special scope. Fig. 2 shows a development-centric view to stakeholders inside and outside the IT division.

None of our stakeholders forced us to introduce agility. Thus, we – as the driving force – had to "sell" agility to all stakeholders. In the following paragraphs we summarize our related activities.

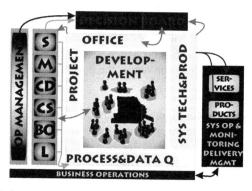

Fig. 2. Stakeholders inside and outside the IT division (frame).

Stakeholder: IT Management

The management in the IT division consists of the division director and four managers, three leading a department, one leading a supplementary unit attached to the division. While we take the point of view of the development here, the *System Technique and System Production* (STSP) yet is a stakeholder. Holding the stakes of the company for data center concerns this department contracts the hosting partner and controls all service level agreement matters as system monitoring, backup, security maintenance, load balancing and more things that are important in the production environment. Deploying a new system to production machines for these colleagues is a task that is triggered by a production-ready new system release, packaged by the development. Less new releases means less work with that task and leaves more time to anticipate intrusion attempts, network capacity problems, to be renewed certificates and so on. Rising headcount in the STSP department rapidly also had its limits. Thus, it was not easy to gain them as allies for short release cycles and early deployments.

The department *Process & Data Quality* (PDM) was easier to infect. With SCHUFA, this department is not just the quality assurance but also the domain experts for all credit bureau business processes, some kind of product development (not to be mistaken as development in the sense of software development) and revision inside IT. While agility easily can be argued to emphasize quality and bringing new products online in short cycles is also highly valued by that fraction the PDQ manager became a strong ally inside IT for agility.

One of the compromises worth to be exposed targeted the above mentioned different environments. The development was set to be in charge for two of them and PDQ took responsibility for one. Being in charge for the two production systems left enough responsibility for STSP and pulled away the thread of continuous or even daily deployments to be handled and managed, projected to be three a year.

The *Project Office* now is some kind of a department with defined responsibilities and direct strong communication paths to the IT director and all IT departments as well as to all corporate stakeholders outside IT. First established as a project itself, the *Project Office* asked for a lot of reporting data on our process, the actual projects, the consumed man-days and some more. After having learned, that the overall objective is to measure the work that we have done on projects in the department we elaborated an approach that offered a calculation basis to give numbers for workload and workload-based project dispatching and large-scale forecasts for the next two releases. At the end of the day the *Project Office* became a strong ally for objectives of agility and other contemporary improvements driven by the development.

Stakeholder: Top Management

Top managers are usually focused on visions and results and thereby need reports.

With SCHUFA some of the directors and executives from fig. 1 are seated in the *Decision Board*. This is an organizational element we introduced to anticipate top managements information needs. The *Project Office* reports the over all project plan in a recurrent meeting to the *Decision Board* members. If resources are tight these reports may cause the board to terminate or shift projects as well as give more resources or concentrate resources to a distinct project.

For top managers first of all agile development is a new technique. Means: some aspects might be valuable others might not – depends on the promises given.

Thus, we tried to promise not too much and found high expectations combined with some strengthened knowledge and convictions how projects have to be conducted. And we presented the time boxing promise: "we will be in time, will not extend the delivery date but cut features out of the deliverable if we need to; however, we will not shift the deadline".

Stakeholder: Domain Expert

The domain experts with SCHUFA were spread over all divisions (left side, fig. 2) and also were strongly represented in the IT division (mainly in PDQ). From the very start, the PDQ colleagues were tightly integrated in the development process as to be questioned experts in interview and modeling sessions.

Being nearby all the time, this department shared and accompanied our way to agility. We considered that as an extraordinary opportunity to have access to on-site customers. However, the ability to join interview sessions and understand prepared models and helping it to correct or improve are not the same as modeling skills. Getting new product descriptions from *Marketing* and process improvements or erroneous functionality from *Business Operations* had to be on an interview or text basis.

Thus, we used that organizational structure with the defined over all development process. PDQ was in charge for the requirements engineering including bug reports preceding our sessions with the PDQ people. The profit for our session was that one single on-site customer is much easier to handle than a bunch of.

Stakeholder: User

There are two types of users of the new system:

Type 1 users are colleagues from the various departments and locations of *Business Operations*, sitting on an interactive user interface to the new system to answer requests or maintain the corporate data base. These users typically use workplaces of the new system. Some of the work places indirectly use SCHUFA products.

Type 2 users are other systems in which architecture the SCHUFA system usually appears as a backend system. Human communication in this case happens between the developers of the front end system and the SCHUFA system. These users are programming access to SCHUFA products.

Expected communication skills and means are completely different. We addressed type 2 users with a SCHUFA-defined and XML-based exchange language for requests and notes to the XML gateway of the new system. We prepared white papers and other developer adequate artifacts and provided a fully available system environment for the development at contract partner site. We designed the overall development process in the way that every new release with enhanced features appears live at the same time on the production environment and the contract partner test environment either. This solution completely fitted our agility-driven development needs.

We had some more to do with the type 1 users. First of all, a smooth transition was very important. And we also had to deal with terminal users that now had to use a browser interface. Thus, we noticed to have two different phases from the point of view of every individual:

1. switching to the new system with the new user interface philosophy and
2. learning additional features of a new release of the system

We addressed phase 1 with an operations team of extra-smart colleagues (pilot team) using the new system while others still used the legacy system for an interim period. Accompanied by *Human Resources* training on the new system was arranged using the acceptance environment. The pilot team was contacted frequently by our project manager and PDQ to learn improvement suggestions and get requirements for the next releases of that workplace.

4 Organizational Options

To organize a software development unit in teams is a good idea if it becomes bigger than – to give a number – ten employees. Basically two orthogonal aspects have to be respected: project and line.

Line
Fortunately, employees tend to stay employed with the same company exceeding finished projects, sometimes even if they are external. That guarantees persistent rising of the department's know how where leaving consultants or internal employees can be seen as a disadvantage while there remains a lack of skills.

A line-based organizational structure is ideal to pass lessons learned from one project to others. It also enables a project-independent work to be allocated. Having an available budget for developing and maintaining e.g. a framework is a good way to build value inside the company – some kind of implemented and project-persistent knowledge.

Of course that position can be a threat for the top management if misused by the department manager. In addition such values tend to be uncountable because nearly no one in the market is asking for such company-specific frameworks. This is not a global valuation of domain-specific frameworks as stand-alone products. However, it's an observation of the authors at least considered to be valid for the German financial industry.

Project
At the same time, success is often aligned to projects. With a smart project organization and a good marketing of the project's results a lot of good news can be disclosed and help the development to be seen as a very useful part of the company. Since development departments use to be cost centers this topic should not be neglected. The next mighty manager who is trying to promote himself by a cost saving suggestion is sometimes just around the corner and definitely no software development department is really strong without an adequate budget.

We know that the four variables cost, quality, time and scope are interrelated in every project. In studying experiences from Kent Beck and other authors on that topic ([3], [9]) and recalling our own we decided to do what software engineers love to do: decompose. Decompose a big project in many smaller ones. Using this practice inside the department meant to get experienced and educated faster because the existing knowledge is applied and refined frequently.

Saying small project we mean that a project should not spread more than two releases of the system. Our projects usually have a project leading board of three individuals and for practical purposes it is usually set up with two managers from the concerned domain departments and one from IT. With the help of the *Project Office* (see below) our *Project Manager* constantly communicates to the board.

Model-Based Development

Applying experiences published in [1] and [12] and adding our own conviction, we saw big advantages in applying agile practices to modeling and in applying intensive modeling to our projects. Both, the internal team matters and the external communication should be positively influenced by using UML models. Thus, we think some Agile and XP publications miss an important thing. E.g. Cockburn correctly names roles like *project manager*, *designer/programmer*, *tester* and *UI expert* but does not name a role like *modeler*, *business modeler* or *business process designer* or something similar (see [8]).

"Think in metaphors, communicate in pictures." This thesis is widely supported by modeling with the Unified Modeling Language we used in the department.

We respect artificial paintings invented ad hoc in meetings. However, graphically refer to an existing model or add a diagram in a formal notation way (formal in the UML sense) brings a lot of meeting exceeding and context spanning value to the development. We think, the metaphor background is most valuable if you talk about a constantly refined and completed model and communicate the appropriate aspects to the distinct addressee.

In the given context of SCHUFA it turned out to be useful to grasp the application domain knowledge available at some software developed in the form of UML component and deployment diagrams. By doing so we introduced an over all building plan referred to in all phases of the projects. This model was used as some sort of fix point. All discussions about functional requirements especially with people outside the department were focused on this building plan. This building plan was maintained all the time because it just offered a set of diagrams that opened a key hole to the model for spectators. Of course, we additionally and much more intensively worked with use case, activity and class diagrams, to complete the overall model and inserted needed details for the implementation with these diagrams or with Java means in the programming sessions. Thus, we avoided never-ending discussions about diagram details, communicated the model in different depth of detail to differently skilled people.

Perhaps defining roles is the first step to discipline an XP process. However, if a team is big enough we can afford specialists without loosing agility.

5 SCHUFA Development

While installing an agile development philosophy on the department level we decided to replace a distinct individual based role model by a team based organizational structure. The basic idea is that teams scale up better than individuals and the bandwidth of a team's knowledge can be wider than an individual's.

Organizational Mix
Under these circumstances it is good to have a well-fitted organizational supported process that gives most possible advantages from both worlds: line and project.

We tried to apply learned lessons from project-oriented people with a background of huge projects ([7], [10], [11]), combined it with published experiences from convinced small-project people ([3], [8], [14]) and added our own.

The size of our teams varies over time and from team to team. The weakest team in headcount is the *Web Design Team*. The strongest was the *Development Team* with a headcount of 12, scaled down later on. Some may be astonished to hear that the *Project Management Team* at its high time had seven *Project Managers*. We don't want to analyze here what the main reasons for that phenomenon were. Some company based conditions as reporting expectations may have been influential factors and communication (internal and external) capacities could also be considered to be reasons. What we realized is that used terms as "project" imply expectations. Sometimes we felt a lot over-administered with company-processes suitable to monitor two or three huge projects in a period of two or three years. Having 15-30 smaller projects per year forces these huge-project expectations to scale down.

Project Office
With the *Project Office* we anticipated some major needs: the top management could not afford to sit in five or more *Project Leading Boards* but needs to keep informed especially on extraordinary events. The managers of the SCHUFA divisions sometimes felt to compete with their colleagues in occupying development resources. By shifting the responsibility from IT to top management to set priorities for the next to be conducted projects meant for some of us to escape the crossfire of "but-my-project-is-the-most-important-for-the-company" accusations. The kind of *Project Office* the SCHUFA established is far more than the fulfilling of needs described here. However, it's mainly destination and intention still is a headquarter-located information center for projects.

6   Living the Process

There are many books on project management out there. Some just focus on a particular sequence as [12] or write novels about virtual experiments in that domain [9]. Others have an overall understanding of projects from outside [7] or inside [2] the development team.

Inside the Software Development
From an internal point of view of the department projects realize versions of components delivered in a release of the new system (see fig. 3). Components can be of stereotype *system* or *user interface component, workplace component, organizational component, product* and *access component*. Additional development actions have to

be taken to develop and maintain the framework that realizes the architecture. Only the development of product and workplace components is published as projects company-wide.

Projects take place in time slices called iterations. Selected stakeholders can see and feel the current development status at the end of the iteration (at least then). A pre-released version of the component will be deployed to the integration test environment inside a development release of the new system. With such previews we keep the stakeholders informed continuously. This avoided unexpected surprises.

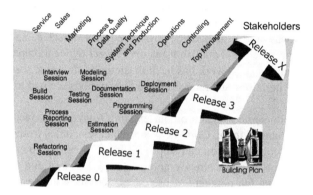

Fig. 3. Building the New System in Releases.

New requirements will be given full respect. However, they can only be implemented in the current release if they arrive before a so called baseline. Our baseline was a date in the middle of the release period (four iterations per release). Late arriving requirements may and usually were shifted to the next version of the component which could be the same or a following project.

The team wrote session cards to a tool to describe a bunch of work to do for realizing a demanded feature. A session card had to contain little tasks that could be taken and fulfilled in a short period of time like one or two sessions.

We classified our sessions. One worth to be mentioned is of type *Estimation Session*. At least at the beginning of each iteration to every project one session of that kind had to be planned. Another session type is called *Refactoring Session*. While easy refactorings happened in "standard" sessions as *Programming* or *Modeling Sessions* more complex ones (e.g. affecting the architecture) had to be written in a separate session card. Some similar session card is created for *Architecture Sessions* but they usually were originated in architectural extensions. *Presentation Sessions* tended to be planned at the end of an iteration phase. *Documentation Sessions* were created whenever an external documentation of an implemented piece of software such as a white paper was required. *Interview Sessions* could be demanded out of a *Programming* or *Modeling Session* and could be planned by the *Project Manager*.

Modeling Sessions use UML as language of choice, *Programming Sessions* use Java. Both are usually arranged as paired sessions what means that two people work together on one computer. During the work they nearly constantly talk to each other.

Main results are skilled up employees and high quality code. *Inspection Sessions* could be demanded and described by any developer to point to an observed phenomenon that was under suspicion to or already had caused problems. Usually in such sessions at least one participant was from the *Architecture Team*.

Measurement
Usually project oriented organizations use to count in man days or man months. They use this method or some derived calculations as key performance indicator (KPI). The big disadvantage on calculation based on man-days is, that work time is just time not result, not work that has done or has to be done.

Our intention was to give an even better indicator for ourselves and later on to put it in a management report and publish it via the *Project Office* as capacity plan. Thus, the *KPI* has to show if more work has been mastered in the same time. Having fixed the time slices for iterations and releases these time periods seemed to be ideal for our purpose.

We decided to do some research on our existing source code over the last months to find out what changed there. Good help in such cases comes from your configuration management tool where you can step back in the time line to earlier builds. We mainly used the tools that we already applied (the UML tool and the Java IDE) to count and wrote down the numbers of use cases, activities, classes, beans and some more. The problem with counting is: whatever you count can be manipulated. Using lines of code as a calculation basis may cause programmers to change their notation style or add garbage comments. In the same way using classes could probably result in many tiny classes some times. More complicated formulas could also solve the problem but we liked to have a simple measure.

Thus, we decided to use session cards (SC) as the basic number and started without weighting different types of session cards different. We then decided that it is easier to understand for people outside the department if we avoided using more terms like session, e.g. iteration or release and simply took "month" instead as a time period indicator. We named the unit of the resulting number SDP for software development performance.

```
SDP perfMar04;
// …
perfMar04 = SD.calcPerformance(2004,3);
```

We further decided to intentionally hide the concrete formula for *calcPerformance* (work per time) because we may change it in the future from today's *number of session cards worked on per month* to *number of session cards completed per month* or some completely different. However, the SDP as a unit should persist.

This indicator expressed in one number, how good the software development performed in a given period of time. Based on the development of that number over time further analysis of de- or increases of that unit could be taken. Having an exact number of the overall costs of the department provided by the company's controller we were able to report how expensive a single iteration or a single release was.

With that calculation basis we looked into the past. Project stakeholders and company leaders were even more interested in the planning. So they liked to have a good estimation that meets the future reports exactly if possible.

Capacity Planning

Capacity planning was a main task of a *Project Office* like ours at SCHUFA. Some of the guys there had lots of experiences with that topic based on man-day calculations. The basic idea was to have a trunk of internal employees and supplement these guys by external employees if more work has to be done in the same time. You run into a big problem with this approach if you engage external staff that is able to stretch a particular amount of work to be done over a much longer period of time. It's not easy to detect that by the *Project Office* or the management because the calculation basis is time not work (or effort).

Our SEP approach fulfilled the need to have forecasts in capacity also and we had a work-based calculation. However, you still have estimations instead of exact predictions. In addition you need to experience that kind of performance measurement a considerable time period to approximate reality with the prediction.

To start an example calculation we first had to estimate the amount of work to be done in session cards (SC): "Today we assume that realizing the component 'contract partner' is 32 SC of work to be completed."

Our experience is that this first estimated number rises by ¾. About ½ of it is discovered before the baseline is reached. That in mind we say: "We expect the organizational component 'contract partner' release 1 to be 46 SC of work."

As a further measure of experience we know that about ¼ of the features on session cards is not crucial to the success of a workplace or product component. Having that in mind we said: "34 SC have to be planned to be done if we like to go live with the contract partner component in the next release's iteration 1 and 2 of the new system."

Having our calendar-based planning in mind, social effects like holiday-time in various concerning states could be considered to make our next estimation step more realistic. A good estimation basis was the last year's months of the two iterations. E.g. we planned for February and March 2004 where Feb03 may have had a SDP of 43.7 $^{SC}/_{month}$ and Mar03 may have had a SDP of 52.7 $^{SC}/_{month}$. With this in mind we decided: "Let's plan to do 15 SC of 'contract partner' in the February iteration and 18 SC in the March iteration. That leaves 13 SC more for April and Mai for that component."

This calculation example showed a free capacity of 28.7 SC for February and 34.7 SC for March for other projects of the department.

These are the numbers we and the *Project Office* were interested in. We could then pick the next project from the priority list and go ahead the same way.

What we have learned from this easy calculation basis – to be honest – is: some people are used to calculate man days and costs for years. It's sometimes hard for them to accept the advantage of a new KPI as ours. While we strongly believe in the advantage of our KPI we keep convincing others outside step by step and go on planning this way inside the department.

Performance Results

After many months of practicing the described approach we have seen that influences from early adoption phases decrease and the amount of work described in session cards does not vary as much as in the beginning any more. However, there was still a wide range dependent from level of understanding and the individual author of the session card.

In capacity planning we are still trying to improve our predictions and forecasts in the *Project Management Team*. While *Project Managers* are individuals they tend to pack more or less work to be done in a single session card. Sometimes the first *Interview Session* completely redefines the PM's or the team's view to a feature or application that has to be realized. Since we have comparably small projects we might be able to learn quicker and to become experienced faster in that domain. We still see some more work to be done in the team especially concerning lately joined team members or external *Project Managers*. It's reassuring if you have a comprehensible calculation basis as our KPI offers. You just do not feel like a gambler in the role of a *Project Manager*.

Team Building Results

Some of the colleagues in the department felt like sort of lonely hackers in the beginning. A freshly started department has its own rules, of course. Accompanied by team building events the colleagues – one after the other – discovered our applied XP practices for themselves and also found their roles in the teams and the all together working process. However, that takes time. With us, about one year passed until all accepted the new way of building software and there are still some traps in the corridor in the offices. One must carefully maintain that spirit to keep the engagement, employee's satisfaction, and after all: stakeholder's satisfaction.

7 Conclusion

We accomplished two major projects and numerous smaller ones with agility in use as described in this article. In a period of about two years the described organizational structure was developed and helped us to arrange the processes with development participation. The team and the managers still have to "sell" agility – to the stakeholders and some team members as well. However, we have seen a huge commitment to the approach at the end of that period if we compare it to the limitations and barriers we faced in the beginning – personally and organizationally.

This approach was particularly worthwhile in the SCHUFA context, because software staff was heterogeneously qualified and because a new architecture was introduced. On the other hand, the agility approach showed its shortcomings with respect to quickly grasping the application domain knowledge and in communicating it to many developers. In order to overcome this drawback, we introduced teams of specialists in the department. Here we gained benefits from model driven approaches. That means, UML models were used to communicate the application domain knowledge and session cards to dispatch the work.

In the given situation, this combination turned out to be useful and an appropriate compromise. Future work will be devoted to describing more precisely under which circumstances a combined software engineering process as that described above can help to reconcile agile practices with organizational needs. We also intend to elaborate how the approach from SCHUFA could be applied to companies with similar constellations willing to add lightweight agility to their software engineering process.

References

1. Ambler, Scott W., Agile Modeling, Wiley: New York, 2002
2. Beck, Kent, Extreme Programming Explained, Addison Wesley: Boston, 2000
3. Beck, Kent and Martin Fowler, Planning Extreme Programming, Addison-Wesley: Boston, 2001
4. Boehm, Barry and Richard Turner, Balancing Agility and Discipline, Addison-Wesley: Boston, 2004
5. Brooks, Frederick P., jr., The Mythical Man-Month, Anniversary Edition, Addison-Wesley: Boston, 1995, pp. 231-239
6. Burkhardt, Rainer, UML Unified Modeling Language, 2nd ed., Addison-Wesley: Bonn, 1999
7. Cantor, Murray R. Object-Oriented Project Management with UML, Wiley: New York, 1998
8. Cockburn, Alistair, Agile Software Development, Addison-Wesley: Boston, 2002
9. Crispin, Lisa and Tip House, Testing Extreme Programming, Addison-Wesley: Boston, 2003
10. DeMarco, Tom, The Deadline, Dorset House: New York, 1997
11. DeMarco, Tom and Timothy Lister, Peopleware, 2nd ed., Dorset House: New York, 1999
12. Erikson, H.-E. and M. Penker, Business Modeling with UML, Wiley: New York, 2000
13. Jeffries, R., A. Anderson, and C. Hendrikson, Extreme Programming Installed, Addison-Wesley: Boston, 2001
14. Wallace, Doug, Isobel Raggett and Joel Aufgang, Extreme Programming for Web Projects, Addison-Wesley: Boston, 2001

Ercatons: Thing-Oriented Programming

Oliver Imbusch, Falk Langhammer, and Guido von Walter

Living Pages Research GmbH
Kolosseumstrasse 1a, 80469 Munich, Germany
{flabes,falk,guido}@livis.com

Abstract. Thing-oriented programming (TP) is centered around the concept of a "Thing". A thing in an executing software system is bound to behave like an object does in our real world. TP is an emerging programming model which overcomes some of the limitations of current practice in software development in general and of object-oriented programming (OOP) in particular. Ercatons provide an implementation of the model. TP does not describe a new programming language. The so-called "ercato virtual machine" or "ercato engine" implements the ideas discussed and has been used to validate the concepts described here.

1 Motivation

The development of ercatons was inspired by the way we all deal with real-world objects and how recent object-oriented techniques have deviated from this ideal. An anecdote may illustrate this best.

"One morning, we noticed some workers tile our office's backyard. The day before, piles of square tiles had been delivered and the workers now seemed to make good progress covering the backyard's middle section. All of a sudden, loud noise stopped us working. What had happened? The workers had finished to cover about 90% of the surface with square tiles and had started to *cut* tiles using a stone saw. Due to corners and the irregular shape of the backyard, the produced tiles had all shapes one could possibly think of. The end of the day, the entire backyard was nicely tiled."

What if the tiles were software objects? We would have two options: First, the textbook option with *tile* as a base class, *square*, *rectangular* and *polygon-bounded tile* as its derived classes (where we already encounter and avoid the meaningless discussion if *rectangle* should be inherited from *square*...). Or second, the pragmatic option of a *generic tile* with appropriate constructors. And we would have to create objects on demand while tiling or we would have to algorithmically solve the tiling problem in order to create all required classes upfront. Still, we probably would miss cases where we need a hole in the tile etc. And still, our software objects do not model tiles – the defined classes model a *factory* which produces them.

In the real world, we use square tiles and cut to fit. In the software world, we use tile factories which must be able to produce tiles of all shapes we analyzed beforehand to be required.

M. Weske and P. Liggesmeyer (Eds.): NODe 2004, LNCS 3263, pp. 216–237, 2004.

This example, as trivial as it appears to be, does matter. Initially, the problem seems to go away if we look how software is really being built: We may always modify a generic tile class and recompile and test until the software is finished. Source code modification then is what corresponds to "cut-to-fit" in the real world. At a second analysis however, this is not true anymore for large enough systems. First of all, complex systems are never finished. But more fundamentally, complex systems must be layered and modular with lower level modules considered stable at some point. And now the problem of a lack of reusability of objects emerges even *within* a single system, if only complex enough.

The best technologies to cope with this situation are a combination of waterfall methods (specify as much as possible as early as possible), model-driven architectures (same reasoning), and powerful modules with well-defined contracts (increase chances of reusability as much as possible). However, projects must, by definition fail to scale linearly with size this way. Interestingly, real-world engineering projects do not.

Thing-oriented programming (TP) is the attempt to overcome the limitations of OOP. The philosophy behind it may be summarized by the following "manifesto".

The Ercato Manifesto of Thing-Oriented Programming:

§0 *The exception is the rule.*

§1 *Our world is **rich** and complex* rather than well-structured and simple.

§2 *Software must cover **irregular**, changing patterns* rather than regular patterns.

§3 *A software system is an **organic** being*
rather than a set of mathematical algorithms.

§4 *Software components are an **integral part** of our rich world*
rather than entities at some meta level.

§5 *Software engineering evolves from small to **large***
rather than from concrete to abstract.

We will not go into too much detail regarding the manifesto here. While the first three points are widely accepted within the OO community, the latter three points may be what constitutes the essence of the emerging TP model.

Ercatons are a development aimed at addressing *all* of the points of the Ercato manifesto. Ercatons have been developed over the past four years and this paper aims at presenting its core ideas and to set it into a larger context, namely that of Thing-oriented programming.

2   The Emerging Thing-Oriented Programming Paradigm

We distinguish between a mainstream trend within OOP and an emerging Thing-oriented trend.

Mainstream. The mainstream trend is dominated by generative methods such as model-driven architecture (MDA), aspect-oriented programming (AOP), various wizards in IDEs and an increasing level of abstraction. It is also characterized by pattern frameworks (such as Struts for the MVC paradigm for the web or J2EE for business logic) and a strong emphasis on an architecture which is as complete as possible upfront.

The evolution of programming languages has long be characterized by an attempt to conceptualize real-world entities into software entities – object-oriented languages being the current end point. Modeling languages such as UML2 are no exception as they emphasize visualization without escaping the limitations of an object-oriented language. Component-based software is a facet. Aspect-oriented programming deviates a bit as it depends on formal aspects such as grammar. Both are pushing those limitations a bit. Altogether, we found it disappointing how different software objects still are from real-world entities after a quarter century of research. They are poor when it comes to representing them while *using* or *growing* a system, as opposed to representing them while modeling.

The mainstream seems to disagree, given the movement for model-driven architectures (MDA) or executable models; or the generation of executable systems from models. The promise is: Once you have the model, you are done. And if objects are fine to model a system, where is the problem? The problem simply is that it may be impossible or too hard to ever create this model!

We believe that it may be possible and worthwhile to create a model for a simpler, special case such as a given algorithm, or some important processes, or a less accurate one for better overview; but not in general for an entire problem, not within time and budget, not without mistakes. We are convinced that being forced to model every detail of a system is against the general engineering principle of keeping things as simple as could possibly work.

Thing-Orientation. The trend towards Thing-oriented programming may first have emerged in 1979 with "ThingLab" [1]. The publication of the programming language "Self" [2] in 1987 and of prototype-based languages in general were important milestones. The language "NewtonScript" [3] was inspired by Self and led itself to "JavaScript" [4]. Both are prototype-based. More recently, XML-based language "Water" [5] and Java-based system "NakedObjects" [6] emerged. Water is another prototype-based language linking every XML-tag with an object and calls its top-level ancestor "Thing" rather than "Object". NakedObjects is not a language (it uses Java) but drops the MVC pattern in favor of the idea that every object should expose an intrinsic user interface (i.e., that every object should be usable by itself). We notice growing interest in plugin architectures as well, as recently demonstrated by the popularity of Eclipse [7]. A plugin has some characteristics of a Thing which an object does not.

Orthogonally, new engineering methods emerged, with Extreme Programming [8] and the Agile Manifesto [9] being examples. Those methods contradict the mainstream trend towards even more abstract and complex models or architectures as well as the waterfall method. All of these developments address some points of the Ercato manifesto. Ercatons are meant to address *all* aspects of the Ercato manifesto and to be fully Thing-oriented. First information about it was released in 2003 [10].

As we are not aware of a publication bringing all of the above developments into the single context of a trend towards Thing-orientation (as opposed to model-driven), we would like to start with our definition of the notion of a Thing.

3 Definition of Thing-Oriented Programming

The basic idea behind a "Thing" is to be able to represent a real-world entity without the absolute requirement to model it. If we do not model, we still describe, visualize, compare etc. Document-like properties of a Thing acknowledge this. During usage of a system, while we learn more about various aspects, Things are designated to morph and formalize aspects to reflect the increase in knowledge. Also, models can still be expressed by projection of knowledge "to the essentials" where what is essential and what is not may be a function of time.

Definition: A "Thing" is a software entity within a production software system with the following properties:

1. **Uniqueness** – It is unique and no two Things can be *exactly* equal:

   It has exactly one unique "name" and two Things are always distinguishable.

2. **Structure** – It has *inner structure* which is both state *and* behavior:

   Its *state* is a data tree or structure of equivalent complexity, not restricted to slots. Its *behavior* is defined by reaction to received messages, or events such as elapse of time.

3. **Object** – Its inner structure is inherited, polymorphic, delegated and encapsulated:

   Inheritance: a Thing may inherit (or clone) inner structure from another Thing. *Polymorphism*: two Things may behave qualitatively different for the same message. *Delegation*: a Thing's inner structure may refer to other Things. *Encapsulation*: a Thing defines how much of its inner structure is exposed to another Thing.

4. **Document** – It is human-readable:

   There is an equivalent externalizable and human-readable form accessible by name. It has one owner controlling its visibility and encapsulation. It determines its life-cycle, incl. infinite life (persistence). It has a (non-perfect) memory of previous inner structures it had over time (versioning).

5. **Morph** – Its behavior, state, owner, inheritance relation etc. may change during lifetime.

6. **Projection** – It defines its interactions with components of a production software system:

   It has one or more representations when manipulated by algorithms (programming interface). It has one or more representations when manipulated by humans (user interface). It determines its formal properties such as search index entries it may contain.

7. **Deterministic** – It will only temporarily maintain inconsistent inner structure (transaction safety).

Definition: A "production software system" is a real-world system comprised of hardware, software and humans currently solving or able to solve the problem the software is being crafted for. Such systems may be distributed or not. A program source editor or IDE is no such system.

To support Things, such systems will most likely be composed of a grid of virtual machines executing one or several flavors of a Thing execution environment. The semantics of a Thing may and should be independent of a production software system.

Definition: "Thing-oriented programming" is the art of creating software composed of Things. Because this activity resembles growing and building rather than modeling and programming, we sometimes call Thing-oriented programming "to *build* rather than *model*".

Note that some of the properties of a Thing are common properties for object instances, other for documents. The following simplifying statement shall summarize the above points for the rest of this paper: *"A Thing is unification and super-set of an object instance and a document."*

A remark is in order: It is of course true that a document could be created or an object could be instantiated that has all claimed properties, e.g., a generic object instantiated from a Java class. However, a second such instance inheriting from the first would not be inherited in the Java sense. This means that Java as such lacks some of the required properties and could be used to *implement* an environment for Things only. To make this clear: *"Objects are not Things. Documents are not Things."*

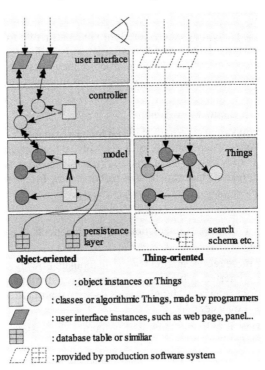

Fig. 1. A Thing defines all relevant aspects within a software system, i.e., every single instance does. There is no intrinsic difference between a user's and a programmer's view.

Untyped object-oriented languages such as Smalltalk are closer to Things than strongly typed languages such as Eiffel or Java. Prototype-based languages such as Self are even closer because they do not depend on classes and are able to change their behavior during lifetime. Many properties we deem important for Thing-oriented programming are missing from prototype-based languages and therefore, we do not classify TP as prototype-based.

The discussion so far left open the question why we call the approach "Thing-oriented". Both, objects and documents are normally combined to represent real-world entities. But there has been no unifying concept. Therefore, the fact that Things must be a superset of objects and documents immediately follows from the initial question: *"What is the software entity which most closely represents a real-world entity?"*

In Fig. 1 we conclude this section with an overview about how a Thing-oriented software system differs from a traditional object-oriented one.

4 Definition of Ercatons

Ercatons are specified to be Things and to address all of the points of the Ercato manifesto, hence the name.

Ercatons separate inner structure from algorithm. Inner structure is expressed in one language (such as XML) with algorithms being expressed in another (such as Java or XSLT). This separation could easily be removed by creation of yet another language. The most elegant way to do so would be by treating code-closures [11] as ercatons. However, this would not be in line with both clauses of §3 of the Ercato Manifesto. All typical OOP features (such as polymorphism, inheritance, encapsulation, method signatures etc.) are features of an ercaton independent of algorithms. Actually, any piece of code written in a language which has XML syntax is an ercaton and a closure and removes the separation. It is just that currently, we do not recommend this style.

The specification of an ercaton is such that the difference between itself and the real-world entity described by it are reduced to an absolute minimum. As a consequence, any ercaton describing a *virtual* real-world entity (such as a bank account) *is* the entity. Algorithms are ercatons in turn, because code implementing an algorithm *is* a virtual real-world entity.

Definition: An "ercaton" is a Thing (as previously defined) with following additional properties and specifications:

1. **Name** – an ercaton has a structured local name:

   The local name is a string of the form "~owner/path[,version]" and follows Unix shell conventions.

2. **Syntax** – its equivalent externalizable and human-readable form is XML:

   Every XML document (if it includes a valid name) is an ercaton. It uses ercato markup (XML elements and attributes in given separate namespaces) to alter its semantics. This markup is not bound to an XML schema and will coexist with most XML applications. The ercato markup may be considered the syntax of an ercaton. Syntax exists to express all of the semantic properties of a Thing.

3. **Flavors** – ercatons come in seven flavors or more:

   plain: an ordinary ercaton. **role:** a user, owner, or rôle; **user** is a sub-flavor. Users must be authenticated. **prototype:** has reduced semantic power, e.g., serving as a template to be cloned. **resource:** contains binary data such as a movie or a code archive (the XML form of a resource ercaton is, as an exception not equivalent to it). **index:** a formal data schema or other formal information; ercatons are able to index part of their state in relational databases; persistence of ercatons must not depend on formal information. **version:** a history of versions of an ercaton. Ercatons may change flavor (morph), but cannot be of more than one flavor at a time.

4. **Commutativity** – federations of ercatons form unordered sets:

   The state of an *ercato engine* is fully defined by all ercatons, independent of the order they have been manipulated in. This implies that an ercaton action cannot store data outside of ercatons, i.e., in a database.

5. **Algebra** – ercatons may be added (+) and subtracted (-):

   Inheritance is supported where syntax is as general as XML (the infoset tree). The algebra is defined such that inheritance corresponds to addition. Let a and b be ercatons, then it holds true:

   $$a = a + b \qquad \Leftrightarrow \qquad a \text{ inherits from } b$$

   Subtraction is defined to be the inverse operation, $(a - b) + b = a$, and $a - a = 0$.

6. **Behavior** – ercatons contain actions, triggers, targets and objects:

   action: specifies behavior upon receipt of a message; consumes and produces ercatons; actions are protected by sets of rôle-based permissions; an ercato engine must be able to discover and export actions as WebServices. **trigger:** specifies behavior upon an event; events include elapse of time, change of state, asynchronous events such as receipt of email. **target:** pipeline specifying projection onto a named user interface; an ercato engine must support at least a web-based interface. **object:** specifies projection onto named API for an algorithm; an ercato engine must support at least a Java-based object model.

   Behavior may be specified by a closure (in some XML language such as XSLT), delegated to an action of another ercaton, or implemented by an algorithm. An algorithm may be a resource ercaton containing a Java jar-file and is then identified as ercaton/class/method().

7. **Permission** – ercatons encapsulate their inner structure:

   State and actions are guarded by the following rôle-based permissions: **r:** readable state. **w:** writable – ercaton can be morphed or deleted as well. **b:** browsable; state which isn't browsable for a rôle cannot be retrieved indirectly, i.e., by a database query performed by that rôle. **x:** action is executable. **s:**

substitute rôle by owner of action before executing it (s-bit); permissions are carried along action delegations forming a capability chain. **t:** action is executable and may modify this ercaton (2nd s-bit).

Permissions provide both the rôle-based business logic and the package/module-based OO encapsulation (private, package-private, public, friend, etc.) – using package names as rôles.

8. **Distribution** – ercatons may be distributed:

Access or invocation of actions is not bound to one address space and ercatons may freely migrate (using a global name). The transmission protocol is HTTP or SOAP [12] using the externalized form. The transmission of authentication depends on the trust between two ercato engines. The ercato engine employs an optimistic locking strategy for concurrent operations. It may optionally use the XOperator (c.f. below) to avoid detection of false collisions.

Definitions: An "ercato engine" is a production software system supporting ercatons as Things. An "ercatoJ engine" is the ercato engine we have implemented on top of J2EE [13]. Note however, that ercatons are language-independent. The ercatoJ engine exists and is in mission-critical production use, e.g., at Henkel KGaA [14].

All of the above 8 points are to be discussed in more detail elsewhere. This paper, however, aims at providing an overview and introducing into the general idea. We will therefore now highlight and give examples for the aspects we deem to be particularly interesting.

5   Examples

Some examples may clarify things and introduce into the syntax, the ercato markup.

Example 1. A hello ercaton in its XML form (below, we will leave out the erc: namespace).

```
<?xml version="1.0" encoding="ISO-8859-1"?>
<hello xmlns:erc="http://ercato.com/xmlns/ErcatoCore">
  <erc:id>~sample/hello</erc:id>      <!-- the name or ercato-id   -->
  <p>Hello, world!</p>                <!-- the ercaton's only state -->
</hello>
```

Example 2. An improved hello ercaton. It returns a variable string.

```
<hello>
  <erc:id>~sample/hello2</erc:id>
  <erc:action> /bin/echo (text=xp{concat('Hello, ',$name,'!')})
  </erc:action>
</hello>
```

This example uses another ercaton, `/bin/echo`, to delegate the implementation. Beforehand, the argument within the `xp{...}` clause is evaluated as XPath [15] expression. To see the result, the expression `~sample/hello2(name="world")` must be executed.

Example 3. A counter ercaton which updates its state.

```
<counter xmlns:erc="..."
xmlns:xsl="http://www.w3.org/1999/XSL/Transform">
  <erc:id>~sample/count</erc:id>
  <count>0</count>                           <!-- state -->
  <erc:action name="main">
    <erc:arg name="amount">1</erc:arg>       <!-- default value -->
    <erc:native lang="Xslt">                 <!-- a closure     -->
      <xsl:template match="count">
        <count><xsl:value-of select=". + $amount"/></count>
      </xsl:template>
    </erc:native >
  </erc:action>
</counter>
```

This simple ercaton contains the entire logic required to maintain a counter to be incremented, stored, viewed and used (in a transaction-safe way). This unique counter is identified as `~sample/count`. This example uses a closure in order to be self-contained (not referring to any other ercaton). However, real usage would more be like

Example 4. Counter ercaton rewritten (after incrementation is refactored).

```
<counter>
  <erc:id>~sample/count</erc:id>
  <count>0</count>
  <erc:action name="main"> /bin/increment (xpath="//count")
  </erc:action>
</counter>
```

Fig. 1. The count ercaton of Example 3/4 in its default web browser look&feel (after three clicks onto 'main').

Its owner (or another ercaton) may do the rewriting during production. There is no big difference between the rewrite and an invocation of an action like `main`. The `amount` argument is implicitly passed down the delegation chain.

Due to the properties of an ercato engine, ercatons may be displayed in a browser window with one URL per ercaton-id. In the ercatoJ engine, the counter `~sample/count` looks as in Fig. 1.

A click onto the "main"-button would increment the count to 4, equivalent to expressions `~sample/count!main (amount=1)` or just `~sample/count()`. *Every* ercaton has, by definition, a "look&feel" as is seen here. In a different context, an ercaton may be displayed by a panel window within a GUI, or in a console window. We will now discuss some selected features in more detail.

6   The Programming Model

Rather than featuring a programming language, ercatons are programming language-independent. It is therefore necessary to show how ercato programs are written. It is obvious that the ercato programming model is centered around the idea of creation, modification and use of ercatons. An ercaton may be used by inspecting its state, executing its actions, sending it to the user as part of the user interface, or sending it to another system.

Because ercatons may contain triggers which fire upon elapse of time, ercatons may also show autonomous behavior (or life). This is useful to implement agent-based patterns. Ercatons are meant to directly implement entities of the real world also known as the problem domain or business logic. Most ercatons do. Their names are like `~flight/booking/1h6361/ma34`. Other ercatons provide utility services. Their names are like `/bin/cp`. We call the former *business ercatons* and the latter *service ercatons*. When it comes to implementation of actions, we distinguish between three typical cases:

- Structural, administrative tasks such as editing state etc.: Delegated to service ercatons.

  Note that delegation to an ercaton such as `/bin/increment` does only look like a shell script call. Upon invocation, the delegation chain will actually be followed and its end will be invoked. Final invocation is also cheap as it normally takes place within the local address space. Typical programming language primitives (instance creation, copy, a full edit cycle, print, change of part of its state, queries, etc.) are all provided by service ercatons.

- Preparation of state for a user interface or exchange: Implemented by service ercatons which are XSLT stylesheets.

- Algorithmically non-trivial tasks: Implemented in an OO language (Java) after projecting the state of involved ercatons onto appropriate object instances.

  There is a language binding which maps ercatons to Java objects (incl. their inheritance relation) together with an API to expose more features. Using this language binding, any framework to bind Java objects to XML and back may be used. The Ercato API for Java includes a light-weight framework for this task. Within the ercatoJ engine, invocation of an action implemented in Java incurs minimal overhead only.

Example 5. The counter ercaton is again rewritten, now with a Java implementation.

```
<counter>
  <erc:id>~sample/count</erc:id>
  <count>0</count>
  <erc:object lang="Java">
    <erc:archive> ~sample/lib.jar </erc:archive>
    <erc:class> sample.Counter </erc:class>
  </erc:object>
  <erc:action name="main">
    <erc:arg name="amount">1</erc:arg>
    <erc:native lang="Java">
      <erc:method> increment </erc:method>
      <erc:parameter name="amount" type="int"/>
    </erc:native>
  </erc:action>
</counter>
```

with (complete and working) Java code as follows:

```
package sample;
import com.ercato.core.*;
import org.w3c.dom.Text;

public class Counter extends ErcatonObject implements Action {
    public void increment (int amount) {
        count += amount;
        if (amount != 0) touch ();
    }
    protected void evaluateElement (EvaluationContext ec, String tag,
                                    String ns) {
        if (!"count".equals (tag)) return;
        counter = ec.getTextNode (false);
        count   = Integer.parseInt (counter.getData ());
    }
    protected void approve () {
        counter.setData (String.valueOf (count));
    }
    private Text counter;
    private int  count;
}
```

Support for other languages may be added later provided the language supports a sandbox security model. The permission model is such that a user must not gain additional privileges by creating an ercaton with a malicious action written in any language. The implementation language of actions is hidden and actions may invoke each other even when implemented in different languages.

It is important to observe that the `Counter` Java-class is reusable within *any* ercaton which contains a count-tag with numeric content. This is a general observation and the following relationship is deduced:

Construct:	Thing-oriented language:	Object-oriented language:
Signature for algorithms	**OO-class**	OO-interface
Signature for state	Missing or XML-schema	**OO-class**

Ironically, this shift of usage of OO-classes in a Thing-oriented system makes them small and reusable.

7 Inheritance

Inheritance may be the most exciting single aspect of ercatons. It is supported where syntax is specified to be as general as XML (the infoset tree). The general idea is to provide an algebra for infoset trees defined such that inheritance corresponds to addition. Let a and b be infoset trees (ercatons except resource ercatons), then it holds true:

$$a \equiv a + b \quad \Leftrightarrow \quad a \text{ inherits from } b \qquad \textbf{(Eq. 1)}$$

Subtraction is defined as the inverse operation, and the following equations hold true:

$$a \equiv a + a \qquad \textbf{(Eq. 2)}$$

$$a - a \equiv 0 \qquad \textbf{(Eq. 3)}$$

$$(a - b) + b \equiv a \qquad \textbf{(Eq. 4)}$$

$$\exists\, a,b\colon a + b \neq b + a \qquad \textbf{(Eq. 5)}$$

This way, object-oriented inheritance turns out to be just a special case of a more powerful mathematical operator which we call the "XOperator" [16]. Morever, ercatons can continue to be stand-alone entities unrelated to each other and be unrestricted by a type system or type-safety.

An ercato engine must not make a difference between two ercatons a and a' where the left clause of Eq. 1 holds true for a' and b, and where a declares *"to be clone of"* b. In the latter case, b is called *"clonebase"* of a. An ercato engine is required to maintain Eq. 1 to hold true over changes of a clonebase, i.e., clone and clonebase must be kept synchronized.

This model provides full support for situations where no instance is like any other, but does support several classical OO techniques for more regular situations too. These techniques include: (1) an object inheriting from an ancestor, (2) an object instantiated from a class, (3) two objects sharing a "common part", and (4) instance data filled into a template, or overriding default data.

To illustrate the above, we will evolve the counter ercaton example. We define an ercaton `~sample/count2` which is kept *similar* to `~sample/count` except, of course for its ercato-id which must be unique. Ercaton `~sample/count` is now clonebase of `~sample/count2` and every change to the clonebase is a change to `~sample/count2` as well. Both ercatons being similar means that accessing their XML form yields almost equal results. This implies that the XML form of `~sample/count2` must differ from the listing in after creation when inspected. At most one clonebase is allowed. However, an arbitrary number of "bases" is allowed. A base is like a clonebase except that changes after creation are not tracked.

An ercaton may have rich inner structure (as demonstrated by the `<action>`-element and may be declared clone of another ercaton which has rich inner structure too. The XOperator-addition of infosets of both ercatons results in the following rules:

1. Clone *a* and clonebase *b* are compared.
2. What in *a* is missing is inherited from *b*.
3. What in *a* is an extension of inner structure in *b* extends that inner structure.
4. What in *a* is additional is an extension of *b* altogether.

Annotations and additional rules refine the rules. We found that the XOperator is roughly as powerful as XSLT transformations. Lets present a simple example of non-empty inheritance:

Example 6. An ercaton inheriting from another. The `~sample/count` ercaton was defined in Example 3.

```
<counter>
  <erc:clone>~sample/count</erc:clone>
  <erc:id>~sample/count2</erc:id>
  <erc:action name="main">
    <erc:arg name="amount">2</erc:arg>
  </erc:action>
</counter>
```

This definition is equal in effect to the definition of the following ercaton:

```
<counter xmlns:xsl="http://www.w3.org/1999/XSL/Transform">
  <count>0</count>
  <erc:id>~sample/count2</erc:id>
  <erc:action name="main">
    <erc:arg name="amount">2</erc:arg>
    <erc:native lang="Xslt">
        ... detail from Example 3 ommitted here ...
    </erc:native>
  </erc:action>
</counter>
```

Note that the default value for the action argument is overridden only. It would have been equivalent to first create the clone from an empty declaration and then to change the default value in the resulting ercaton; or to first copy and change, then to declare it clone of another ercaton. It is therefore not necessary to model the inheritance relationship – it is discovered automatically. In doing so, the XOperator-subtraction is used to invert inheritance. An ercaton of prototype flavor may be used if its sole purpose is to act as a clonebase. This corresponds to an abstract class in a class-based OO system.

The above example of inheritance has been very object-oriented, just overriding (part of) an action. A very Thing-oriented example is one where two ercatons containing state expressed as scalable vector graphics (SVG) do inherit from each other.

~sample/whiskers-extends-plaintiger =   ~sample/whiskers extends ~sample/plaintiger

Fig. 2. A "whiskers" ercaton inheriting from a "shaven tiger". Ercaton `~sample/whiskers-extends-plaintiger` differs from ercaton `~sample/whiskers` by a single `<erc:clone>`-tag only.

8 Indexing

A long-lasting problem of object-oriented programming has been the tedious mapping of objects to relational databases and the insuffience of object databases. Thing-oriented programming should have the same problem. However, Thing-oriented programming allows *every* Thing to be persistent. Therefore, the problem is reduced to the use of databases for structured queries across relations. *"Persistence and Structured Queries are orthogonal and shall be implemented independently."*

The internet is a good example that virtual real-world entities already obey this rule (a network of websites for persistence, "Google" for queries). However, we are not aware of a publication about this as a deeper insight. In order to serve both ends, the ercato programming model includes a powerful mechanism to fully get rid of the "persistence problem". It is composed of three cornerstones:

1. Index ercatons.
2. Index attributes in arbitrary ercatons.
3. Query ercatons for structured queries across relations and API for supported OO-languages.

A small example illustrates this:

Example 7. A index ercaton defining two indices where one points to ercatons.

```
<goods>
  <erc:type>index</erc:type>
  <erc:id>~sample/goods</erc:id>
  <erc:index>
    <erc:name>name</erc:name>
  </erc:index>
  <erc:index>
    <erc:name>price</erc:name>
    <erc:index-type>idref</erc:index-type>
  </erc:index>
</goods>
```

The first index is for a name, the second for a reference to an ercaton holding a price. Index ercatons may also contain references to other index ercatons themselves, from one index to another. This is the equivalent of SQL join statements and inner as well as outer joins can be modeled.

Example 8. An arbitrary ercaton indexing name and price for later retrieval.

```
<article>
  <erc:id>~sample/learjet</erc:id>
  <name erc:index="~sample/goods">Learjet</name>
  <erc:idref erc:index="~sample/goods#price">~prices/lj</erc:idref>
</article>
```

Arbitrary XML nodes may be indexed this way. Normally, such an index annotation is not marked explicitly but is inheriteded. Index operation does not need any XML schema to work. If an XML schema does exist for a given ercaton, it may of course be used to manage its index annotations automatically. However, we do not recommend to rely on a schema in a programming task.

Example 9. Retrieving all articles more expensive than 1799 €/$ from the ~sample/items index ercaton which acts as a view joining goods and prices.

```
/bin/simplequery (index="~sample/items" name="price" value=">1799")
```

The programmer is not exposed to SQL, EjbQL, XQL, and the like. The result is a list ercaton holding a list of ercato-ids satisfying the constraint and additional indexed information. Information about ercatons which the user has no browse capability for will not be found. Support exists to manage hierarchical catalogs and to index cumulative data for commutative operations (such as the sum of values).

When index annotations or indexed data within an ercaton is inherited from a clonebase which is being changed, index information does change accordingly and the result of queries will change as well. This change is allowed to happen asynchronously with implementation-defined worst-case delay.

The ercato engine specification can be updated to include support for forthcoming dataspace structuring techniques such as the semantic web in such a way that existing ercatons can profit.

9 Kernel vs. User Space

The ercato engine may be regarded an operating system managing ercatons as a resource. If this point of view is used, the ercato engine represents the kernel space of the operating system and everything said so far applies to the kernel.

There is a constant battle to minimize kernel functionality in favor of user space and the ercato programming model is no exception. Therefore and not unlike Unix, a large set of functionality is found in standard actions within service ercatons owned by ~root, the so-called system ercatons.

Example 10. A standard action 'cp'.

```
/bin/cp (from="~sample/count" to="~sample/count4")
```

The ercaton /bin/cp has a main action able to copy ercatons. And ~root can do so for all owners.

Many actions named similar to the Unix /bin directory exist. /bin/ls may be used, for instance, to browse catalogs such like the catalog of ercato-ids. Much of the power comes from the many standard actions in system ercatons available, and their number keeps growing. As has been said before, ercatons are *not* separate executable files executing in a separate address space or script files.

~userA-ercatons	~userB-ercatons	~userC-ercatons
/root-ercatons		
ercato extension layer (erx:)		
ercato **engine** (erc:)	ercato **engine** (erc:)	ercatoJ **engine** (erc:)
		J2EE application server
	Operating system	
Processor		

Fig. 3. Different components of an ercato programming environment. The three engine-pillars represent three options to implement the engine. The ercatoJ engine uses the right-most option. The lower half represents the kernel as described in this paper while the upper half represents the user space.

All ercatons depend on the kernel while many ercatons additionally depend on system ercatons (the erx-layer) to facilitate implementation.

An ercaton containing algorithms referred by system ercatons plays a role similar to a shared library. The resource ercaton containing most system actions' code is /lib/erxlib.jar. Actions in system ercatons are additionally aware of annotations in the erx-namespace (ErcatoExtensions). This paper cannot describe the erx-layer here due to space limitations. Fig. 3 visualizes how the components fit together.

In the case of the ercatoJ engine (the rightmost pillar), every ercaton is represented by an Enterprise JavaBean (EJB) entity bean instance during runtime. Note that deployment of business logic is independent of EJB deployment, though.

An address ercaton being part of an address management application may serve as an example how both, the erc- and erx-layers interact.

Example 11. The address of Easter Bunny.

```
<address>
    <erc:id>~sample/adr/bunny</erc:id>
    <erc:clone>~sample/adr/base</erc:clone>
    <name>Easter Bunny</name>
    <street>Wiese 7</street>
    <zipcode>12345</zipcode>
    <phone>0190 666 666</phone>
</address>
```

Assume that we want address searching to be available and offered in a navigation as well as administration operations such as edit, copy, delete and verification of address data. Additionally, we want other users to be able to find and use this address without necessarily the right to alter it. A corresponding address manager application containing Easter Bunnies address may roughly look like Fig. 4.

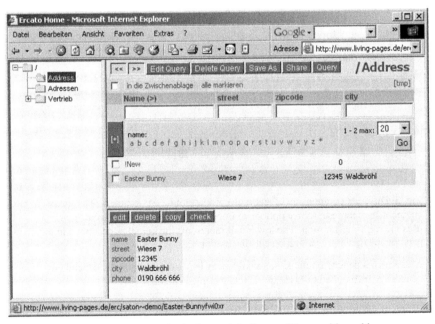

Fig. 4. The Easter Bunny ercaton in the lower right frame of the resulting address manager. Navigation and search facility are provided by a navigation and a query system ercaton.

In order to achieve this, we specify a suitable clonebase as listed in Example 12. It contains annotation attributes of elements like `erx:field-ref="string"`. It contains an action reference to the system ercaton `/bin/edit`, too. The annotation is used by the system ercaton to provide a suitable implementation of an edit cycle and it is used by the implicit system view target ercaton to provide a suitable view of the ercaton.

This interaction between ercatons and annotation is a typical pattern within the erx extension layer. The ercato engine requires no notion about view or edit or any Thing.

Example 12. The address ercaton used as Easter Bunnies clonebase.

```
<address xmlns:erc="..."
xmlns:erx="http://ercato.com/xmlns/ErcatoExtensions">
    <erc:id>~sample/adr/base</erc:id>
    <erc:type>prototype</erc:type>
    <erc:catalog category="/Address" id-ref="~sample/catalog"/>

    <name    erx:field-ref="string" erc:index="~sample/catalog"/>
    <street  erx:field-ref="string" erc:index="~sample/catalog"/>
    <zipcode erx:field-ref="int"    erc:index="~sample/catalog"/>
    <city    erx:field-ref="string" erc:index="~sample/catalog"/>
    <phone   erx:field-ref="string"/>

    <erc:action name="edit">   /bin/edit        </erc:action>
    <erc:action name="delete"> /bin/rm!wizard   </erc:action>
    <erc:action name="copy">   /bin/cp!forEdit </erc:action>
    <erc:action name="check">  ~sample/check.xsl
        <erc:arg name="default">Waldbröhl</erc:arg>
    </erc:action>
    <erc:trigger name="on-change">!check</erc:trigger>
</address>
```

10   Patterns – Or Lessons Learned

We have now been working with ercatons for years and we are amazed how much our thinking about software engineering has changed since. In particular, we and our partners have successfully used the J2EE-based ercatoJ engine in a number of projects.

Like a migration from procedural to object-oriented, the migration from object-oriented to Thing-oriented has led us to develop a number of patterns and best practices which are worth mentioning here.

The Firewall Pattern. Because an ercaton may contain both code, even source code, and business data, it may be difficult to understand how the two could be kept separate. First of all: there is no need for it. An ercato engine serves as a perfect repository for source and/or binary code. However, with possibly millions of ercatons in a system it may be reassuring to know which ercatons are structurally most important. The firewall pattern provides a way to achieve this.

A firewall is composed of empty proxy ercatons. The pool of ercatons not protected by a firewall shall be small and mostly contain prototypes, resources, service and test ercatons. This pool is called "the software" and may be stored into CVS or replicated. Whenever the software is modified, all modified ercatons are copied into the ercato engine and tested. After all tests succeeded, the firewall proxies are copied.

Formally, the firewall pattern recreates the distinction between "data" and "text". However, an ercaton may be moved between both sides of the firewall (by inheriting from the proxy or not) without altering its semantics. Thing-oriented programming therefore provides a unification of both.

The Face Pattern. Ercatons and their actions always have a user interface. Ercatons specify targets to provide arbitrary user-interfaces. The face pattern is used to create alternate user interfaces without the need to create or customize targets. An alternate user interface may be provided by an alternate ercaton but same target. Such an ercaton is called an alternate "face" of the original ercaton and may be returned by an action or another target.

The Doctor Pattern. Ercatons may modify each other. Ercatons which modify other ercatons in order to improve them in a rather general way or to remove a defect are called doctor ercatons.

A particular doctor ercaton is an ercaton which queries ercatons for cross-cutting properties and modifies their closures or action delegation chains. In this particular case, the doctor pattern is known as aspect-oriented programming. A garbage collector removing unreferenced ercatons which mark themselves as volatile is another example of the doctor pattern. Unreferenced ercatons are not removed by an ercato engine because ercatons, being Things, may exist alone.

The Workflow Pattern. Ercatons gather information during lifetime. This makes them good candidates to be passed along the edges of a workflow. Such ercatons are work ercatons.

To represent the next possible states reachable in the workflow, actions represent each possible transition and permissions are set such that only legal transitions are executable at a given state. Actually, different rôles may see different legal transitions which is just fine. Because an ercaton has a unique id while traveling along the workflow, a catalog entry which may change over time is used for navigation. The workflow pattern is also useful when invoking a series of actions on a single ercaton.

Aggregation. An ercaton is used as a container. A car with four wheels may be *five* objects in Java but is only *one* ercaton. Multiple list elements may inherit from a single element in a clonebase.

Association. An ercaton may refer to another associated ercaton using an `<idref>`-tag. A target may eliminate the difference between aggregation and association by using an `<expand>`-attribute. The use of such a pseudo aggregation is required for a many-to-one relation or a tighter permission for the associated part.

The Structure Constraint Pattern. In the XML world, structure constraints are often implemented by an XML schema. In an OO language, a class serves this purpose. While both may be used with ercatons (by use of a schema or object tag), the structure constraint pattern provides an alternative.

The ercaton contains constraint markup which is used to validate an ercaton against its constraints within a trigger fired by the on-change event. The trigger may raise an exception to veto change. The trigger is synchronized with the transaction. Besides structure and types of values, structure constraints may check referential constraints and dynamic conditions and may normalize inner structure. Structure constraints may be refined by inheritance.

Lessons Learned

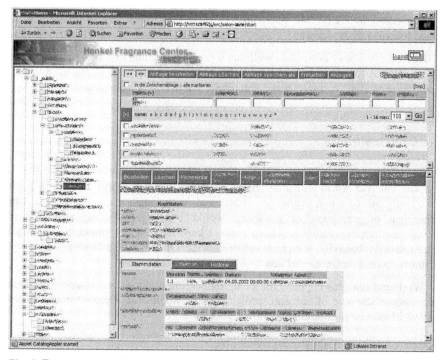

Fig. 5. Ercato-based application in production at Henkel. Five ercatons are seen (i.e., their user interfaces as specified by their declared target pipelines).

The left hand frame contains a catalog ercaton. The lower right frame shows a recipe ercaton with some action buttons. The upper right frame shows a query ercaton with result for its current query.

The users of this application run demanding operations involving recursive retrieval of ingredient information, updating lists or doing complex searches. The system, on average, serves about thousand transactions per minute & processor and has good reserve for peak loads. Our analysis shows that certain optimizations in current DOM tree implementations could yield at least one order of magnitude overall performance improvement. Performance on complex retrieval operations already is on equal with a native SQL implementation.

The ercatoJ engine is and was successfully used in a number of J2EE-based enterprise projects, by us and our partners. Most notably, it now implements a large software system at the chemical corporation Henkel KGaA, Düsseldorf, Germany. The system is used for the development and partly also production of new chemical recipes. It interacts with a farm of SAP/R3 systems and replaces a host system with about a million lines of code. The system went productive with great success [14]. Fig. 5 shows a screen shot for a part of the application, released for publication.

A general observation we have made is that development really focusses on the business logic. Despite the fact that a special ercato development environment does not exist, we observe an increase in developer productivity by a factor of three or better (compared to J2EE/CMP plus Struts). Altogether, much less programming language source code is required.

However, we have noticed as well that a good style guide or a best practice example is essential for success in a larger team. There are simply too many ways to work with ercatons and a common sense about best practice is yet to emerge.

11 Conclusion

Things in general or ercatons in particular provide a concrete way to bridge the gap between our real world and programs. Transforming a real-world entity into a software entity can be a non-mathematical task and "authoring", "building" or "growing" rather than "programming" or "modeling" would be the right wording. Still, ercatons provide enough expressive power to express knowledge about similarities or inheritance relations, behavior, structural constraints etc. Of course, the formulation of algorithms remains a mathematical task.

We found that this copies traditional engineering methods and is able to dramatically reduce the size of software projects where traditional object-oriented systems may yield too complex solutions.

The current implementation certainly falls short with respect to language elegance, performance and tool (IDE) support when compared with an object-oriented language like Java, Smalltalk or Self. The concept does not. Especially when comparing the approach to EJB- or .NET-based alternatives, or an XML-based persistence approach [17], then ercatons have some very interesting features.

The current mainstream heads for more and more abstract language technologies, combined with graphical tools to hide them from ordinary programmers. We believe this trend will reverse.

Think Thing.

References

1. Alan Borning: *"ThingLab – A Constraint-Oriented Simulation Laborator"*. XEROX PARC report SSL-79-3, July 1979.

2. David Ungar and Randall B. Smith: *"Self: The Power of Simplicity"*. OOPSLA '87 Conference Proceedings, pp. 227-241, Orlando, FL, October, 1987. http://research.sun.com/research/self/

3. Walter Smith: *"SELF and the Origins of NewtonScript"*. PIE Developers magazine, July 1994. http://wsmith.best.vwh.net/Self-intro.html

4. Netscape: *"Core JavaScript Reference"*. http://devedge.netscape.com/library/manuals/2000/javascript/1.5/reference/

5. Mike Plusch: *"Water: Simplified Web Services and XML Programming"*. (2002) John Wiley & Sons. ISBN: 0764525360. http://www.waterlang.org/

6. Richard Pawson and Robert Matthews: *"Naked Objects"*. (2002) John Wiley & Sons, Ltd. ISBN: 0470844205. http://www.nakedobjects.org/book.html

7. Azad Bolour: *"Notes on the Eclipse Plug-in Architecture"*. http://www.eclipse.org/articles/Article-Plug-in-architecture/plugin_architecture.html

8. Kent Beck: *"Extreme Programming Explained: Embrace Change"*. (1999) Addison-Wesley ISBN: 0201616416.

9. *"The Agile Manifesto"*. http://agilemanifesto.org/

10. Jürgen Diercks, Falk Langhammer: "Bauen statt modellieren". iX-Magazin 2/ 2004, p. 100-103. Heise Verlag. http://www.heise.de/kiosk/archiv/ix/2004/2/100

11. Gerald J. Sussman and Guy L. Steele, Jr. *"Scheme: An Interpreter for Extended Lambda Calculus"*. MIT AI Lab. AI Lab Memo AIM-349. December 1975. ftp://publications.ai.mit.edu/ai-publications/pdf/AIM-349.pdf

12. W3C: "Simple Object Access Protocol (SOAP) 1.1". W3C Note 08 May 2000. http://www.w3.org/TR/SOAP/

13. Bill Shannon: *"Java 2 Platform Enterprise Edition Specification, v1.4"*. (2003) Sun microsystems. http://java.sun.com/j2ee/j2ee-1_4-fr-spec.pdf

14. Joachim Buth and Falk Langhammer: *"Ercatons – XML-based J2EE project at Henkel"*. iX-Konferenz 2003, Heidelberg, Germany. Proceedings http://www.heise.de/newsticker/meldung/43691

15. W3C: *"XML Path Language (Xpath) Version 1.0"*. Recommendation 16 November 1999. http://www.w3.org/TR/xpath

16. XOperator evaluation kit. http://www.living-pages.de/de/projects/xop/

17. Tamino XML server home page. http://www.softwareag.com/tamino/

Author Index